ARCHBISH
CW00346897

The Archbishops of Canterbury Series

Series Editor: Andrew Chandler, University of Chichester, UK

Developed in association with Lambeth Palace Library archives, this series presents authoritative studies on the Archbishops of Canterbury. Each book combines biographical, historical, theological, social and political analysis within each archiepiscopacy, with original source material drawn from the Archbishop's correspondence, speeches and published and unpublished writings. The *Archbishops of Canterbury* series offers a vital source of reference, of lasting importance to scholars, students and all readers interested in the history of the international Church.

Other titles in this series:

Archbishop Pole
John Edwards, University of Oxford, UK

Archbishops Ralph d'Escures, William of Corbeil and Theobald of Bec
Heirs of Anselm and Ancestors of Becket
Jean Truax

Archbishop Anselm 1093–1109
Bec Missionary, Canterbury Primate, Patriarch of Another World
Sally N. Vaughn

Archbishop Fisher, 1945–1961
Church, State and World
Andrew Chandler and David Hein

Archbishop Ramsey

The Shape of the Church

PETER WEBSTER

ASHGATE

Published by
Ashgate Publishing Limited
Wey Court East
Union Road
Farnham
Surrey, GU9 7PT
England

Ashgate Publishing Company
110 Cherry Street
Suite 3-1
Burlington, VT 05401-3818
USA

www.ashgate.com

British Library Cataloguing in Publication Data
A catalogue record for this book is available from the British Library

The Library of Congress has cataloged the printed edition as follows:
Webster, Peter, 1974-
 Archbishop Ramsey : the shape of the church / By Peter Webster.
   pages cm. -- (The Archbishops of Canterbury series)
 Includes bibliographical references and index.
 ISBN 978-0-7546-6589-2 (hardcover) -- ISBN 978-0-7546-6596-0 (pbk.) -- ISBN 978-1-4724-5794-3 (ebook) -- ISBN 978-1-4724-5795-0 (epub) 1. Ramsey, Arthur Michael 2. Church of England--History--20th century. 3. Anglican Communion--History--20th century. 4. Religion and politics--History--20th century. I. Title.
 BX5199.R22W43 2015
 283.092--dc23

2014039112

ISBN: 9780754665892 (hbk)
ISBN: 9780754665960 (pbk)
ISBN: 9781472457943 (ebk – PDF)
ISBN: 9781472457950 (ebk – ePUB)

MIX
Paper from
responsible sources
FSC® C013985
www.fsc.org

Printed in the United Kingdom by Henry Ling Limited,
at the Dorset Press, Dorchester, DT1 1HD

Contents

Acknowledgments

My thanks are due to Clare Brown, Andrew Chandler, Ian Jones, Matthew Grimley and Patrick Harrigan who read and commented upon substantial drafts at various stages. I benefitted greatly from many conversations with John Maiden on Ramsey and the 1960s, and from the comments of Philip Williamson and of conference audiences in Belfast, at Wycliffe Hall, Oxford, and at the annual meetings of the Ecclesiastical History Society.

Particular thanks are due to Clare Brown, Rachel Cosgrave, Matti Watton and all the staff at Lambeth Palace Library, including the late and much missed Melanie Barber. It is by the kind permission of the Librarian of Lambeth Palace that the Ramsey Papers are here cited and reproduced.

Thanks are also due to Andrew Atherstone, Clyde Binfield, Perry Butler, Alister Chapman, Alec Corio, David Hart, Tim Hudson, Bill Jacob, Diarmaid MacCulloch, Douglas and Lis McCormick, Stephen Parker, Mark Smith, Todd Thompson, John Webster, Sarah Webster, John Wolffe, and Martin Wellings.

I am very grateful to Andrew Chandler as series editor for the opportunity to engage with Michael Ramsey in this book. Thanks are also due to Sarah Lloyd and all at Ashgate for their patience and assistance at every stage.

List of Abbreviations

BCC	British Council of Churches
CIO	Church Information Office
GCC	Ramsey, *The Gospel and the Catholic Church* (London, 1936)
H. C. Deb.	House of Commons Debates
H. L. Deb.	House of Lords Debates
ODNB	Oxford Dictionary of National Biography
WCC	World Council of Churches

PART I
Years in Office

Introduction

Arthur Michael Ramsey was Archbishop of Canterbury from 1961 until 1974, the hundredth occupant of the office. As perspectives on the period have lengthened, his term of office appears more and more to have been pivotal in the history of the Church of England and of the nation as a whole. Ramsey's time coincides with Arthur Marwick's 'Long Sixties', in which nothing less than a cultural revolution occurred in British life.[1] Part of that revolution was in the relationship between the British and their religion, and Callum Brown and others have located the crucial shifts in the religious imaginary in this period.[2]

At the same time, all the churches were reassessing their relationships with each other, as part of a process with a longer pre-history but given urgency by the times. These parallel movements in popular religious sentiment and within the churches called into question several key relationships that had seemed very settled, and the role of the archbishop in the articulation of those relationships. Ramsey's time saw the removal of much of the Christian content from the law as it touched matters of public and private morality. Also under scrutiny was the constitutional relationship of Crown, Parliament, people and the established Church. And as the tectonic plates moved at home, so did the role of the archbishop as leader of the global Anglican Communion.

The career of Michael Ramsey provides then an important perspective on each of these broader movements. The present work is no biography, but rather an assessment of Ramsey's tenure as archbishop; but a brief biographical conspectus of Ramsey's path to Canterbury is necessary nonetheless. When viewed in outline, the shape of Michael Ramsey's life and career offers few surprises. He was born in Cambridge in 1904, the second of two sons and brother to two younger sisters. His father Arthur Ramsey held a fellowship in mathematics at Magdalene College; his mother Agnes was the daughter of an Anglican clergyman, and a teacher, published author, socialist and suffragette.

---

[1]   Arthur Marwick, *The Sixties. Cultural Revolution in Britain, France, Italy and the United States, c.1958–c.1974* (Oxford, 1998), p.7.

[2]   Callum Brown, *The Death of Christian Britain. Understanding Secularisation 1800–2000* (2nd ed, Abingdon, 2009), pp.170–92; Hugh McLeod, *The religious crisis of the 1960s* (Oxford, 2007), *passim*.

Arthur Ramsey was the son of a Congregationalist minister, and the family attended Emmanuel Congregational Church, in which Ramsey's father was a deacon for a time.[3]

After stints in several schools – some unhappy; some, like that at the choir school of King's College Cambridge, much brighter – in 1918, Ramsey won a scholarship to Repton School. Here he discovered history and the classics, the benefits of a well-stocked library, the excitements of debate in a politically exciting time and the attractions of the worship of the Church of England, into which he was confirmed at the age of 16. The man responsible for preparing the young Ramsey for confirmation was Geoffrey Fisher, headmaster of Repton, and later to be Ramsey's predecessor as Archbishop of Canterbury.[4]

In 1923 Ramsey entered Magdalene College, Cambridge, with a Classical scholarship and a room directly above those of his father. Here he was first secretary and eventually president of the Cambridge Union, the university's debating society. He was to know well several men whom he would encounter professionally in later life: Selwyn Lloyd, who was to be a Conservative Home Secretary, whose room was next to Ramsey's; and Patrick Devlin, the eminent lawyer and jurist, and a Lord of Appeal from 1961.[5] It was here that he imagined a career in Liberal politics (of which more below). But a more profound reorientation was taking place in Ramsey's thought and feeling, away from the classics, law and politics, and towards ordination. Ramsey had developed an attachment to the Catholic wing of the Anglican church in stages: under the influence of Eric Milner-White, dean of King's College Cambridge, while a pupil at its school, and then by his own investigation while at Repton. In Cambridge, he learned from men such as Edward Wynn and E.C. Hoskyns, and from hearing William Temple, then Bishop of Manchester, at a mission to the university in 1926.[6] After a change in his direction of study, he left Cambridge with first class honours in theology, and entered Ripon College, Cuddesdon, to begin preparation for ordination in the summer of 1927. A year later he was

---

[3]   The facts of Ramsey's early formation and career are to be found in the biographical studies by Owen Chadwick and James B. Simpson; Owen Chadwick, *Michael Ramsey. A life* (Oxford, 1990); James B. Simpson, *The Hundredth Archbishop of Canterbury* (New York, 1962). See also the entry in the *Oxford Dictionary of National Biography* by Alan Wilkinson.

[4]   On Fisher's time at Repton, see Andrew Chandler and David Hein, *Archbishop Fisher, 1945–1961. Church, State and World* (Farnham, 2012), pp.15–22

[5]   On the later interaction of Ramsey and Selwyn Lloyd, see John Maiden and Peter Webster, 'Parliament, the Church of England and the last gasp of political Protestantism, 1961-4', *Parliamentary History* 32; 2 (2013), 361–77, at pp.370–71.

[6]   Chadwick, *Ramsey*, pp.22, 25, 27.

ordained deacon, and took a position as curate in the church of St Nicholas in Liverpool. He was ordained in the church at Farnworth in September 1929.

Ramsey's gifts had already been noted, however, and so he was to leave Liverpool before the planned time to become sub-warden of Lincoln Theological College at Easter 1930. Neither his bishop nor his rector favoured the move, but it was inevitable that they should bow to the combined pressure of the theologians Charles Raven and E.C. Hoskyns, backed up by William Temple, by now Archbishop of York. It was to be at Lincoln that Ramsey erected for himself what Owen Chadwick described as a 'structure of thought', and where he was to produce his first major work, *The Gospel and the Catholic Church.*[7]

That structure of thought was constructed in part by dint of preparing for teaching, at which his hearers recalled him to be outstanding. The traces of his time at Lincoln are also to be found in his lifelong special concern for priests in training, some of which can be seen in his classic *The Christian Priest Today*. But these six years were most marked by the irresistible rise of his profile in the Church away from Lincolnshire. Amongst many invitations, one that he accepted was to be examining chaplain for the Bishop of Chester; none other than Geoffrey Fisher. Perhaps most surprising was that a member of staff of a provincial theological college, and not even the most senior, should find himself in the company of the foremost theologians from Europe and America, at a meeting in preparation for Temple's 1936 Oxford Conference on Church, Community and Society.[8]

Given this growing national renown and the appearance of *The Gospel and the Catholic Church* – a work recognised as significant even if not universally accepted – Ramsey might well have expected to move closer to the centre of the academic world. But instead, for reasons that remain unclear, Nugent Hicks, Bishop of Lincoln, thought Ramsey needed further parish experience,[9] so in 1936 Ramsey moved to the Boston Stump, otherwise known as the parish church of St Botolph in Boston, Lincolnshire, as the most senior of four curates, although his position was in name that of lecturer. There he was to stay until, after a short spell as incumbent of the small parish of St Benet in Cambridge, he went to Durham in January 1940, as Van Mildert Professor of Divinity and canon of the cathedral.

After his native Cambridge, the city and county of Durham were to be Ramsey's next great love. There he met Joan Hamilton, whom he married in the

7   Chadwick, *Ramsey*, p.45.
8   Simpson, *Hundredth Archbishop*, pp.78–79.
9   Simpson, *Hundredth Archbishop*, p.80; Chadwick, *Ramsey*, pp.51–52.

cathedral in April 1942. Much has been made of Ramsey's social difficulties and
of his incapability in practical things. Joan was to provide the companionship
that ameliorated the former, and organisational support in the latter.[10] In the
faculty he was a popular lecturer and an effective leader, placing it firmly in the
first rank in Britain.[11] Ramsey continued to write, with the 1949 volume the
Transfiguration his major achievement from Durham. At the first meeting of the
World Council of Churches, at Amsterdam in 1948, Ramsey found himself on
a commission with Karl Barth, Richard Niebuhr and others; the very top flight
of world theological talent.[12] When in 1950 he was appointed as the Regius
Professor of Divinity in his beloved Cambridge, there was nowhere further to
go in British theological life. At the age of 45, he had found what he and Joan
thought would be his final home.[13] Within 11 years he would be Archbishop
of Canterbury.

He was to reach Lambeth Palace in two steps. After less than two years, the
letter arrived from Prime Minister Churchill offering him the see of Durham,
confronting him with what Chadwick has rightly described as the most difficult
decision he had ever faced. On one side was his great love of Durham; an
affection which the selection process showed was reciprocated. But was it wrong
to leave Cambridge after such a short time, he wondered, with a job only just
begun and certainly not finished? Both archbishops privately thought that it
might be. More generally, were his gifts and desires really best suited to the work
of a bishop, rather than to the scholarly life, at the peak of which he had only
just arrived? Was it to be, in the phrase of his best man, a 'candle-snuffer'?[14] After
much deliberation he accepted, and was consecrated in September 1952, and
enthroned in Durham the month after. He felt very strongly that to be a scholar,
a leader in thought as well as in administration, was central to the function of
a bishop. There were few enough of these, he thought, and so it was important
that he took the opportunity now it had arisen.[15]

A number of key preoccupations mark Ramsey's time at Durham, and
as Archbishop of York from 1956. Two of these were the ecumenical and the
international. During this time he was joint chair of the committee for the
relationship between the Anglican churches and the new Church of South

---

[10]   Simpson, *Hundredth Archbishop*, p.115.
[11]   Simpson, *Hundredth Archbishop*, pp.107–108, 111, 114–15.
[12]   Simpson, *Hundredth Archbishop*, pp.113–14.
[13]   Simpson, *Hundredth Archbishop*, p.114.
[14]   Chadwick, *Ramsey*, p.75; Simpson, *Hundredth Archbishop*, pp.117–18.
[15]   Chadwick, *Ramsey*, pp.72–77. On his view of the role of the bishop, see 'The bishop'
in his *Canterbury Essays and Addresses* (London, 1964), pp.161–64.

India.[16] Ramsey travelled to Evanston, Illinois, for the 1954 meeting of the World Council of Churches, as he had to Amsterdam in 1948.[17] In 1956 he led an Anglican delegation to meet leaders of the Russian Orthodox Church in Moscow.[18] At the 1958 Lambeth Conference, at which Fisher was Canterbury to his former pupil's York, the elderly George Bell, bishop of Chichester, thought Ramsey the outstanding figure.[19]

In a place like Durham it was easy for Ramsey to give free rein to his imaginative sense of history. The collection of *Durham Essays and Addresses* is shot through with the interplay of present with both the city's and region's spiritual past. Twice he led pilgrimages to Holy Island, from both Durham and York. In Durham Cathedral he found, in the words of Owen Chadwick, an 'ecstasy, of history speaking out of sanctified stones'.[20] At Auckland Castle, historic residence of the Bishops of Durham, 'the past was so alive, and my great predecessors seemed like daily companions.'[21] Although he was to develop no great attachment to Lambeth Palace as a building, he had a great affection for the palace at Canterbury, as he did for Bishopthorpe, his residence at York, in the garden of which William Temple had often meditated.[22]

Another central preoccupation was with the clergy, and particularly with young ordinands. One of Ramsey's biographers taxes him with inattentiveness to the practical needs of his diocese and his staff, and of carelessness over the proprieties of appointments.[23] Although there is some justice in this, on occasion he could be practical, such as his move to ensure that the expenses for bishops moving into ancient and enormous houses and acquiring elaborate new costume did not prevent talented men from taking up the role.[24] Yet it is a paradox of Ramsey's career that, despite this lack of sensitivity to practical need, he was

---

[16]   George Bell to Ramsey, 5 January 1956, reproduced at Chadwick, *Ramsey*, p.91. Ramsey presented the report of the committee to the Convocation of York in July 1955; his speech is given in his *Durham Essays and Addresses*, (London, 1956), pp.73–80; R.C.D. Jasper, *George Bell. Bishop of Chichester* (London, 1967), pp.350–51.

[17]   His thoughts on Evanston were published in *Durham Essays and Addresses*, pp.81–84; Chadwick, *Ramsey*, pp.85–86.

[18]   Simpson, *Hundredth Archbishop*, pp.148–53.

[19]   Jasper, *George Bell*. p.384.

[20]   Chadwick, *Ramsey*, pp.84, 96, 80.

[21]   Chadwick, *Ramsey*, p.79.

[22]   Chadwick, *Ramsey*, p.94.

[23]   Michael De-la-Noy, *Michael Ramsey. A Portrait*, (London, 1990) pp.162–65.

[24]   In this, Ramsey's experience of becoming Bishop of Durham conditioned his actions as archbishop; Andrew Chandler, *The Church of England in the twentieth century: the Church Commissioners and the politics of reform, 1948–1998*, (Woodbridge, 2006), pp.183–84.

acutely sensitive to the spiritual needs of the clergy. Perhaps his greatest delight was to spend time with clergy in retreat, and he spent much effort while at York in the development of the retreat house Wydale Hall.[25] The foreign trips often involved meetings with students of all kinds, whether at Nashotah House in the United States, or at the (Roman Catholic) English College in Rome in 1966.[26] A useful study in its own right would be the impact of Ramsey's classic *The Christian Priest Today*, first published in 1972 and dedicated to all those men he had ordained in two decades as a bishop and archbishop.[27] Revised in 1985, at the time of writing it remains in print, still being read by at least some ordinands.[28]

Ramsey the Anglo-Catholic

If there was one thing the Protestant wing of the Church of England thought they knew about Ramsey when he came to Canterbury in 1961, it was that he was a Anglo-Catholic. Ramsey had chaired the group charged by Geoffrey Fisher with defining the catholic nature of the Church of England; and indeed the report the group produced, *Catholicity* (1947) bears many of his fingerprints.[29] In international theological summitry, dominated as it was by the Protestant churches, it was often the Church of England that represented the Catholic tradition in the absence of Rome and the Orthodox. Ramsey, often the Anglican representative at such gatherings, had come to be seen as one of the most persuasive advocates of catholicity.

Some observers thought that Ramsey had ruled himself out of contention for Canterbury by agreeing to address the highly visible Eucharistic Congress, organised by the partisan Church Union on the eve of the 1958 Lambeth Conference.[30] As archbishop, he was to find himself in trouble for suggesting that any world church would necessarily be headed by the bishop of Rome. But Ramsey's catholicity was not simply that of the Anglo-Catholic movement of his time; not the catholicism which thought the only barrier to the return of the

---

[25] Chadwick, *Ramsey*, pp.95, 357.
[26] Chadwick, *Ramsey*, pp.213–14, 319. See also the impressions of one Nashotah student of Ramsey in retirement in Dale Coleman's foreword to Michael Ramsey, *The Anglican Spirit* (London, 1991), pp.5–6.
[27] Published by SPCK. The revised edition went through six impressions in its first 12 years.
[28] I am grateful to Andrew Atherstone of Wycliffe Hall for information on this point.
[29] *Catholicity. A study in the conflict of Christian traditions in the West* (London, 1948), *passim*.
[30] Chadwick, *Ramsey*, p.98.

Church of England to the Roman fold was Rome's pronouncement on Anglican orders, *Apostolicae Curae*. Ramsey was no papalist; his was a generous and global catholicity, involving both East and West, in which Rome was only one component part, albeit vital, of a wider enterprise of reunion. No one institution possessed the fullness of the catholicity Ramsey had in mind, and true reunion would see none of the churches unchanged by the process. All the churches needed 'a penitence of a thoroughly practical kind', which was not defensive of this or that thing, but that could hold to those things whilst trying to learn to look from a narrow outlook to a wider one. It required a 'sanctification in the truth' after the Lord's own prayer.[31]

If Ramsey was an Anglo-Catholic, he also sat very lightly to its ritual. His own devotion was centred on and anchored by the Eucharist, but paid only limited attention to the Virgin Mary, and was little concerned with the details of ceremonial.[32] When Cardinal Suenens celebrated the Eucharist privately during his visit to Lambeth in 1967, Ramsey especially appreciated the simplicity and lack of minor ceremonial that Suenens used.[33] One episode while he was Bishop of Durham showed him unwilling to fight older battles over ritual discipline. The vicar of the most Anglo-Catholic parish in the diocese appealed to his new bishop in 1953 for support for various ritual practices to which some in the parish had objected. Whilst working to achieve reconciliation between the parties, Ramsey gave his sanction to much of the pattern of worship, although elements of it were clearly illegal. The action was not forgotten, and it formed the basis of Protestant objections to Ramsey's election to York.[34] But the objections, whilst explicable in their polemical context, did not reflect Ramsey's position correctly. He sanctioned the ritual at St Mary Tyne Dock not because he himself particularly relished it, or because he thought it normative for others. Rather, it was in keeping with the tradition of the particular congregation; and continuity in the worship of the Body of Christ in its local setting mattered more than the strict interpretation of canon law. Ramsey, then, held to the substance of English Catholicism without concerning himself with its accidents.

---

[31] *Catholicity*, p.48
[32] Chadwick, *Ramsey*, p.47.
[33] Ramsey memorandum on the visit of Suenens to Lambeth, 19 May 1967, at Ramsey Papers vol.120, ff.283–85, at f.283.
[34] Chadwick, *Ramsey*, pp.83–84, 92.

The Nonconformist Ramsey

It is the fate of archbishops to disappoint nearly everyone in the Church at one point or another. The correspondence in the Ramsey Papers reveals close and affectionate regard between Ramsey and many Anglo-Catholics. There was, however, one key moment of rupture between Ramsey and the party, over his support for the proposed union between the Church of England and the Methodist Church (on which see Chapter 1). A friend and ally, Victor Stock (later dean of Guildford), noted the conspicuous absence of many of the party from Ramsey's funeral in 1988, thinking it evidence of the 'strangulated disapproval' still felt towards him.[35]

The evangelicals within the Church had no such high expectations of Ramsey when he came to office. Protestant disapproval centred on his failures at Durham, as already noted. The suspicion of a younger generation of evangelicals went back to 1955, when Ramsey had involved himself in a dispute about 'fundamentalism', in connection with a university mission in Durham led by John Stott, rector of All Souls' Langham Place.[36] As well as taking issue with this particular view of the Bible, Ramsey had also criticised the type of missionary methods that he had witnessed in Cambridge as a student, which was taken to be an oblique criticism of the American evangelist Billy Graham who had visited London the year before and on whom many evangelical hopes had rested. But there were greater theological sympathies between Ramsey and the evangelicals than many supposed. They lay in his emphasis on the Bible, on the cross, and on the need for the Church to overcome its preoccupation with its own internal affairs, and to pay greater attention to renewed mission.[37]

This element of Ramsey's make-up must be understood in light of his childhood and youth. The Ramsey family religion in Edwardian Cambridge was as part of Emmanuel Congregational Church. Ramsey was later to recall with gratitude the influence of the minister of Emmanuel, H.C. Carter, while on retreat before his ordination.[38] Emmanuel was no backwater: visitors to the house included the prominent Nonconformist laymen Bernard Manning and

---

[35]   Victor Stock, *Taking Stock. Confessions of a City Priest* (London, 2001), p.51.

[36]   Alister Chapman, *Godly ambition. John Stott and the evangelical movement* (Oxford, 2012), pp.40–48.

[37]   Peter Webster, 'Archbishop Michael Ramsey and Evangelicals in the Church of England' in *Evangelicalism and the Church of England in the Twentieth Century: Reform, Resistance and Renewal*, ed. Andrew Atherstone and John Maiden, (Woodbridge, 2014), pp.172–92, at pp.180–84.

[38]   Chadwick, *Ramsey*, p.41.

G.G. Coulton,[39] and it is possible that Ramsey there encountered P.T. Forsyth, one of the most significant theologians writing from within English nonconformity. Ramsey was to cite Forsyth throughout his career; few other Anglo-Catholic divines could have thought to recommend Forsyth's writings on ministry to new ordinands.[40]

Had not Ramsey shed this skin when preparing for confirmation as an Anglican at Repton? Whilst Ramsey was to move in adulthood towards a Catholic view of Church order and of the Eucharist which would hardly have been acceptable at Emmanuel, he was never to develop the half-conscious superiority of many senior clergy brought up as Anglicans. Ramsey knew something of what it cost to be a religious minority from the history of his native church. The Methodists in the diocese of Durham noticed this and appreciated it, as did the two Nonconformists on whose votes he was elected to the regius chair at Cambridge.[41] One of his most significant appointments to the staff of the Durham theology faculty was the Methodist C.K. Barrett, showing an openness to Nonconformist theology not common in 1945.[42] The Ramsey Papers show a great warmth between Ramsey and the leaders of the Free Churches with which he dealt, and the 'tumultuous welcome' he received at the inauguration of the United Reformed Church in 1972 showed the degree to which some Nonconformists regarded him as 'our archbishop'.[43]

Ramsey the Politician

Had events, and Ramsey's mind, taken a different course, historians might have been considering the legacy not of Michael Ramsey the archbishop, but of Ramsey the career politician. Until part way through Ramsey's time as an undergraduate, his mind was firmly set on pursuing a career in Liberal politics. The Ramsey home had been political in its atmosphere. Agnes Ramsey was a socialist and campaigner for the enfranchisement of women, active in the Labour party.[44] The Ramsey family religion had in it a large dose of social conscience. Once at Cambridge, Ramsey attracted attention as a debater, becoming president of the Union in 1926. Just as Liberalism in Parliament was being squeezed between

---

[39] Chadwick, *Ramsey*, p.7.
[40] Michael Ramsey, *The Christian Priest Today* (2nd ed., London, 1985), p.4.
[41] Chadwick, *Ramsey*, pp.82, 69.
[42] Chadwick, *Ramsey*, pp.61–62.
[43] Chadwick, *Ramsey*, pp.341–42.
[44] Chadwick, *Ramsey*, p.5.

the Conservatives and the new force of Labour, Ramsey embraced a liberalism without the strait-jacket of doctrine: pragmatic, individualist, anti-imperialist and with a concern for the weak and the poor. Herbert Asquith witnessed Ramsey on a campaign platform, and thought him one day likely to lead the party. Had his studies not intervened, he might have accepted the invitation of the party in Cambridgeshire to be its parliamentary candidate.[45]

Despite this promise, by a gradual process that was complete by 1926, Ramsey came to the conviction that his future lay in ordination and not in politics, or rather, that his motivation to political service was most completely realised in the context of a wider vocation. He later dismissed his politicking as an 'adolescent enthusiasm'. Here the historian must dissent from his subject, as Owen Chadwick observed.[46] Ramsey's whole career must be read in part as a working-out of those political convictions, in which their ethical substance was first incorporated in a wider vision of the divine plan for humanity, which vision was then applied theologically to particular problems. In many cases a Christian concern with the social ineluctably became political. Of some significance here was a fortnight spent working amongst the poor of the East End of London in 1926, at the time when his mind was moving towards ordination. While at Liverpool, he saw similar deprivation and social tension as he had in the East End.[47] When at Durham, he regularly attended the miners' gala, that show of trade union strength, mindful that his predecessor B.F. Westcott had mediated between miners and mine owners in the strike of 1892.[48]

As we shall see in Chapter 5, Ramsey was to speak fluent politics with a strong religious accent, but by the 1960s the Liberal Party was in eclipse, and some of its most distinctive concerns had been redistributed between the Labour and Conservative parties. Ramsey thus had no obvious home amongst the main parties, in contrast to the identification with Labour of a figure such as Mervyn Stockwood, Bishop of Southwark, or the reflex Conservatism of many of the other bishops.[49]

---

[45]   Chadwick, *Ramsey*, pp.20–21.

[46]   Chadwick, *Ramsey*, p.26.

[47]   Chadwick, *Ramsey*, p.43.

[48]   Chadwick, *Ramsey*, p.82; see also his address to a congregation of miners in Durham Cathedral at *Durham Essays and Addresses*, pp.99–102.

[49]   On Stockwood's political views, see Michael De-la-Noy, *Mervyn Stockwood. A Lonely Life* (London, 1996), *passim*.

Ramsey's Theology

Ramsey was a professional theologian before he was a bishop, and he continued to write prolifically during his time in office, and indeed for several years after retirement. A word is necessary about the limits of this study's concern with Ramsey's work *qua* theology.

The present author was born just a few days after Ramsey retired in 1974, and was still at school at the time of Ramsey's death. As such, I had no personal acquaintance with or memory of Ramsey whatever, and so had no stock of 'Ramsey stories.' These stories – anecdotes of Ramsey's clumsiness, 'otherworldliness', shyness and awkwardness in company – are legion.[50] Michael De-la-Noy laid much of this to Ramsey's charge, thinking that the apparent indifference to his staff and the painful silences in conversation were willed, a moral failing.[51] I intend to show at length elsewhere that much of this apparent eccentricity can be accounted for by a retrospective 'diagnosis' of autistic spectrum disorder. Yet for Ramsey, at least one kind of otherworldliness was a critical part of the Christian life and was, in its right measure and context, something to be cultivated. At the consecration of a bishop in the United States in 1962, he contrasted the 'superabundant activity' of the modern Church with the need for a 'readiness to go apart in quietness, waiting upon God'. Of course the Church must be 'deeply involved with the present age, studying it, learning its techniques, sensitive to its aspirations and fears', yet this is best enabled when there is 'that otherworldly strain of which All Saints Day is the reminder.' The Church needed to 'see our present tasks in the light of our heavenly goal'.[52] It was not by accident, therefore, that unlike Fisher, Ramsey by and large eschewed any involvement in the public affairs of the Church after his retirement, writing rather less on the nature of the Church and its doctrine, and much more on the life of prayer and the work of the Holy Spirit. Ramsey lived some 13 years in retirement, first back at Cuddesdon, then at Durham once again, and then briefly at York.[53] From this relative seclusion emerged two studies in particular: *Holy Spirit* (1977) and *Be still and know* (1982).[54] Here was an indicator of Ramsey's true priorities.

---

[50] Chadwick, *Ramsey*, pp.112–22.

[51] Michael De-la-Noy, *A day in the life of God* (Derby, 1971), pp.37–40 and *passim*.

[52] 'The Bishop' in Michael Ramsey, *Canterbury Essays and Addresses*, pp.161–64, at p.162.

[53] Chadwick, *Ramsey*, pp.382–97.

[54] *Holy Spirit* was published by SPCK; *Be still and know* by Fount Paperbacks in association with the Faith Press.

However, it is Ramsey's theology written during his time at Canterbury which is more visible in this study. Ramsey's most systematic theology has attracted modest but significant attention in more recent years, most notably in studies such as that by Jared Cramer and the collection of essays edited by Robin Gill and Lorna Kendall.[55] Ramsey's theological writing appears extensively here, including long-form academic writing such as *The Gospel and the Catholic Church*,[56] but also his sermons (both published and unpublished), addresses to the Church Assembly, occasional pastoralia, book reviews and all kinds of other forms, all of which contain or flow from Ramsey's theology, broadly defined. The present work, however, is one of history; and so all Ramsey's writing and speaking is here deployed in order to explicate Ramsey's actions as archbishop and to assess their coherence as a whole. It necessarily sets Ramsey's theology in the context of the state of Anglican self-understanding of the time, but sets aside any questions of the degree to which Ramsey's thought was typically 'Anglican'.

Insofar as a consensus is visible, it would seem to be that Ramsey's most enduring extended work, and most rewarding of continued reading, is his first, *The Gospel and the Catholic Church* (hereafter GCC).[57] This work figures prominently here, since its concern with the nature of the Church is closest to the main preoccupation of this study. Whether it is Ramsey's most innovative or enduring work of theology proper, when examined as part of the development of the discipline, is beyond the concern of this study. It will become apparent that the central preoccupation of GCC with the shape of the Church and its fundamental purpose was one which gave Ramsey categories of analysis with which to deal with the fundamental questions that the 1960s posed.

Those difficult questions that pressed in upon all the churches are examined at length in Chapter 4. Ramsey seemed imperturbed in the face of issues that engendered panic and despondency in others, and it was the view of providence and of history laid out in GCC that was his protection. There had been an optimism in liberal Anglican theology in the early part of the twentieth century, the history of which Ramsey knew intimately, as his 1959 Hale memorial lectures showed.[58] According to this view, human nature was essentially good,

[55]   Jared Cramer, *Safeguarded by Glory: Michael Ramsey's ecclesiology and the struggles of contemporary Anglicanism* (Lanham, MD, 2010); Robin Gill and Lorna Kendall (eds), *Michael Ramsey as Theologian* (London, 1995).

[56]   London, 1936.

[57]   See Rowan Williams, 'Theology and the Churches' in *Michael Ramsey as Theologian*, ed. Robin Gill and Lorna Kendall (London, 1995). pp.9–28.

[58]   Published as *From Gore to Temple. The Development of Anglican Theology between Lux Mundi and the Second World War 1889–1939* (London, 1960).

and perfectible given the right tools; society and its institutions embodied in some rather vague way the right order of things, and all was progressing, evolving, according to the divine plan. Despite his great affinity with the liberal theologian F.D. Maurice, Ramsey's apprehension of the course of human and divine history was darker and more textured. It was the theology of GCC that protected him from the shocks of the 1930s and the 1939–45 conflict that were to destroy the more naïve optimism of the earlier period, and prepared him for the different but related challenges of his time as archbishop.[59]

GCC is concerned not with what the Church of Christ could be if only it were more efficiently managed. It is not concerned with what the Church should *do*, in social action or in the cause of peace. Its concern is with what the Church *is*; what its very existence shows to the world of the saving work of Christ, and the business of sin and judgment. Just as the New Testament shows a Church 'scandalous and unintelligible to men', the Church in every age should, and indeed is able to do little more than 'teach men to die to self and to trust in a Resurrection to a new life'. For the Church to meet the philanthropist and the reformer on their own terms, and to speak of its purpose in those terms, was to miss its deeper purpose. The Church 'amid its own failures and the questionings of the bewildered ... with its inconsistencies and its perversions and its want of perfection' exists only to point beyond itself.[60]

As Rowan Williams has noted, there was an extremism, even an impossibilism in the picture Ramsey painted in GCC which, if unchecked, threatened to render any action of Christians within it superfluous, even futile.[61] But there was a counter-balance in Ramsey's very present sense of the action of God in history and of the sureness of God's help to His people. Even if the Church could do little by its own efforts, the study of the sweep of the Church's history showed that the gates of hell would indeed never prevail against it. Ramsey's article on the authority of the Bible for Peake's commentary of 1962 is shot through with a vivid apprehension of the Scriptures as the record of God's sovereign direction of history, and His mighty acts of redemption of His people.[62] It was this conviction that enabled Ramsey to keep his head as the consciousness of religious crisis of the early 1960s was combined with a wider sense of societal upheaval, culminating in conflict in Ulster, economic crisis and political instability in the early 1970s. On a retreat to Iona, as the West found itself increasingly set around

---

[59]   For some of what follows, I am indebted to the suggestive essay by Williams, 'Theology and the Churches', pp.9–28.

[60]   Ramsey, *Gospel and the Catholic Church*, pp.3–8.

[61]   Williams, 'Theology and the Churches', pp.11–12.

[62]   Reprinted as *The Authority of the Bible* (Edinburgh, 1962), *passim*.

by the threat of nuclear extinction, 'ecological doom and the restive poor' in the developing world, and with Christianity 'in retreat, and near rabble', Ramsey could transport his hearers with the serene prospect of 'the great Christian centuries to come'.[63] This was no mere piety, no rallying call to a faltering army, but a conviction of the nature of God and His relationship to His church.

There is, however, a tension, if not quite a paradox, in Ramsey's thought, between this great salience of the corporate Church on the one hand, and on the other, a very personal sense of the individual soul as of equal weight in the divine plan. Ramsey had a particularly vivid apprehension of the interrelatedness of individual Christians both between churches and across nations. As Chapter 1 will show, although Ramsey yielded to none in his holding to Catholic essentials when thinking institutionally, he knew that at a local level, fellowship, worship and prayer between Christians in divided churches would always outpace, and should indeed lead, structural change nationally. The sources edited for this study show that Ramsey often reached for examples of local co-operation as examples of where the churches should be heading, in Northern Ireland, or in South Africa, or between Anglicans and Methodists or Roman Catholics.

This connection was not only geographical. Rowan Williams has noted the lack of 'hermetic seals' between believers in the past and in the present: they are 'involved with and in a community of believers extended in time and space, whose relation to each other is significantly more than just one of vague geographical connection and temporal succession. In theological shorthand [they are] a member of the Body of Christ.'[64] This sense of the reality of the communion of saints is key to understanding Ramsey's thought. Everywhere in his writing does the reader find Ramsey reaching for the life of an individual: in relation to Northern Ireland, it is St Patrick; on pilgrimage to Whitby, it is St Hilda.[65] Chapter 1 shows him dealing with the diplomatic complexities of the commemoration of the English Roman Catholic martyrs; but it is to the saints and martyrs common to all English Christians that he directs attention. For Williams, the study of the Christian experience of the saints of the past has a different quality for Christians: 'our immersion in the ways in which *they* responded becomes part of the way we actually hear the call ourselves.'[66] For

---

[63]   The words of Christopher Martin, editor of *Great Christian Centuries to Come. Essays in honour of A.M. Ramsey* (Oxford, 1974), p.1.

[64]   Rowan Williams, *Why study the past? The quest for the historical Church* (London, 2005), pp.26–7.

[65]   See, for instance, his reference to Patrick in an address in Westminster Cathedral, 14 March 1972, Ramsey Papers vol.319, ff.63, at f.63.

[66]   Williams, *Why study the past?* p.31.

Ramsey, both the saints of old and the places in which they lived and worked were ever-present in imagination and in prayer. The 'great cloud of witnesses' that the writer to the Hebrews had seen was more than purely metaphor.[67]

Ramsey's Biographers

As with all the archbishops, the business of assessing Ramsey's record began before it had ended, and indeed before it had begun. A pattern has developed of biographical studies of the archbishops appearing as they arrive in office, such as Margaret Duggan's study of Robert Runcie, published in 1983.[68] Ramsey had his, *The Hundredth Archbishop of Canterbury*, which was published in the United States in 1962.[69] Perhaps the first extended attempt at an assessment was the collection of essays edited by Christopher Martin and published in 1974, *Great Christian Centuries to Come*. Three of the contributors to the collection were associated with the radical monthly *Prism*, and Martin thought Ramsey a 'man of vision ... Not for him the prudential foresight of the politician, balancing achievement the year after next with compromise today; not for him the ancillary voice to the best intentions of public men'. For David L. Edwards, a participant in much of what he described, Ramsey's time would come to be seen as 'a chapter in the triumph of the Christian gospel over English conservatism.'[70]

Not all commentators on Ramsey have been as positive. One of the two full-length studies of Ramsey's life and career which appeared simultaneously in 1990 is that by Michael De-la-Noy.[71] Already a biographer of figures as various as Elgar, Denton Welch and Edward Sackville-West, De-la-Noy had particular acquaintance with many of the events he described. He also had edited *Prism* and been a member of the House of Laity of the Church Assembly; but most importantly De-la-Noy had been Ramsey's press officer between 1967 and 1970. The book is well stocked with eye-witness testimony, and is supplemented with varied and useful interview evidence, including interviews with members of Ramsey's family, and from Ramsey himself. It is an opinionated and entertaining read, adding much in the way of colour which Chadwick tended to eschew.

De-la-Noy made no claim for the status of authorised biography for the book. Indeed it is called a Portrait rather than a Life, and the strengths of the

---

67 The phrase appears in the Authorised Version translation, at Hebrews 12:1.
68 Margaret Duggan, Runcie. *The making of an archbishop* (London, 1983)
69 Simpson, *Hundredth Archbishop*
70 Martin, *Great Christian Centuries*, pp.2, 7.
71 De-la-Noy, *Ramsey*.

book are also its weaknesses. De-la-Noy did not have access to the official papers at Lambeth, and makes limited and superficial use of easily accessible printed sources. As such, it depends heavily on the memories of interviewees, and is more dogmatic in its judgments than the sources ought to allow. It is also critical where *Great Christian Centuries* was not, representing the disappointment of radical hopes when viewed at a greater distance. De-la-Noy also left his position at Lambeth after some controversy, as documented in 1971 in his own *A Day in the Life of God*.[72] That earlier book is an indictment of the state of the established Church of England from a young radical Anglican, marred by a tendentious attempt to justify the manifest error of judgment on De-la-Noy's part that led to his dismissal. The copy in my possession is a pre-publication copy sent to the Ramseys, but despite this particular olive branch, Ramsey thought it a tragic shame that it should ever have been published. The later study, even with the Ramseys' co-operation, shows signs of old scores being settled; arguments lost with Ramsey in person being re-joined from a distance, but without full possession of the necessary information.

The other study of Ramsey to appear in 1990 is the one with which every student of Ramsey must reckon; *Michael Ramsey. A life* by Owen Chadwick. One would need to read the book carefully to notice (such is his self-effacement), but Chadwick was himself involved at the very centre of several of the events he describes. He had been part of the delegation that had accompanied Ramsey to Moscow in 1956.[73] He was a member of the commission on synodical government, and chairman of the influential commission on Church and State which reported in 1970.[74] Even less well-known was their contact over scholarly matters. Ramsey read and appreciated Chadwick's *The Victorian Church* when it appeared in 1966.[75] He also sought Chadwick's counsel upon the draft pamphlet *Image Old and New*, Ramsey's reply to John Robinson's *Honest to God*, which Chadwick gave in a state of 'doubt and difficulty'.[76] As with many others, Ramsey had had an effect at a more personal level. 'He was a warm man. He was very close to God' Chadwick wrote shortly after Ramsey's death. 'To be near him was to be near Someone above and beyond him.' It was Chadwick who preached at the memorial service for Ramsey in Westminster Abbey in June 1988.[77]

[72] De-la-Noy, *A Day in the Life of God*.
[73] Simpson, *Hundredth Archbishop*, p.148.
[74] Its report appeared as *Church and State* (London, 1970).
[75] Ramsey to Chadwick, 30 August 1966, at Ramsey Papers 94, f.299.
[76] Chadwick to Ramsey, 6 March 1963, at Ramsey Papers 50, ff.62–63.
[77] Stock, *Taking Stock*, pp.49, 56.

Of course there is room for more work on Ramsey. Naturally, Chadwick did not deal directly with the debates about secularisation and the 1960s that have since been prompted by the work of Callum Brown and others in recent years. He also tended to underplay the force and significance of conservative opinion, and particularly conservative evangelicalism. More prosaically, having been completed before the Ramsey Papers were catalogued, it has no references to the papers which a scholar could follow, and an inadequate index. That said, the debt that this current study owes to Chadwick will be evident on every page. But where Chadwick seeks to document, this study looks to interpret; and its burden is with the shape of the Church.

Chapter 1 starts where Ramsey himself began, with the relationships between the constituent parts of the Body of Christ, the different Christian denominations, both at home and abroad. As the Church of England moved closer to the other parts of the Anglican Communion, and the Communion towards other churches at the global level, so did the Church of England move closer to other churches in the United Kingdom. This movement was both prompted by and necessitated change in the relationship between the Church and the State in the UK, in the matter of the House of Lords, the crown appointments to Church offices, and more fundamentally. This renegotiation is the subject of Chapter 2.

That change was partly a recognition that Britain had changed since the constitutional arrangement of Church, State and law had been put in place. Chapter 3 deals with Ramsey's reaction to the radical series of reforming legislation in the matter of the moral law. Ramsey saw more clearly than many that the distinction between crime and sin needed to be clearer, if an increasing number of those subject to the law had ceased to recognise the category of sin at all. It was in the interest of both Church and State that the boundaries of their respective disciplines were clear.

But these changes were not made in an atmosphere of leisure. The long 1960s have been read as a time of simultaneous crises in multiple spheres of national and international affairs. Within the churches there was a mounting sense that the language of the Church, both in worship and in theology, was not being understood. Chapter 4 examines Ramsey's role in the revision of the Book of Common Prayer (the Church's worshipping language), and in the celebrated case of John A.T. Robinson, Bishop of Woolwich, and his *Honest to God* (1963). The sense of crisis was also to spread to the nation at large by the last years of Ramsey's office, and the chapter also considers his actions in relation to Northern Ireland, and the expectations that at least some of the public had of the archbishop as a national figurehead.

Archbishops of Canterbury had long had opportunities to speak truth to power; to speak prophetically against the powerful and in favour of the weak, both at home and abroad. Chapter 5 shows that this, in part, suited Ramsey's politics very well, but also that how that prophetic voice could be heard was changing as the shape of the Church changed. The Church of England needed to learn to sing the Lord's song in a strange land.

Chapter 1

The Church and the Churches

The Anglican Communion

Although the fact was not always central in the vision of many in England, the Church of England was part of a wider Communion of all the Anglican provinces worldwide. All of those provinces, in Africa, North America, Australasia, India, the Middle East and elsewhere, had come into being as a result of English missionary effort, but as the British Empire was gradually dismantled, the relationship between home country and colony was changing, as was the relationship between Canterbury and the churches to which it had given birth.[1]

Writing in 1974, John Howe, Secretary General of the Anglican Executive Council for the Communion, thought the situation in 1961 had been one made for a figure with Ramsey's gifts.[2] Fisher had overseen the process by which much direct jurisdiction over parts of the worldwide church had been repatriated to local churches, most particularly in Africa and Australia. Fisher had also overseen the appointment of Stephen Bayne as the first executive officer in 1959, giving the Communion the resources to maintain its life between Lambeth Conferences without dependence on the staff at Lambeth.[3] The chief structural change under Ramsey came about as a result of a resolution of the 1968 Lambeth Conference: the Anglican Consultative Council, the first global body for the Communion with a continuing nature, which first met in 1971.[4]

---

[1]   William L. Sachs, *The Transformation of Anglicanism. From State Church to Global Communion* (Cambridge, 1993), *passim*; W.M. Jacob, *The Making of the Anglican Church Worldwide* (London, 1997), *passim*.

[2]   John Howe, 'The future of the Anglican communion', in Martin (ed.), *Great Christian Centuries*, pp.113–34, at p.114.

[3]   Chandler and Hein, Fisher, pp.87–91; Stephen F. Bayne, *An Anglican Turning Point. Documents and Interpretations* (Austin, Texas, 1964), pp.3–20, and *passim*.

[4]   The ACC comprised clerical and lay representatives from around the whole Communion, and met every two years. On the formation and functions of the ACC, see John Howe and Colin Craston, *Anglicanism and the Universal Church* (revised edition, Toronto, 1990), pp.85–91.

The role of the archbishop had thus become less an executive one, and more personal; a change that suited Ramsey perfectly. As air travel became steadily more affordable, so the travels of twentieth century archbishops became more frequent and further in reach.[5] In his travel, Ramsey encountered the diversity of the Anglican Communion in its local contexts, a diversity which Anglicans in England were apt to overlook, and so while his relations with the worldwide Communion are not treated in depth here, Ramsey's actions were always and everywhere conditioned by his awareness of the churches as a worldwide fellowship.

Many Anglicans overseas also found Ramsey a fortifying presence. The papers relating to his travels show intense interest from the media, but also from the crowds who came to meet him, as he preached, lectured and visited. Ramsey's staff had to fight hard to keep sufficient space in packed itineraries for an elderly man to rest between engagements, but the appetite for him was insatiable and the disappointment at any cancellation acute.[6] When in England, Ramsey's correspondence was full of news, good wishes and requests for counsel on each and every issue, to which Ramsey was assiduous in response.

The sense of crisis in domestic Christianity which will be explored in Chapter 4 had its parallels worldwide.[7] Howe tried to describe why Ramsey, through his travel and his writings, was an important steadying influence. For Howe, Ramsey's stature as a theologian before he was a bishop was a reassurance in itself. But as well as that, Ramsey was crucial in showing which were 'the things that are not shaken' (his own words, from *Canterbury Pilgrim*) whilst not pretending that all was well and that nothing need change. For Howe, Ramsey had 'shown, amongst things new and old, what is sand and what is rock.'[8] The theologian John Macquarrie thought Ramsey's greatest achievement to have been his general theological stance, in a time of bewilderment amid rapidly changing theological fashion: a stance open to new ideas, but at the same time 'profoundly attached to and respectful towards the tradition.'[9]

There was still some work left over after Fisher in the creation of independent churches within the Anglican Communion, and removing the last vestiges of control from Lambeth. One such situation was Jerusalem, where the Englishman George Appleton was archbishop of an diocese surrounded on all sides by the

---

[5]   Chadwick, *Ramsey*, pp.401–403.

[6]   Chadwick, *Ramsey*, pp.209–210.

[7]   For an overview, see Jeremy Morris, *The Church in the Modern Age*, (London, 2007), pp.73–136.

[8]   Howe, 'Future of the Anglican Communion', p.123.

[9]   John Macquarrie, 'Whither Theology?' in Martin, *Great Christian Centuries*, p.157.

mainly Arab diocese that included Palestine, the Lebanon and Syria. Ramsey sent the trusted and recently retired Bishop of London, Robert Stopford, to arrange for the absorption of Jerusalem into the bigger see.[10] Not without difficulty did he also give independence to the Anglican dioceses in South America in 1974, including the Falkland Islands.[11]

Ramsey did not relish large gatherings such as the Lambeth Conference, the World Council of Churches or the General Synod; there was little room for the kind of debate that was possible in the House of Lords or the Cambridge Union, or the personal connection possible with a gathering in a small room.[12] But he knew that the Conference, which it was his turn to host in 1968, was important to the Anglican Communion, even if he intervened little from the chair. Important was the extent to which it was a conference focussed on theology. Ramsey took up a suggestion made to Fisher for 1958, but rejected, that the agenda in part be set by theologians, as seen in the three volumes of preparatory essays.[13] Also present was a small army of observers from other churches, including many friends from ecumenical work in England and abroad.[14] As so often elsewhere, Ramsey's real impact at the 1968 Conference was in its atmosphere, created by the Ramseys' hospitality and the times of reflection he led. One bishop thought it 'more truly religious' than Fisher's conference of 1958.[15]

To what extent was Ramsey the first post-colonial archbishop? That is to say: was his idea of the Anglican Communion one of a fellowship of sister churches of equal stature? Or was the vision still a paternalistic one – of children newly given independence in name, but remaining under the sway of Lambeth in fact? As we shall see, Ramsey's background was a preservative against a reflex Anglican superiority in relation to the other churches; and there are parallels in his instincts in relation to churches overseas. Although he had disliked the meeting of the WCC at Evanston in 1954, he had come away already convinced of the growing into leadership of African and Asian churches. Those churches certainly needed resources and technical expertise from the West, as did their countries at large. 'But neither the Churches nor the countries will suffer

[10] Chadwick, *Ramsey*, pp.223–24.
[11] Chadwick, *Ramsey*, pp.233–34.
[12] See his reflections on the 1954 meeting of the WCC at Evanston, Illinois, at 'Evanston', in *Durham Essays and Addresses*, pp.81–82.
[13] *Lambeth Essays on Ministry*, *Lambeth Essays on Faith*, and *Lambeth Essays on Unity*, all published the following year by SPCK; W.M. Jacob, *The Making of the Anglican Church Worldwide* (London, 1997), pp.284–85.
[14] See the list in *The Lambeth Conference 1968. Resolutions and Reports* (London, 1968), pp.151–54.
[15] Chadwick, *Ramsey*, pp.274–76. The words are those of Chadwick.

Western domination: they are rising to adult stature, they are the teachers and we are the learners.'[16]

Ramsey went to Evanston in 1954 when only a diocesan bishop. Under greater pressure as archbishop, did this sense of the worldwide communion influence decision-making in London and Canterbury? As we shall see, Ramsey took considerable personal trouble in order that it be abundantly clear that the Anglican-Roman Catholic conversations that were taking place were between Rome and *worldwide* Anglicanism, and not with the Church of England, as the Roman Catholic bishops in England were apt to think. In 1971 he sought, as far as he was able, to restrain Gilbert Baker, Bishop of Hong Kong, from ordaining women to the priesthood, as Ramsey was concerned that the whole Anglican Communion had not yet reported on the issue as the Lambeth Conference had requested, and because of the likely impact on ecumenical progress.[17] The papers at Lambeth are also replete with correspondence with the archbishops with regard to matters in England. In the wake of the first negative vote on the Anglican-Methodist unity scheme (of which more below), the papers contain news from Cape Town to Cardiff of concern over the impact on local co-operation with Methodists; Ramsey told the English bishops of 'deep grief and bewilderment' at the vote throughout the Communion.[18]

It may be that some of this may be described as information-as-consultation, rather than a more collegial engagement. That said, it is hard to see what better mechanisms were available to achieve such an end, with a Lambeth conference only every decade, a tiny central staff and the Anglican Consultative Council only from 1971. Even then, although he had enjoyed the ACC's first meeting at Limuru in Kenya, Ramsey came to view the Council as no substitute for a regular meeting of all the archbishops, which had been the function of the Lambeth Consultative Body which it had succeeded, and which meetings were reinstated in 1979.[19]

To the contemporary reader, it is hard to see the optimism of Fisher's later years other than through the prism of the travails of the Communion in the early twenty-first century. There was a feeling that, with the right machinery, the Communion could not only survive in radically changed circumstances,

---

[16] 'Evanston', in *Durham Essays and Addresses*, p.83.

[17] Chadwick, *Ramsey*, p.281.

[18] Archbishop of Wales to Ramsey, 26 Nov 1969, at Ramsey Papers 167, f.93; copy of Archbishop of Cape Town to John Howe, probably from July 1969, at Ramsey Papers 166, f.269; minutes of Bishops' Meeting, 25 July 1969, at Ramsey Papers 166, f.286.

[19] Chadwick, *Ramsey*, p.277–78; Howe and Craston, *Anglicanism and the Universal Church*, pp.92–93.

but take on a 'greater and perhaps more dangerous responsibility' to meet the problems of the world.[20] In retrospect, such optimism did not, and could not, have reckoned with the cross-currents of liberalism in ethics in the Anglo-Saxon branches of the Communion, and greater conservatism elsewhere.

Did Ramsey hasten the rupture by his support for the liberalisation of the moral law in England, described in Chapter 3? It may be that, had Ramsey consulted more widely as the reforms proceeded through Parliament, he may have more clearly seen the possible worldwide ramifications of the apparent support of the Archbishop of Canterbury for what some saw as the legalisation of sin. But Ramsey would not have accepted that the changes altered the moral discipline of the church one iota, and the reports and resolutions of Lambeth 1968 are wholly conservative when dealing with moral issues.[21] The decriminalisation of male homosexuality in England undoubtedly created the space in which a liberal Christian understanding of gayness could be developed, but in Ramsey's time conservative Anglican evangelicals were not yet as strong or as interconnected as they would become, nor as exercised by the change in the moral law.[22] It would be hard indeed to tax Ramsey with responsibility for the consequences for Anglican unity four decades later.

Orthodoxy

To the majority in England, the oldest and most fundamental division in Christendom was the least visible. Ecumenical effort with Roman Catholics and with the Nonconformist churches was conditioned by the presence of those separated brethren in every town and many villages. Of the churches of the east, most Anglicans knew little, and the Orthodox churches in England were few. As such, there were no domestic schemes of union between Orthodoxy and the Church of England to match the Anglican-Methodist unity scheme, and no international event to match the second Vatican Council. The mass of the Orthodox remained distant, both in space and in mind, many of them trapped behind an impenetrable iron curtain.

---

[20]   The words of the committee of the Lambeth Conference 1958 on overseas missions, known as the Gray Committee, as quoted by Bayne, *An Anglican Turning Point*, p.12.

[21]   *The Lambeth Conference 1968. Resolutions and Reports*, p.37, on marriage.

[22]   Matthew Grimley, 'Anglican Evangelicals and Anti-Permissiveness: The Nationwide Festival of Light, 1971-1983' in Atherstone and Maiden, *Evangelicalism and the Church of England*, pp.183-205.

To be sure, there were exceptions within the Church of England. Anglican orders had been formally recognised by the autocephalous churches of Greece and the Middle East after 1922, and there had been Orthodox representation at the Lambeth Conference of 1930. Within the Church of England, both the Anglican and Eastern Churches Association and the Fellowship of St Alban and St Sergius worked to foster contact and understanding. But that there was much work still to do was evident from a relatively unremarked work of Ramsey's, published in 1946, in which he asked the reader to 'hearken to the less familiar cause of unity with the East'.[23]

This particular essay, *The Church of England and the Eastern Orthodox Church. Why their unity is important,* rewards some extended consideration, since it indicates much about Ramsey's vision of the whole ecumenical cause. English readers were familiar with divisions between Anglican and Roman, and between church and chapel; but few felt the tragedy of the initial schism in which 'the seamless robe of Christ received its greatest rent.' All the churches of the West thus inherited a 'maimed Christendom' without true wholeness, which brought 'a thwarting of the inward life.'[24] Latin Christendom had lost sight of crucial balancing elements in Eastern theology, necessary for a truly catholic understanding; the moralistic and legalistic had overwhelmed the mystical and metaphysical. Church history since the schism had as a result been marked by successive imbalanced, lopsided presentations of Christianity in reaction to each other: Luther reacting to medieval Catholicism, Methodism coming into being as a reaction to the eighteenth century Church of England. The Schism had thus been 'the parent tragedy of many later tragedies of Christian division.'[25]

What was to be done about it? The 1947 report *Catholicity*, of which Ramsey was the principal author, argued that all of the churches of East and West would need to go beneath and beyond their own understandings of the nature of the church, bent out of shape as it was by the schisms that had brought the separate churches into being. Unity could not be achieved by a mere 'fitting-together of broken pieces, but must spring from a vital growth towards a genuine wholeness or catholicity of faith, thought and life.'[26]

There was of course already in 1948 a growing impetus in England towards unity between the Protestant churches, the outworking of which in Ramsey's time at Canterbury is examined below. Ramsey saw danger in this movement,

---

[23]   *The Church of England and the Eastern Orthodox Church. Why their unity is important* (London, 1946). It was published for the Fellowship of Saints Alban and Sergius.

[24]   *The Church of England and the Eastern Orthodox Church*, pp.5–6.

[25]   *The Church of England and the Eastern Orthodox Church*, p.4.

[26]   *Catholicity*, p.10.

since unity on a pan-Protestant basis would most likely make a wider unity impossible. National movements for union held similar dangers if they proceeded without reference to the churches overseas. Ramsey thought that it would be 'disastrous if it were a unity in terms of a sort of "national Christianity" representing the lowest common measure of English religious sentiment'. The unity of English Christians 'must be the expression in this land of the One, Holy, Catholic and Apostolic Church in its richness. This richness cannot be realised so long as East and West are separate. The quest for unity at home must go hand in hand with the quest for unity far beyond home.'[27] And the Church of England was uniquely placed to act as a bridge between East and West, Protestant, Catholic and Orthodox. By recovering 'the ideal of non-papal catholicity she looked instinctively to a Catholicism which embraces both East and West.' The Church of England could 'point beyond the controversies of the West to that truer and earlier catholicity whereof the entire West is never more than a part.'[28] As we shall see, few in England were able to see the matter from so wide a perspective.

The World Council of Churches

The movement towards pan-Protestant unity at home had its global counterpart in the World Council of Churches (WCC). Ramsey had been a consultant to the first post-war meeting of the WCC at Amsterdam in 1948, and so was not new to its workings when he became one of its presidents in 1961. After returning from the assembly at New Delhi as president, he had an opportunity, at a meeting organised by the British Council of Churches, to reflect on its development.[29] At Amsterdam it had not clearly known its own purpose. At Evanston in 1954 there had been a greater sense of its purpose, but for Ramsey that purpose had been too Western, and too much concerned with pan-Protestant unity. New Delhi had seen a greater influx of the Orthodox churches, and Roman Catholic observers, both of which had been missing at Amsterdam. Most importantly, the goal had become for Ramsey the correct one: anything that stopped short of organic unity between the churches was not enough. At Evanston, many in

---

[27]   *The Church of England and the Eastern Orthodox Church*, pp.13–14.

[28]   *The Church of England and the Eastern Orthodox Church*, p.7

[29]   Typescript address to meeting at Westminster Central Hall, 11 January 1962, at Ramsey Papers 12, ff.299–304.

the Council had seen it as 'a sort of super-church or Protestant Vatican'[30]; in its maturity it had realised its true role, as the servant.

As we have seen, Ramsey disliked the large conference format that the Council's assemblies took, and doubted its usefulness as a means of dealing with complex issues.[31] But he did value the more informal contacts that were made in the interstices of such events. His press officer thought him at his most relaxed at these meetings, at which he could mingle without emphasis on his rank. He refused an official car at Uppsala in 1968 for fear of appearing the great archbishop among churches that had no bishops at all.[32] He came back from Evanston conscious of what such free intercourse between Christians of diverse backgrounds could achieve.[33]

On being elected president of the WCC, Ramsey had been disinclined to take much lead in the administration of the Council, but was keen to help shape the theological agenda.[34] This balance is borne out by the papers at Lambeth, and Ramsey was at times criticised for not involving himself more in the work of the Council's committees.[35] Ramsey's preferred approach is more clearly seen in his visit to the WCC in Geneva, on his way back from Rome in March 1966. Ramsey visited the Council's secretary general Visser 't Hooft in the Council's new headquarters building, and discussed the interaction between Anglican dialogue with Rome and that between Geneva and Rome. Although the press thought the visit a mere addendum to the larger business of meeting the Pope, 't Hooft thought it of real significance. Ramsey's words preached in Holy Trinity, the English church in the city, had found a 'very strong echo' and had been a great encouragement.[36] For his part, Ramsey was grateful to 't Hooft, who was soon to retire after nearly three decades as secretary general, for 'understanding that though I am a very bad Committee man my heart is strongly with you.'[37]

---

[30]   'Evanston' in *Durham Essays and Addresses*, p.84.
[31]   'Evanston', pp.81–82.
[32]   De-la-Noy, *Ramsey*, pp.149–50; Chadwick, *Ramsey*, p.85.
[33]   'Evanston', p.83.
[34]   Chadwick, *Ramsey*, p.400.
[35]   Herbert Waddams to Ramsey, 21 June 1965, at Ramsey Papers 90, ff.22–23, and reply following.
[36]   Visser t'Hooft to Ramsey, 6 April 1966, at Ramsey Papers 106, f.219.
[37]   Ramsey to t'Hooft, 28 March 1966, at Ramsey Papers 106, f.218.

Rome

The Church of England was born of a rejection of the authority of the church of Rome. As such the Roman Catholic church had been throughout Anglican history the reference point by which much of Anglican identity had been triangulated; and it was a history freighted with political intrigue, civil disability and martyrdom. As the political and social heat gradually went out of Catholic-Protestant relations in the twentieth century, those Anglicans who looked most readily towards Rome as a necessary partner in the project of Christian unity had some occasions of hope. The Malines Conversations of 1922–26 hinted at channels through which a genuine theological conversation might be conducted. The joint letter of Archbishop William Temple and Cardinal Hinsley to *The Times* in December 1940 seemed to suggest that a united voice in economic, social and political concern was achievable.[38]

After the crisis of the war years, however, though informal contacts continued, the Roman Catholic Church remained the single and largest missing piece in the official ecumenical jigsaw, not least at the WCC. In the eyes of some, two events in 1959–60 seemed to signal real and significant change. In December 1960 Geoffrey Fisher, on his return from visits to Jerusalem and Istanbul, met with the Pope in Rome; the first such meeting since the sixteenth century. The visit was made in the context of great anticipation of the event that was to become known as the Second Vatican Council, which had been called in 1959 by Pope John XXIII.[39]

Such was the context when Ramsey arrived at Lambeth. If his predecessor had been closely identified with the cause of unity with the Free Churches in Britain, Ramsey was much more clearly known as part of the catholic wing of the Church of England. The closeness to his heart of the ultimate goal of union with Rome was poignantly demonstrated at his death in 1988 with, on his finger, a ring given him by Pope Paul VI.[40] He was however never persuaded by the Anglo-Papalist position of a minority within the Church of England, to whom the only significant obstacle to immediate reunion was the Papal denial of the validity of Anglican orders.[41] Ramsey knew that the issue of Anglican

---

[38] For a survey of Anglican-Roman Catholic relations, see Bernard and Margaret Pawley, *Rome and Canterbury Through Four Centuries* (London, 1974).

[39] On the significance of these two events, see Bernard Pawley, *An Anglican View of the Vatican Council* (New York, 1962), pp.6–8.

[40] Chadwick, *Ramsey*, p.399.

[41] Pawley and Pawley, *Rome and Canterbury*, pp.250–51.

orders, whilst an obstacle, was the wrong point at which to start; the issues were much wider and deeper.

Despite Ramsey's clear-sighted view of the imperfections of the Roman church and the very real difficulties in achieving union with it, the perception that his sympathies lay on the catholic side made it necessary to proceed warily in what was still a combustible polemical climate. Whilst the emotions that catalysed the Prayer Book Crisis of 1927–28 had abated, when Ramsey came to Lambeth there was still some sensitivity in the Protestant nation at large to any suggestion of 'Romanisation' in the Church of England. There was tension generated by even the most seemingly innocuous changes in the canon law of the church in relation to clerical dress and the communion table in 1963–64. As late as 1968 Ramsey, along with all the bishops, was petitioned by the fringe Protestant Truth Society against too close an involvement with a Roman church that, whilst it might have changed its mode of presentation, had not shifted an inch in fundamentals.[42] As in most things, the Archbishop of Canterbury was required to maintain a precarious balance of appearances.

It was also the case that, even amongst those English men and women who did not concern themselves with the theological difficulties, the public image of Rome was freighted with associations of intellectual philistinism and political partiality. Both Oxford and Cambridge universities had in recent years debated Rome's apparent enslavement of the intellect to arbitrary authority; and one sympathetic observer urged the Fathers of the Vatican Council to be mindful of the effect of episodes such as the arrests of Protestants in Franco's Spain for the import of "subversive" copies of the Gospels.[43] Finally, the Vatican itself also remained a political entity as well as a religious one; a state of affairs with its own purchase in public opinion.

Ramsey was then faced with the task of handling both private and public relations between Lambeth and Rome, and also between Lambeth and the archbishops of Westminster, in such a way that encouraged moves towards unity without either undue public protest or compromise on matters of genuine difference. There were a series of positive public affirmations. After some initial consultation in private with Mgr. Jan Willebrands, secretary of the Vatican's Secretariat for the Promotion of Unity among Christians, a team of Anglican observers, nominated from Lambeth, were invited to attend the session of the

---

[42]   Peter Webster and John Maiden, 'Parliament, the Church of England and the last gasp of political Protestantism, 1963–4', *Parliamentary History* 32:2 (2013), 361–77; *To the Bishops of the Church of England. A Memorandum on Ecumenism from the Protestant Truth Society*. [no date], at Ramsey Papers 141 ff.111–12.

[43]   Pawley, *An Anglican View*, pp.107–108.

Second Vatican Council; an invitation of the greatest symbolic importance.[44] Cardinal Augustin Bea, president of the Secretariat for Unity, later reflected that they had 'helped to create a better understanding and deeper esteem between brothers in Christ', and had been able to suggest ideas and so to a limited extent had influenced the Council.[45]

John XXIII died in June 1963, in the midst of the Council that he called. Unable to attend the funeral, Ramsey issued a heartfelt statement on the 'passing of a great Christian leader [who by the] freshness of his vision, the simplicity of his devotion to God and his concern for the unity of all Christians [had had] a creative impact upon the story of our times.'[46] On 17 June Ramsey held, in private at Lambeth Palace, what was described as a 'Requiem celebration of the Holy Communion' for the late Pope. This brought forward strongly worded protests from a widely representative group of evangelical and Protestant voices both within and outside the Church of England, despite Ramsey's protestation that the service was in line with the Book of Common Prayer with only the slightest deviations.[47] Ramsey's sermon spoke only of commending the late Pope to God, and gave thanks for his life, whilst expressing grief 'that as today's liturgy here reminds us we are not yet one in the eucharistic feast.'[48]

Ramsey's address at that service is suffused with the quiet fervency of his hopes for eventual unity with Rome. Perhaps the single most symbolic expression of those hopes was his visit in March 1966 to Rome, and the meeting with John XXIII's successor, Paul VI. Once again, the visit attracted Protestant opposition, including the spectacular gesture by the Ulster Protestant Ian Paisley of invading Ramsey's plane.[49] The visit has been described at length by Owen Chadwick, and need not be elaborated here; but the symbolic effect of the meeting in the Sistine Chapel and the gift from Pope to Archbishop of a ring needs to be reckoned.[50] Chadwick stressed the important effect of the personal warmth between the two men; a fact borne out by the subsequent and regular correspondence between them. The visit had a great effect in encouraging the catholic wing of the Church,

44   The correspondence is at Ramsey Papers 26, ff.137–62.
45   Bea to Ramsey, 14 December 1962, Ramsey Papers 26:140.
46   TS statement, at Ramsey Papers 46, f.238.
47   The correspondence is at Ramsey Papers 46, ff.241–67, 276–307; see also *The Times* 10 June 1963, p.23. Chadwick rather underplays the volume and representative nature of the objections; Chadwick, *Ramsey*, p.316.
48   Typescript address at Ramsey Papers, 46, ff.270.
49   Chadwick, *Ramsey*, pp.318–19.
50   Chadwick, *Ramsey*, pp.319–23.

and in cementing Ramsey's reputation amongst Protestants as leaning further towards Rome than in the other direction.

Aside from the very public displays of increasing understanding, Ramsey, as with so many things, was also assiduous in private in the cultivation of improving relationships. Among the visitors at Lambeth were the Czech cardinal Josef Beran in November 1966; and the theological friendship with Cardinal Suenens of Malines-Brussels was to issue in the jointly written *The Future of the Christian Church* of 1970.[51] There were warm relationships and regular contact with the Roman diplomats charged with managing the Anglican-Roman relationship. Ramsey regularly received Willebrands at Lambeth, although without fanfare. Cardinal Bea was also a visitor to Lambeth, as was the Apostolic Delegate to London, Igino Cardinale.[52]

The evident ease with which Ramsey was able to communicate directly with the Vatican had a less positive effect on the often uneasy working relationship with the English Catholic bishops. As the events at the Council progressed, Anglican insiders came to perceive a marked disparity between, on the one hand, the positive atmosphere in Rome and in the relationship with Bea and, on the other, some apparent intransigence amongst the English hierarchy.[53] The theoretical freedom of Bea from any need to refer to the English bishops while dealing with Lambeth was not easy to justify, and John, Cardinal Heenan later recalled some suspicion of the relationship amongst the English bishops. Some suspected a private agreement between Bea and Ramsey to delay the progress of the canonisation of the English Roman Catholic martyrs in the cause of unity (of which more below). Heenan had felt some personal embarrassment that Bea had not been accommodated by Cardinal Godfrey at Westminster when in England in 1962, largely because of Bea's insistence on visiting Ramsey at Lambeth.[54]

The relationship between Ramsey and Heenan is worth pausing over, as it illustrates the pressures under which both men laboured whilst attempting to hold together very different shades of opinion within their churches. Chadwick suggested that Ramsey suspected Heenan of lukewarmness towards ecumenical

---

[51]   On Beran, see the correspondence of November 1966 at Ramsey Papers 107, ff.96–97; *The Future of the Christian Church* (London, 1971), *passim*.

[52]   Memorandum of Bea's visit to Lambeth in August 1962 at Ramsey Papers 26, ff.123–25; Chadwick, *Ramsey*, p.315.

[53]   See the correspondence between Ramsey and Eric Mascall at Ramsey Papers 103, ff.107–120.

[54]   Heenan, *A Crown of Thorns. An autobiography 1951–1963* (London, 1974), pp.325–26.

endeavour; of being comfortable with 'the old certainties' and nervous of change.[55] Although partly justified by some of Heenan's reactions to the pressures from the radical wing of his own church after the Council, this view downplays the pressure on Heenan not to make concessions to the old enemy, and his genuine commitment to ecumenical progress.[56] Although the relationship between the two men was always cordial, and developed genuine warmth over time, Ramsey was under no illusions about the diplomatic realities of the three-cornered relationship between Rome, Canterbury and Westminster. Ramsey took pains to make sure that relations with Rome were visibly a global matter - a meeting between the Pope and representatives of the Anglican Communion - and not a playing-out of English domestic ecumenism on foreign fields. Arrangements for his visit to the Pope were made directly with Rome, with Ramsey making sure that he was visibly quartered at the English College as a guest of Paul VI, rather than at the hospitality of the English hierarchy.[57] The new Commission on Anglican-Roman Catholic Relations, set up in 1964 to take advantage of the momentum created by the Council, was explicitly a visible means of carving out a space for direct progress with Rome; it was important 'that the Roman Catholic hierarchy in England does not take control of these matters on their own terms'.[58]

Ramsey felt the significance of the visit to Rome very deeply; it was with 'longing in my heart' that he addressed the Pope in the Sistine Chapel. However, he was careful not to downplay the considerable difficulties that remained. 'On the road to unity' Ramsey saw 'formidable difficulties of doctrine' as well as practical matters 'about which the consciences and feelings of Christian people can be hurt.'[59] Not least to retain the confidence of all wings of the Church of England, Ramsey was ready to speak frankly in public when the occasion demanded. One of these occasions was the 1970 canonisation of the English Martyrs.

Recent work by Andrew Atherstone has explored the ecumenical significance of the campaign to canonise 40 English and Welsh Roman Catholics martyred

---

[55]   Chadwick, *Ramsey*, pp.328–29.

[56]   Heenan, *Crown of Thorns* pp.326–28; Heenan (ed.), *Christian Unity: A Catholic View* (London, 1962).

[57]   See the note of a meeting with the Apostolic Delegate, January 1966, at Ramsey Papers 106, ff.97–100.

[58]   Ramsey to David Paton, 3 January 1964, at Ramsey Papers 65, f.124.

[59]   As reported in *The Times* 24 March 1966, p.12.

during the sixteenth and seventeenth centuries.[60] The cause, begun in the nineteenth century, had been revived in 1960 and reached its culmination in Rome in October 1970. Atherstone rightly emphasises the dilemma presented by a renewal of an older mode of English Roman Catholic self-assertion in an unprecedented ecumenical climate. Ramsey had attempted in private to dissuade the English Jesuits of Farm Street in London from pressing the cause of 'controversial canonisations' from the outset,[61] and was to continue to oppose the move, in private and then in public.[62] Ramsey was sure that Anglicans ought to be asking whether there were not exemplars of Catholic devotion from whom they might learn. Growth together in the communion of saints was possible, desirable, and already happening elsewhere; but now was not a propitious time to be raising these individuals in particular, in England. In both the 'ultra-Protestant' and in some Roman Catholics, there was yet a 'polemical self-consciousness' that made an open reception of the ecumenical significance of these individuals impossible. Amongst some English Catholics, at least, there was a 'siege mentality' which was 'bound up psychologically with a persecution and martyrdom complex deeply rooted in history.'[63] Ramsey feared precisely the kind of Protestant agitation that did in fact accompany the canonisation when it came.

It of course suited those who were opposed to closer relations with the Vatican to portray Ramsey as a dupe or a poodle; one Baptist minister thought the visit to Rome a propaganda victory for the Pope, and Ramsey a nervous schoolboy before his master.[64] However, an examination of Ramsey's diplomacy in private shows a clear-sighted appreciation of the real barriers to progress towards unity, and a willingness to address them vigorously. One such area was the status of the Vatican in international diplomacy. On more than one occasion, the question was raised of increasing the diplomatic relationship between the British government and the Vatican to that of full embassy status, in both London and Rome. Ramsey was very clear that the passions generated by such a move would be harmful to the significant progress being made in relations between the churches, and in securing the safe passage of church Measures

[60]   'The canonisation of the Forty English Martyrs: an ecumenical dilemma', *Recusant History* 30 (2011): pp.573–87.

[61]   At a private dinner of November 1962, as reported by Philip Caraman, S.J., one of the vice-postulators of the cause; Atherstone, 'Ecumenical dilemma', p.577.

[62]   Ramsey contributed to the Roman Catholic newspaper *The Tablet* on 29 November 1969, as cited by Atherstone, 'Ecumenical dilemma', p.579.

[63]   Ramsey to Philip Walsh, S.J., 28 June 1966, Ramsey Papers 107, ff.12–13.

[64]   Revd. Percy Nuttall to Ramsey, 24 Mar 1966, Ramsey Papers 106, f.267.

through Parliament. On this basis, Ramsey advised prime ministers Macmillan and Wilson against it, against the view of the Foreign Office, but not without tacit support from Rome itself.[65]

Ramsey was also active in private to press the Anglican case in relation to several vexed issues: chief among them the questions of Anglican orders and of 'mixed marriages'. Ramsey was sure that the problem of the decision of the aged Pope Leo XIII to declare Anglican orders 'absolutely null and utterly void' was not the best issue on which to lead. However, it loomed large in the minds of many Catholics within the Church of England, and Ramsey kept in close touch with Bernard Pawley, observer of the Vatican Council, as to whether and when approaches might profitably be made.[66] However, perhaps the single most pressing issue in day-to-day local relations in England was that of the Roman policy towards marriages between Catholics and other Christians: the so-called 'mixed marriage'.

Considerable bitterness had been attendant over the years on the enforcement of Roman discipline in relation to marriage. Roman Catholics had on occasion been excommunicated for being married in an Anglican church, and were sometimes described as 'living in sin' if they did. Anglicans opting to marry in a Catholic church were required to make very specific promises about the raising of children as Roman Catholics. Ramsey recognised these matters as very great barriers to improved relations, and with Heenan's qualified support, pressed both upon the Pope during their private meeting in 1966.[67] A new Instruction appeared from Rome soon afterwards, which gave some ground; but Ramsey and Paul VI agreed that Ramsey might hope in public that the Instruction was not the last word, and that appeals could be made to Rome. The situation remained tense after the very public affair of the wedding of the daughter of John Phillips, Anglican Bishop of Portsmouth, in a Catholic ceremony at which Phillips was permitted to play no part.[68] However, October 1967 saw the beginnings of relaxation of the tension with the institution of a theological Sub-Commission

---

[65] Ramsey to Macmillan, 15 March 1963, Ramsey Papers 46, f.192; Ramsey to Wilson, 18 June 1965, Ramsey Papers 86, ff.340–41; Council for Foreign Relations memorandum, 9 November 1965, Ramsey Papers 86 ff.354–45.

[66] See the exchange of September-October 1963 between Ramsey and Pawley at Ramsey Papers 46, ff.328–33.

[67] Note of meeting at Ramsey Papers 106, ff.147–52.

[68] *The Times* 29 June 1966, p.12; see also the correspondence at Ramsey Papers 103, ff.1–15.

to consider the matter.[69] Further relaxation was to come from Rome in 1970, in the shape of the apostolic letter, *Matrimonia Mixta*.

In all these various aspects of the Anglican-Roman Catholic relationship, Ramsey had needed to perform a balancing act of the greatest delicacy. Personally and emotionally committed to the ideal of unity with Rome, he knew that many in his own church, the other churches in Britain, and the nation at large, found such a prospect alarming. In public and private, he was encouraging and cautious by turns as the particular matter and the context demanded. And after 13 years, and a significant weakening of the anti-Catholic reflex of the English, Anglican and Roman churches both in England and globally were a good deal closer than they had been when Ramsey arrived at Lambeth.

Intercommunion

One of the solid achievements of the ecumenical movement had been the recognition of unity, albeit limited, between Christians of all the mainline churches by reason of their common baptism. To be sure, there were occasional incidents of rebaptism by Roman Catholic clergy of converts from the Protestant denominations; but Paul VI had assured Ramsey in Rome that this was not the policy of the post-conciliar Vatican.[70] There remained, however, a single massive obstacle: the sharing of the Eucharist. In all the proliferating local ecumenical initiatives, and national and international conferences, sooner or later there loomed the impossibility of shared communion. As the 1968 report of the commission set up by the archbishops to consider the issue put it, 'the eucharist, given to unite us to God and to each other, has become the place at which we are most conscious of our divisions.'[71]

The Anglican Church was already in full communion with several churches overseas, allowing members of each to communicate in the other as a matter of course, and for the interchange of ministers. It was at home, however, that the barrier was most keenly felt. No clearly defined relationship existed between the Church of England and the Free Churches for such fellowship; and certainly none with the Catholic Church. And opinion was sharply divided as to what, if anything, should be done about the issue. For many Anglo-Catholics, as represented by the Church Union, no such intercommunion could

[69]   CIO press release, 20 October 1967, at Ramsey Papers 118, f.31.
[70]   Typescript note of Ramsey's meeting with the Pope, at Ramsey Papers 106, ff.147–52.
[71]   *Intercommunion To-day: being the Report of the Archbishops' Commission on Intercommunion* (London, 1968), p.3

be contemplated with churches whose minsters had not been ordained by a bishop of the historic episcopate. For them, intercommunion was consequent on unity: get the ordering of the ministry right, and unity in the sacrament would follow. For others, including many enthusiasts for unity, this put the cart before the horse. Surely (went the argument) greater sharing of the sacrament (with some limitations) would foster the unity of spirit that would eventually issue in the organic union of the institutions. Every opportunity for deliberate intercommunion ought to be seized as a means to unity.[72]

Within the framework of the church's law and custom, there was room to create such opportunities. In 1933 the Convocations of Canterbury and York had made regulations to allow Christians separated by distance from their own services to communicate in the Anglican church; but it also allowed occasional hospitality at the communion table in services 'definitely intended to promote the visible unity of the Church of Christ', at the discretion of the local bishop.[73] At the 1961 meeting of the World Council of Churches in New Delhi, Ramsey himself had received communion in just such a service under the 1933 regulations, although without being the celebrant.[74]

The issue pulled Ramsey in two directions. He had experienced at first hand the power of shared fellowship as a solvent of the barriers of heart and mind that perpetuated division, and none could accuse him of a lack of commitment to the goal of union. At the same time, Ramsey felt the importance of order. Unity was fundamentally an objective matter of church order, and the emotional effect of inter-denominational fellowship could carry one only so far. Writing to a bishop from the United States, who had welcomed the fact that Ramsey had stood slightly apart from the open communion service in New Delhi, Ramsey was sure that 'general intercommunion must wait until real unity is being brought about on the true principles in which we believe.'[75] Until that time, it needed to be infrequent, and carefully ordered. This was important not only in principle. Ramsey well knew that the longer-term cause of reunion would be damaged amongst Anglo-Catholics if the pace of change was too fast, as his correspondence clearly showed. As we shall see, he was to be proved right.

For the first years of his time at Lambeth, Ramsey was helped by the 1933 regulations, in that they provided room for experimentation within clear limits.

---

[72]   *Intercommunion To-day*, pp.46–63.

[73]   H. Riley and R.J. Graham (eds), *Acts of the Convocations of Canterbury and York 1921–1970* (London, 1971), p.157.

[74]   Ramsey to W.P. Shortland, 15 January 1962, Ramsey Papers 22, f.15.

[75]   Ramsey to Edward R. Welles (bishop of West Missouri), 19 December 1961, Ramsey Papers 8, f.208.

The early years saw a steady trickle of requests for advice about ecumenical events both at home and abroad, which were handled case-by-case without undue contention, but not entirely. An open communion service at a youth conference in Leicester in 1962 provoked a public statement of opposition from the Church Union, thinking the service an offence to the convictions of many and damaging to the cause of unity.[76]

Pressure came not only from the Anglo-Catholic wing of the church, however. All Saints' Day 1961 saw the publication of an open letter, signed by 32 influential theologians, arguing for much greater openness. The letter caused consternation both in England and amongst Anglicans elsewhere. Ramsey's great friend, the theologian E.L. Mascall, was concerned that a letter signed by such an influential group might be thought to be the settled view of the Church of England, rather than simply one side of a contested debate.[77] Others reported simple confusion and distress, particularly amongst theologically-minded students.[78] Ramsey's response, the only realistic one available to him, was not to respond publicly. The church needed a process by which a common mind may be reached, and he privately regretted that the open letter hindered that process.[79]

For many evangelicals, however, there was no such confusion. Such an extension of regular Eucharistic hospitality to members of the other Protestant churches did nothing but regularise a right already claimed by many, in principle and in fact. The rubric in the Book of Common Prayer at the end of the Order of Confirmation stated that 'there shall none be admitted to the holy Communion, until such time as he be confirmed, or be ready and desirous to be confirmed'; but this had been read by many as applying only to members of the Church of England, and not to occasional visitors. A good number in the other churches identified with the Church of England as the national church sufficiently strongly that any withdrawal of such a customary right was important. It was important too to Anglican evangelicals, who thought that the profounder unity already existed between Christians by reason of common baptism, and that to erect such a barrier was a sectarian act.[80]

---

[76]   F.P.Coleman to Ramsey, 29 June 1962, Ramsey Papers 22, ff.73–74.

[77]   Mascall to Ramsey, 4 November 1961, Ramsey Papers 8, f.209.

[78]   Gordon Phillips (chaplain to the University of London) to Ramsey, 10 November 1961, Ramsey Papers 8, f.214.

[79]   Ramsey to G.W.H. Lampe, 6 November 1961, Ramsey Papers 8, f.211.

[80]   One evangelical statement of the matter is Gervase Duffield, *Admission to Holy Communion* (Abingdon, 1964). For a Methodist view, see George W. Underwood, *Intercommunion and the Open Table* (London, 1964).

There was, however, just such a threat of withdrawal in the offing. One of the many canons that had been making slow progress through the decision-making processes of the church was canon B.15. The Church Assembly Legal Board had ruled that, despite archiepiscopal opinion in previous years, the communion rubric should indeed be read exclusively.[81] The canon asserted that occasional communion by non-Anglicans had been in point of fact illegal all along, and attempted to recognise that fact whilst providing for greater flexibility of practice on a more explicit basis. Thought to be a considerable relaxation of the law, it was one of several revised canons intended to clarify the existing state of practice in the church, such as those on ministerial vestments and the communion table. To Ramsey, it was an attempt to further the cause of unity on a basis that took greater account of the theological necessities of church order, thus standing a better chance of taking all within the Church with it. For many evangelicals, however, it was but one part in a broader campaign of piecemeal steps, designed to move the Church of England further away from Protestant brethren and closer to Rome.[82]

By February 1964 it was becoming clear that a wider view was needed. The Church Assembly had only narrowly passed a draft of Canon B.15, and it had been causing a disturbance in the Nonconformist press, not least the mainstream *Baptist Times*. Cyril Black, Conservative MP and Baptist layman, thought the Measure stood a good chance of being rebuffed by Parliament if it were brought forward, quite apart from the division that seemed likely within.[83] Rather than include the provision in an impending and rather miscellaneous administrative measure concerning liturgical reform, it was set aside, and referred to a new Commission that had been formed to consider intercommunion more widely, which began work late in 1965. This conveniently avoided the kind of agitation in Parliament that previous Measures had provoked. However, circumstances had changed in any case, such that a much wider consideration of the issue was needed, both in relation to imminent and concrete developments in relations with Methodism, and to the episcopal churches, including Rome.[84] From this point on, despite the existence of two quite separate Commissions, the two issues of intercommunion and Anglican-Methodist unity were inextricably intertwined.

By the time the Commission published its report in 1968, the two opposing and mutually incompatible approaches to the question were so clearly pointed that a chapter was devoted to an exposition of each. However, there was also in

---

[81] Reproduced in *Intercommunion To-day*, pp.147–52.
[82] Maiden and Webster, 'Last gasp of political Protestantism', pp.365–67.
[83] Black to Robert Beloe, 20 February 1964, Ramsey Papers 59, ff.64–65.
[84] Ramsey to Coggan, 7 December 1965, Ramsey Papers 79, ff.133–35.

view a third approach, which appeared to offer a way through the no-man's-land, in response to a unique moment in Christian history. For those who held to this third view, the habit of regarding existing church structures as ends in themselves was to place the church ahead of the kingdom, which it was the church's role to serve. The contemporary ecumenical movement was 'a singular work of the Holy Spirit of God', in a time of crisis in which all aspects of the churches' lives were coming under divine judgment. As such, 'certain concepts of valid ministry and sacraments which were once decisive can be transcended within a serious intention to unite.'[85] And it is in this connection that we may detect an extra dimension in Ramsey's thinking on the wider question of unity.

More than one historian has attempted to assess the degree to which Ramsey's mind changed in relation to church order, and moved away from the essentially catholic position expressed in *The Gospel and the Catholic Church*, which could be held without great tension in those calmer times. A more helpful way to view the question would be in terms not of a shift from one position to another, but of a greater salience given to one element of his thinking over others at a particular point in time. Ramsey always cherished the catholic ordering of the church, as a visible sign of continuity and thus as a point around which to unify. However, his own Nonconformist background gave him a sympathy with the view that organic unity was in the final analysis less important than intercommunion, if the latter could be achieved but the former could not.[86] Always alive to the reality of change and development in theology, it would seem that over time the latter assumed a greater prominence in Ramsey's thinking.

Attached to catholic order though he was, Ramsey's attachment to it was always subject to the reality of divine action in the present age. In a situation of crisis in church relations, and indeed throughout the church and the nation from the mid-1960s onwards, many things that had seemed certain in inter-war Cambridge seemed mutable, dispensable. If the greater need of God's church on earth demanded it, then there was little in the ordering of the church, so often thought to be immutable, that could not and ought not to be overturned. What God had instituted, He could surely amend. As we shall see in the next section, there were limits to how far the majority in the Church of England could agree.

[85] *Intercommunion To-day*, pp.63–69, at pp.63–64.
[86] Ramsey to G.W.H. Lampe, 8 October 1964, Ramsey Papers 59, ff.96–97.

Anglican-Methodist Unity

When the twentieth century history of the British ecumenical movement comes into clearer focus with the passage of time, it may be that the single most important event was the failure of the scheme for reunion between the Church of England and the Methodist Church. Begun in earnest after the ending of the Second World War, the achievement of unity had by the crucial year of 1969 taken on immense national and international significance. The authors of the final Scheme were in no doubt as to why. Visible disunity among the churches placed constraints on co-operation at local level, leading to 'frustration, impatience and the gradual cessation of effort.' Not only did it hamper the mission of the churches: there was reason to suppose that the decline in numerical strength in the churches and in new vocations to ordained ministry was also consequent on the same 'pattern of incompetence which [the churches] present in which disunity is a main feature.'[87] Internationally, similar schemes of union from Australia to Pakistan to Nigeria were approaching the stage of decisive action, and looked to Britain, home of the mother churches, for a clear lead.

The precise impact of the failure of the Scheme on all these relations has yet to be gauged, but a failure it was; readers may find elsewhere accounts of the process as it unfolded (although there is yet no comprehensive treatment).[88] The salient fact for Ramsey was that, more than 30 years after the Church of England had invited the Methodist Church to enter into a process of negotiations, it had been the Church of England that in the last instance walked away from the table. Reflecting on the first rejection of the scheme by the Church Assembly in July 1969, Ramsey thought it 'an event in history of an almost incredible kind' that one of the Free Churches should have agreed to enter into union on the basis of the historic episcopate. 'That we Anglicans having already said that the principles of the union are sound, should now say "no" would seem to me to make our Church of England no longer credible.'[89] For the first time, leadership amongst the churches had, in a highly significant way, passed from the established church.

The sticking point was the nature of the ordained ministry. Anglo-Catholics held tenaciously to the importance of episcopal ordination as a *sine qua non* of a valid sacrament. They were thus deeply concerned about accepting Methodist ministers into a united church without having been so ordained. Many

---

[87]   *Anglican-Methodist Unity. Report of the Anglican-Methodist Unity Commission. Part 2: The Scheme* (London, 1968), p.3.

[88]   Paul A. Welsby, *A History of the Church of England 1945–1980* (Oxford, 1984), pp.78–82, 166–73,

[89]   Ramsey to Cecil Northcott, 17 July 1969, Ramsey Papers 166, f.248.

Methodists, whilst able to accept episcopacy as a convenient model for church government, were chary about accepting any such ordination for those who were already ministers, and the aspersions it cast about the apparently inferior nature of their ministry hitherto. Conservative evangelicals in the Church of England, whilst episcopally ordained themselves by dint of being Anglicans, nonetheless were concerned about any implication that that ordination was in any way fundamental to their ministry.[90]

In order to circumvent this obstacle, a Service of Reconciliation was devised, through which all ministers in the united church would pass at the inception. It involved the laying on of hands, but had perforce to leave ambiguous the precise question of how the status, before God, of both the Anglican and the Methodist ministers changed during the Service. Indeed, its advocates had been explicit about this ambiguity, arguing that the important thing was neither the starting point, nor the journey, but the destination.[91] This ambiguity was too much, however, for a significant minority of evangelicals and Anglo-Catholics, and figures such as the conservative evangelical James Packer on one side, and the League of Anglican Loyalists on the other, were to keep up a vigorous campaign against the Scheme to the last.[92]

Such campaigns were not new, of course; and under different circumstances might successfully have been resisted. Quite probably crucial, however, were the trenchant and repeated interventions of Geoffrey Fisher. Ramsey's predecessor was loudly and consistently against the Scheme, in print and in a constant private correspondence with Ramsey and other bishops which eventually went unanswered.[93] In the immediate aftermath of the first negative vote, Ramsey certainly thought Fisher's role had been crucial, many having been persuaded

---

[90]   On the debate as a whole, see Chadwick, *Ramsey*, pp.334–36; on the Anglo-Catholic position, see Ivan Clutterbuck, *Marginal Catholics*, (Leominster, 1993), pp.179–97; on the evangelicals, see Andrew Atherstone, 'Evangelical Dissentients and the Defeat of the Anglican-Methodist Unity Scheme', *Epworth Review* 35 (2008), subsequently republished as *Wesley and Methodist Studies* 7 (2015), 100-16; Peter Webster, 'Archbishop Michael Ramsey and Evangelicals in the Church of England' in Andrew Atherstone and John Maiden (eds), *Evangelicalism and the Church of England in the Twentieth Century (Woodbridge, 2014)*, pp.162-82.

[91]   The 1968 Report includes a chapter responding directly to each of the major objections. *Anglican Methodist Unity. Report. Part 2*, pp.128–35.

[92]   See, *inter alia*, Packer (ed.), *Fellowship in the Gospel. Evangelical comment on Anglican-Methodist Unity and Intercommunion Today* (Abingdon, 1968), and E.W. Trueman Dicken, *Not this way. A comment on Anglican-Methodist Unity* (London, 1968).

[93]   Robert Stopford (Bishop of London) to Ramsey, 24 June 1969, Ramsey Papers 166, ff.59–64. See also De-la-Noy, *Ramsey*, p.200.

'that as Lord Fisher dislike the proposals there must be something fishy about them.'[94]

Fisher yielded to no-one in his commitment to reunion between the two churches, being widely credited with the inception of the whole process in his so-called 'Cambridge sermon' of 1946. However, he had come to reject the Scheme, thinking that each of the successive Commissions had made the same basic error, to suppose that the ministries of the two churches could be reconciled before full communion between the two was achieved. For Fisher, full communion between the Church of England and a non-episcopal church was impossible, and so the Methodists would need to accept bishops before there could be any reconciliation of ministries. For Fisher the ambiguity necessary in the service to circumvent the issue was intolerable: '[t]here is no reconciliation to be found here: and, if I speak my mind frankly, to say that the issue is left in the hands of God, is no more than a pious subterfuge, pious and sincere but still a subterfuge and a tortuous one.'[95]

Far from being a 'pious subterfuge', for Ramsey, the fact that the leeway allowed for divergent understandings of the precise operation of the Service was not merely acceptable, but in some ways positive. Pragmatically, he was certain that the opposition from both conservative evangelicals and Anglo-Catholics risked throwing away the only realistic method of achieving union in their own best interests. If Anglo-Catholics were to reject the Scheme, which 'conserves in essence the very things which the Catholic movement has borne witness to' (episcopacy, mainly), it would expose Anglo-Catholics to trends in the movement for intercommunion unconnected to historic order. Conservative evangelicals, perversely in Ramsey's view, seemed content to pass up the prospect of full communion with evangelical Methodists for the sake of a single service which could be read to imply a view of priesthood which they did not share. 'Hence the double tragedy of two sections of our Church being ready to throw away the things which they most care about through fear of losing their theological tidiness.'[96]

There was more behind Ramsey's acceptance of the Service than mere pragmatism, however. He knew that he himself was already a priest and bishop in the Catholic church, and lacked nothing; and also that Methodist ministers did not possess 'the commission and authority described in our Catholic ordinal'. However, they were clearly 'ministers of the word and sacraments of a

[94] Ramsey to Eric Kemp, 11 July 1969, Ramsey Papers 166, ff.190–91.
[95] Fisher, *Covenant and Reconciliation. A critical examination* (Oxford, 1967), p.12.
[96] Ramsey to David L. Edwards (*Church Times*), 20 February 1969, at Ramsey Papers 165, ff.185–86.

sort and I cannot regard them as laymen.' They themselves might believe 'to be already more than I may suspect', but this gave him no offence since 'I cannot define the exact relative standing before God of our respective ministries.' The rite was ultimately not concerned to resolve the divergence, being concerned to define 'what all those who receive it are when it is over, and it does not define the relative standing of what people are already.' The new rite was to ask God to give both Anglicans and Methodists 'whatever he knows them to need in authority and the gifts of the Spirit to make our ministries equal and identical as presbyters in the Church of God.'[97] Ramsey as a theologian was acutely aware of the gaps and the silences in all speaking about God, and it seems to have caused him no great discomfort to accept this method of avoiding the questions that many raised by asking a different and more important one.

This approach, perceived by some simply as either muddle or as calculated evasion of questions of principle, was not forced on Ramsey by inconvenient circumstance. Ramsey had always known that unity could never be achieved by means of the uncomfortable forcing together of existing churches, aided by some compromise over inessentials whilst leaving each intact: 'a fitting-together of broken pieces'.[98] In dialogue much later with Cardinal Suenens, Ramsey was still sure that the ecumenical task was not 'like the reconstruction of a toy once made in its completeness and subsequently broken.' To attempt merely to harmonise existing churches was, from the prophet Ezekiel, to daub untempered mortar on a cracked wall.[99]

Along with *Honest to God*, the failure of the Scheme was regarded by some as perhaps the greatest failure of Ramsey's time as Archbishop. For his press secretary, Michael De-la-Noy, the process had been 'perhaps his greatest test of leadership so far', which the Archbishop failed. In De-la-Noy's view, Ramsey had waited for too long before finally coming out in whole-hearted public support to the Scheme, during which time the opposition to the Scheme had hardened. There had been an opportunity to win the day by personal example, in the single most immediate ecumenical cause of his tenure, and Ramsey had instead opted for the politic course.[100]

---

[97] Ramsey to Andrew Blair, 31 October 1968, Ramsey Papers 143, ff.149–51.
[98] *Catholicity. A study in the Conflict of Christian Traditions in the West* (Westminster, 1947), p.10.
[99] Michael Ramsey and Leon-Joseph Suenans, *The Future of the Christian Church* (London, 1971), p.41. The image from Ezekiel is from *The Church of England and the Eastern Orthodox Church*, p.13.
[100] De-la-Noy memo of 17 April 69, Ramsey Papers 165, f.242; A Day in the Life of God, pp.85–86.

Ramsey, along with Donald Coggan of York, had indeed very deliberately eschewed direct campaigning on the Scheme until January 1969 for fear of being seen to 'steam-roller' through the changes.[101] However, whether or not earlier intervention would materially have affected the outcome cannot be established; and, as Owen Chadwick noted, for every one advocating greater intervention, there was another who thought that the archbishop should remain above the fray. As on so many other matters, people required different and indeed contradictory things from their archbishop.[102] It might also be noted that in private Ramsey did a great deal to bring wavering Anglo-Catholics nearer to accepting the Scheme; something that he was placed to do where Fisher manifestly was not.[103] One correspondent had moved from a position of utter opposition to one of disquiet but with preparedness to accept a majority view: 'only you could have pulled me as far as I have managed to come.'[104]

There was, however, some realisation amongst Ramsey's closest advisers that mistakes had been made. Eric Kemp, chaplain of Exeter College, Oxford and member of the Commission, thought that there had been insufficient discussion of the 1958 report at diocesan level and too great a level of secrecy. At other points the timetable had been too tight, and the final report had perhaps left too many hostages to fortune in the chapters dealing with the specific objections.[105] A prominent organiser of the Anglo-Catholic opposition also thought that the process had been too much led by academics and the great-and-good, and had not taken sufficient account of the realities of local church life.[106] The interaction of the Scheme with the intercommunion report, and its impact on Anglo-Catholic opinion in particular, is difficult to judge. However, campaigners on both sides certainly addressed the two as part of the same movement, as the two reports appeared within weeks of each other in 1968. Some members of the Commission, including Robert Stopford and Eric Kemp, thought that the intercommunion report should have been delayed, since its recommendations would undo much of the work done in reassuring Catholic opinion.[107]

If Ramsey and his staff made any strategic errors, they were perhaps twofold. Ronald Williams, Bishop of Leicester, later thought that to press on to the second

---

[101] Ramsey to Coggan 31 January 1969, Ramsey Papers 165, ff.124–25.
[102] Chadwick, *Ramsey*, pp.343–34.
[103] Chadwick, *Ramsey*, p.334–35.
[104] Cyprian Dymoke-Marr to Ramsey, 9 February 1969, Ramsey Papers 165, f.154.
[105] Eric Kemp to Ramsey, 10 July 1969, Ramsey Papers 166, f.179.
[106] Clutterbuck, *Marginal Catholics*, pp.184–86.
[107] Stopford to Ramsey, 8 December 1967, Ramsey Papers 134, f.305; Eric Kemp to Ramsey, 13 August 1968, Ramsey Papers 134, ff.329–30.

unsuccessful vote in the new General Synod in May 1972 had been a mistake;[108] and it is indeed hard in retrospect to see why the new governing arrangements for the church should have been thought more likely to produce a positive result. In the intervening time, indeed, it may have been that those opposing the Scheme were given valuable time to stiffen further their resolve; certainly, the appearance of the joint evangelical/Anglo-Catholic manifesto *Growing into Union* (1970) suggests so.[109] However, the Methodists had said 'yes', and that decision was now to go forward to the next stage in their processes; they had shown courageous leadership for which Ramsey was very thankful. In that context, to take a second bite at the cherry seemed the logical course of action. To those who argued that to ignore the verdict of the Anglican assemblies was to ignore the voice of the Holy Spirit, Ramsey replied that to disregard the positive vote from the Methodist Conference might well amount to much the same: who was to know?[110] What was out of the question was to begin unpicking the Scheme: '[w]e have no moral right to do this as they have agreed on proposals in which we originally took the initiative.'[111]

If there was a personal failure at all in the whole matter, it was perhaps Ramsey's limitations in fully understanding the position of those opposing the Scheme. In the immediate aftermath of the first vote, he thought that the opposition had been due to 'the psychology of fear of change deepening and becoming obsessive ... once [that fear] became really obsessive it was, I think, beyond the power of argument to help the situation.'[112] This, for Ramsey, was akin to the 'persecution and martyrdom complex' amongst some English Roman Catholics that manifested itself in relation to the Forty Martyrs (see above). Ramsey was later to encounter a similar visceral sense of religious identity in Northern Ireland; a response only slightly connected to cool rational argument, which he recognised but could hardly understand.

This inchoate opposition to change may indeed account for some of the opposition to the Scheme; the historian struggles to find the kind of sources that would make such a determination possible. But it hardly accounts for the opposition of a figure such as Eric Mascall, Anglo-Catholic theologian and long-time friend of Ramsey's, with whom relations became strained; or

---

[108] Chadwick, *Ramsey*, p.343.

[109] Andrew Atherstone, '"A Mad Hatter's Tea Party in the Old Mitre Tavern?" Ecumenical Reactions to *Growing into Union*', *Ecclesiology* 6:3 (2010), 39–67.

[110] Ramsey to Lionel du Toit (Dean of Carlisle), 24 July 1969, Ramsey Papers 166, ff.278–79.

[111] Ramsey to T.F. Torrance, 21 July 1969, Ramsey Papers 166, f.266.

[112] Ramsey to Kemp, 1 July 1969, Ramsey Papers 166, ff.190–91.

James I. Packer, *de facto* theologian-in-chief amongst the conservative evangelicals. Both were among the authors of *Growing into Union*, an undertaking which, whether successful or not, was nonetheless born of a settled conviction that the Scheme was fundamentally flawed, and that another way was possible. Much research remains to be done on the significance of the apparently unlikely 'unholy alliance' between the two extremes of the conventional spectrum of Anglican churchmanship, and the degree to which it represented the beginnings of the formation of a conservative bloc of previously opposed groups. The two poles were, however, close together in opposition to the general trend towards greater indeterminacy in theology, and whilst Ramsey was no liberal in the mould of John Robinson, for one such as Packer to be comfortable with the ambiguity in the Service of Reconciliation was simply asking too much. Central to the self-presentation of the revivified conservative evangelicals was the matter of 'clarity' and 'certainty' in theology, over against supposed liberal ambiguity and doubt. To have accepted the service would thus have been to dilute the movement's unique selling point. Theological 'tidiness' was not merely a fussy, unnecessary scruple, as Ramsey supposed, but fundamental to the conservative mind.

Ecumenical Success and Failure

In the end, the proponents of organic unity among the churches in England in Ramsey's time had to settle for a single success. The new United Reformed Church, the joining of Presbyterians and Congregationalists in England, was inaugurated in October 1972. Ramsey received a 'tumultuous welcome' at the ceremony, a recognition of his place in the ecumenical movement in England.[113] Ultimately, however, the high hopes that had been raised by Fisher's Cambridge sermon, at the Faith and Order conference in Nottingham and by the Vatican Council were unfulfilled. Was the Church of England really ready for the radical choices with which it was faced? Few seemed to have been able to look beyond local and national circumstance – to think in terms other than of the jagged edges of their own particular piece of the broken toy. Ramsey's vision from the 1940s, of individual churches of West and East changing shape and converging as they drew nearer to Christ in holiness and truth, seemed not to have the imaginative power to energise more than a few.

Even supposing Anglicans had been ready to embrace the wider vision, could the machinery of their church have allowed it? Much was made of the glacial

[113] Chadwick, *Ramsey*, pp.341–42.

pace at which decisions could be made within the Church Assembly, and Ramsey
had limited patience with its detailed and sometimes partisan and ill-informed
deliberations. But the intertwining of the process of canon law revision, inherited
from Fisher (see Chapter 2), with parallel commissions on each and every issue,
ineluctably gave the impression of muddle. And archbishops, whilst their words
were attended to, could not control the Church Assembly, or significantly shape
the independent-minded groups to whom they entrusted those commissions,
or even rely on all their bishops for support. Given this context, to charge
Ramsey or any other archbishop with a lack of 'leadership' would be quite to
misunderstand the role. All he could do was to set a tone of seriousness of intent,
and hope to intervene only as much as was really necessary.

In the final analysis, it may be that by 1969 when the Anglican-Methodist
scheme first faltered, the opportunity for ecumenical progress on the basis of
organic union had passed. In the half-century since, the Church of England has
never again come as close to achieving such a union as it did then, and at the
time some were suggesting that progress could be made in other ways. Lionel
du Toit, moderate evangelical and one of the members of the commission on
Anglican-Methodist union, had felt compelled to vote against the Scheme he
had helped create, and wrote to explain his reasons. Had the times now changed
again, he wondered, since the days of the Cambridge Sermon, leading away from
such organisational schemes? Vatican II had pointed in the direction of a focus
on the existing unity of Christians in baptism, and on the real ecclesial standing
of separated brethren. Could this leaven now not be allowed to work, through
local action with controlled intercommunion? Perhaps, thought du Toit, the
humiliation of 1969 had been necessary for God to point the churches in a
different direction.[114]

Ramsey did not accept, and could not have accepted, that the entire thrust
of the ecumenical movement had been misdirected, but there were broader
currents within the churches that were beginning to sweep organic union
further out of reach. Hugh McLeod has pointed out a marked downturn in
the mood within the Western churches in the late 1960s, and a loss of nerve
amongst reformers as the churches' vital statistics fell.[115] This prompted a general
move to shore up the fragments within each of the churches in the interests of
the remaining faithful. Expansive schemes of reunion, first conceived in times of
greater confidence, became less and less the priority. In retrospect, it seems that
Ramsey's opportunity to see his vision of unity realised simply came too late.

---

[114] Lionel du Toit to Ramsey, 23 July 1969. Ramsey Papers 166, ff.271–72.
[115] McLeod, *The Religious Crisis of the 1960s*, pp.188–214.

Chapter 2

Church and State

Introduction

At the apex of English society sat a monarch on whom the crown was set by the Archbishop of Canterbury. Twenty-six of the Church's bishops sat by right in Parliament; and the five most senior of these were also members of the Privy Council. Those bishops in the Lords had been appointed by the sovereign on the advice of the Prime Minister, as were a great many other senior dignitaries. Unlike the other Christian churches, much of the law of the Church of England was also the law of the land: a tangled mass of ancient legislation and case law. Since the Enabling Act of 1919, the Church had been able to agree with itself, by means of the Church Assembly, that it wished to vary that law, or its liturgy or doctrine; but the final ratification remained in the hands of Parliament. As such, the archbishops found almost every decision to be taken hedged around on every side, and room for manoeuvre at times impossibly limited.

Many words had been spoken and written over the 'problem' of Church and State, among political theorists, churchmen and politicians, over many years.[1] For some within the Church, the fact that bishops were appointed by a politician with or without knowledge of the Church or inclination to learn was adequately compensated by the opportunity to act as salt and light from a position at the heart of the political and social elite. For others, such as the founders in 1917 of the Life and Liberty Movement, the time had come that the balance of cost and benefit had tipped decisively. For William Temple, the Church was 'the Body of Christ, and must be free to obey spontaneously the command of its

---

[1]   See Matthew Grimley, *Citizenship, Community, and the Church of England: Liberal Anglican Theories of the State Between the Wars* (Oxford, 2004), *passim*. A contemporary academic treatment, including a selection of edited resources which remains useful, is David Nicholls, *Church and State in Britain since 1820* (London, 1967). See also several of the essays in Mark Chapman, Judith Maltby and William Whyte (eds), *The Established Church: Past, Present and Future* (London, 2011).

Divine Head, so as to make its witness obvious to the People, and effective for the extension of the Kingdom of God.'[2]

Ramsey's personal view was only stated explicitly at the very end of his time at Lambeth, and so must in part be read off from his statements on several related issues, with which this chapter is concerned: the attempts to reform the system of Crown appointments; the foundation of the General Synod in 1970; the abortive attempt by the Labour government of Harold Wilson at reforming the House of Lords; the Archbishops' Commission on Church and State, which reported in 1970; and, on Ramsey's very last day in office, the passing by Parliament of the Worship and Doctrine Measure of 1974.[3]

'Establishment has never been one of my enthusiasms.' Thus began Ramsey's essay on the issue of Church and State, written specially for his valedictory collection of sermons and lectures, *Canterbury Pilgrim*. Granted, establishment had in the past benefitted the Church. Perhaps against its natural tendency, Ramsey thought, establishment had helped (not to say forced) the Church 'to be theologically comprehensive and to be pastorally involved with the whole community and not only with gathered congregations.'[4] At moments of tension Ramsey would press this need for thinking together as a whole Church against those who seemed inclined to defend a party interest.[5]

However, despite the benefits that had accrued to the Church from the establishment, Ramsey knew that it was not always and everywhere an advantage. Of all the provinces in the worldwide Anglican Communion, only the two in England were established, and the Church of Wales was not obviously suffering for 50 years of disestablishment. Ramsey knew from his own background in Nonconformity of those churches in England that had witnessed for centuries without any such protection. When under pressure from established Church and State, these churches were able to say 'at a great price obtained I this freedom'. And English society was changing, such that to both privilege and burden one church amongst many, and one faith amongst several, became in Ramsey's mind a detriment to both Church and State: 'in the world as a whole Christianity is

---

[2]   F.A. Iremonger, *William Temple, Archbishop of Canterbury. His Life and Letters* (London, 1948), p.224.

[3]   Nicholls, *Church and State*.

[4]   Ramsey, 'Church and State in England' in *Canterbury Pilgrim* (London, 1974), pp.176–84, at p.176.

[5]   Webster, 'Michael Ramsey and Anglican evangelicals', *passim*.

passing into a post-Constantinian phase in which the buttressing of Churches by privilege may hinder rather than commend their witness and claim.'[6]

For Ramsey, that witness and claim was hindered in several ways. Ramsey's status as head of what many would habitually describe as a state church was a distorting lens through which was refracted each and every comment he might make: on race relations or apartheid South Africa; on capital punishment or the Vietnam war. The same words could never be received in the same way when spoken by a cardinal or by the president of the Methodist conference. Ramsey was also sure that the Church desperately needed the freedom to renew its worship and thus its mission. From Parliament it needed at first the freedom to experiment with a renewed language in worship, and also not to be required to return to Parliament for that licence to be renewed.

Elements of the establishment also acted as obstacles, in law and in feeling, to ecumenical work and schemes of reunion amongst the other churches, both at home and abroad. There were practical issues of law and practice: if the Methodists were to join the Church of England, would this mean more bishops, and Methodist ones, and should they sit in the House of Lords? Furthermore, if movement towards the other churches was movement away from the State, what would remain of the particular national role which Anglicans had tended to assume was theirs? The authors of the final scheme for the union with the Methodists had carefully distinguished between an established church and a national church. The latter 'need not regard itself and the nation as coterminous, nor need it be established. Its national character is a matter of how it understands its churchly calling, and does not depend for its reality on the status which the national community gives it.'[7] The order in which Ramsey posed the question was deliberate and important: 'What changes does the cause of church unity in this country require?' The priority was the mission and witness of the churches, jointly and severally, and 'the problems are not for us Anglicans to answer by ourselves alone.'[8]

When the situation was weighed in the balance, then, Ramsey thought '[i]t would not be grief to me to wake up and find that the English establishment was no more.'[9] He was, however, acutely conscious that the relationship between Church and State was delicately poised, with change in any one aspect of it

---

6 Ramsey, 'Church and State in England' pp.176–84, at p.176; on the loss of salience of the inter-war idea of the 'national moral community', see Grimley, *Citizenship*, pp.12–13, 203–22

7 *Anglican-Methodist Unity. Part 2*, p.93.

8 Ramsey, *Canterbury Pilgrim*, p.177.

9 Ramsey, *Canterbury Pilgrim*, p.176.

likely to affect the others. There was also a need for caution, since by no means everyone thought that the Church either needed these new freedoms, or could be trusted with them once they were in hand. Ultimately, however, for Ramsey those freedoms were essential, and if in the process of obtaining them the link of Church and State were broken, the Church would need to accept the fact. There was a need to render unto God the things that were His.

The Monarchy

Ramsey's view on the link between Church and State needs to be carefully disentangled from his view of the monarchy in general. According to ancient privilege, Ramsey as Bishop of Durham was entitled to attend the new Queen Elizabeth at her coronation in Westminster Abbey in 1953. The television footage shows him, massive and impassive, at her right hand throughout the ceremony. Preaching two days before, Ramsey spoke of a 'happy nation', united despite differences of class and wealth, with the 'happiness of a people who know we have a great treasure; and the treasure is the Monarch whose subjects we are.'[10] On the occasion of the birth of Prince Edward in 1964 Ramsey spoke in similarly conventional terms of the exemplary royal family: 'around the throne a Christian family united, happy and setting to all an example of what the words "home and family" most truly meant.'[11]

But the authority of monarchy had attached to it its own obligations. In Christ's washing of the disciples' feet, he had shown the meaning of a 'royalty of selfless service'; a Christian monarchy should derive its tone from 'Christ's own union of the ruler of all and the servant of all.' The monarch not only had a duty to her people, but also to God. The coronation service showed to the nation the newly crowned queen, in all the regalia of sovereignty, kneeling to receive communion 'just where any Christian man or woman or child might kneel ... She knows that to the Crucified King Jesus all monarchies are subject, and by him they all are judged.'[12] As we shall see, loyalty to the Church of England's Supreme Governor did not preclude sharp debate about what that loyalty meant in practice, and its limits.

---

[10] Ramsey, 'The crowning of the Queen', in *Durham Essays and Addresses*, pp.91–94, at p.91.

[11] As quoted by *The Times*, 12 March 1964 ; Ben Pimlott, *The Queen* (London, 1996), p.336.

[12] Ramsey, 'The crowning of the Queen', pp.92–93. See also Chadwick, *Ramsey*, p.142.

Clearing the Decks

That Ramsey's view was settled very early on is apparent from a memorandum prepared for the meeting of the bishops in October 1961, on the subject of Church reform and the State.[13] There was much to be done, but the bishops needed both to avoid becoming unduly concerned with the detail, and to know their own collective mind. The Church must first have decided how to use any new autonomy it might request, since any commission would simply pass the question back to the Church, as would Parliament. As Ramsey put it later, '[d]isestablishment is itself a negative formula. It says what should be discarded. It would be better to ask: *quo tendimus* [towards what are we headed]?' And if the Church came to the mind that what it required for its mission and witness meant change, 'then we should be ready to pay the price.'[14]

But before such fundamental questions could be faced, there were decks to be cleared. The first priority was to conclude the process of the revision of the canon law, a process that had begun between the Wars. The principal report of the commission set up to deal with the matter was now 14 years old, yet the process was nowhere near complete.[15] Ramsey was determined that it be concluded with all possible speed, since it was disproportionately consumptive of time and energy, and since by the preoccupation with the canon law 'the proportion of things is obscured.'[16] Mindful of the effect of the Church's apparent obsession with its own inner workings, he exhorted his bishops that in all things 'regard should be given to the impression of the Church upon the country, for the Church's own preoccupations are part of its witness for God and the Gospel.'[17]

Of a piece with this central concern with the outward face of the Church was Ramsey's attention to the reform of worship (on which see Chapter 4). Significant attention had been paid during the process of canon law revision to the precise nature of 'lawful authority' to authorise variations from the 1662 Book of Common Prayer.[18] However, to treat Prayer Book reform as merely part

---

[13] TS memorandum 'Church Reform in Relation to the State', at Ramsey Papers 9, ff.244–46.

[14] Ramsey, *Canterbury Pilgrim*, p.176.

[15] *The Canon Law of the Church of England. Being a Report of the Archbishops' Commission on Canon Law …* (London, 1947).

[16] Ramsey to the Revd. Michael Bruce, 8 September 1961, at Ramsey Papers 5, ff.315–16.

[17] TS memorandum 'Church Reform in Relation to the State', at Ramsey Papers, 9 ff.244–46.

[18] See the memo on 'Lawful Authority' printed as an appendix to *The Canon Law of the Church of England*, pp.215–23.

of canon law was to denude it, and indeed the public at large had missed its wider importance: the public for whose benefit such reform was largely intended. It was vital that 'the matter of freedom for Liturgical revision may be grasped as a big and vital matter in itself and not as one portion within the many details of Canon Law.'[19]

An instinctive reaction of the twentieth century Church of England, when faced with major and intractable questions of a constitutional nature, was to set up a Commission. At least three such bodies had been convened and had reported since 1918 on issues connected with the Church-State relationship.[20] Ramsey was himself later to set up just such a Commission, which reported in 1970 (of which more below), but he was pressed only months after his translation to Canterbury to institute a group to investigate legislation 'to re-establish the Church of England in such a manner as to remove the embarrassment to Church and State of the anachronisms in their present relationships.'[21] It was, however, clearly the wrong time, and Ramsey prevailed upon the proposer of the resolution in Convocation not to press ahead with it.[22] There were too many processes already ongoing in relation to canon law, the ecclesiastical courts and other matters that could not easily be halted.

Crown Appointments

One such process already in train was the continuing pressure within the Church Assembly and the Church at large to re-examine the system of Crown appointments. In the year before his move to Lambeth the Church Assembly had set up a group to look at the appointment of bishops. Despite Ramsey's lack of appetite for shaking the constitutional tree too vigorously too soon, he saw the need for the removal of some of the more objectionable elements of what he described to Prime Minister Macmillan as a 'humiliating and tiresome' system. Part of this was the issuing of Letters Missive to cathedral chapters to appoint the

---

[19]   Ramsey to Michael Bruce, 8 September 1961, Ramsey Papers 5, ff.315–16.

[20]   The three most wide-ranging reports were: *The Archbishops' Committee on Church and State. Report* (London, 1918); *Church and State. Report of the Archbishops' Commission on the relations between Church and State* (London, 1935), the so-called Cecil Commission, and; *Church and State. Being the report of a commission appointed by the Church Assembly in June 1949* (London, 1952), the report of the Moberley Commission.

[21]   Bruce to Ramsey, 24 August 1961 Ramsey Papers 5, ff.313–14.

[22]   Ramsey to Bruce, 8 September 1961, Ramsey Papers 5, ff.315–16.

man nominated by the Crown, on pain of the ancient penalties of *praemunire*.[23] *Praemunire*, he told the Lords, was 'a terrible penalty', over which he personally should prefer execution 'which was the fate of several of my predecessors and is a penalty which has at least the possibility of a martyr's crown.'[24]

Praemunire, although a spectacular element of the problem, was not of the kernel. It had been part of the coming to independence of Anglican provinces overseas that they had taken on the choosing of their own chief pastors, their bishops, previously exercised from Canterbury. Ramsey thought it a matter of the 'maturity and spiritual health of a Church' that it should do so, and without those powers a church would remain 'warped in its potentiality of growing ... in the practice of Christian wisdom.'[25] He was also clear that the Church Assembly group was not nearly weighty enough to be credible, and so, in an action criticised at the time for its conservatism, stayed the proceedings in the Church Assembly in order that a new Commission be set up instead.[26] The Howick Commission began work in early 1962 and issued its report in December 1964.[27]

When it appeared, Ramsey was not alone in thinking the Howick report largely a failure, in that it failed to face squarely the criticisms of the present system and paid insufficient attention to issues of unity with other churches.[28] In any case, by the time the Church Assembly debated the report in early 1965, the mood had shifted. The failure of the 1964 Protestant campaign in Parliament to muster effective opposition to the Vesture of Ministers Measure had emboldened those who favoured a more radical look at the whole question of establishment.[29] For these reasons and its own, the Church Assembly set the report aside, and called instead for another Commission on the wider question of Church and State. Ramsey was in fact to see no material change in the controverted parts of the appointments system in his time, although the Law Commission was to remove the penalties of *praemunire* on its own initiative in 1967.

---

[23]   TS notes of a meeting with Prime Minister Macmillan, 28 September 1961, at Ramsey Papers 7, ff.80–84. The medieval statute of *praemunire* outlawed the assertion of papal or any foreign power, which was thought to apply to cathedral chapters that did not ratify the Crown's appointment of a bishop. Chadwick, *Ramsey*, p.190.

[24]   H.L. Deb. 16 Nov 1966, vol. 277, col.1263.

[25]   Ramsey, *Canterbury Pilgrim*, p.183.

[26]   Grubb statement to the House of Laity, 3 July 1961, at Ramsey Papers 7, f.26. In the view of Christopher Wansey, one of the most vocal critics of the system, Ramsey 'saw the red light of reform and acted to stop it.' *The Clockwork Church* (Oxford, 1978), p.59.

[27]   *Crown Appointments and the Church* (London, 1964).

[28]   Ramsey to Coggan, 28 November 1964, Ramsey Papers 57, f.84. Welsby, *Church of England*, p.220;

[29]   Maiden and Webster, 'Political Protestantism', at 376.

Synod and Parliament

The relationship with Parliament had by and large been calm for several decades in 1961, mainly because few matters of any controversial importance had been brought before it. However, the events of 1927–28, when Parliament had twice rejected the revised Book of Common Prayer, cast a long shadow over the process of canon law revision, the piloting of which Ramsey inherited.[30]

That the role of Parliament was no dead letter was amply demonstrated by the events of 1963–64, during which time three Measures came before Parliament, designed to reform the byzantine workings of the Church courts, and to clarify some seemingly minor points of detail relating to the communion table and to clerical dress. The consequent agitation from a broad coalition of Protestant and evangelical groups against the Measures showed that the type of political Protestantism which was last visible during the Prayer Book Crisis had still some traction in significant parts of the Church.[31] Parliament was not simply a cipher at best, or a brake on the legitimate freedom of the Church at worst; it was still for some the lay synod of the Church, providing important protection for the residually Protestant mass of the laity against the Catholicising tendencies of the bishops.

But ultimately that agitation ended not with a bang but a whimper. After long and noisy debates and three divisions, all three measures passed without significant votes in opposition. Parliament had signalled its unwillingness to act as umpire in what many parliamentarians had come to regard as matters of the Church's concern alone. The impression was confirmed by the smooth passage of the 1965 Prayer Book (Alternative and Other Services) Measure, which provided for experimental use of newly composed services for a limited period. Those concerned about the direction of change in the Church turned their attention away from Parliament and towards the Church Assembly as the place in which to work. The path to change had opened.

If the Church of England was not to be governed by Parliament, it would need a more effective system of government of its own with which to replace it. The disadvantages of the dual system of Church Assembly and with two Convocations of the clergy, instituted by the Enabling Act of 1919, had been felt acutely long before Ramsey's time at Canterbury, and particularly its separation of laity and clergy.

---

[30]   On the Prayer Book Crisis, see John Maiden, *National Religion and the Prayer Book Controversy, 1927–8* (Woodbridge, 2009), *passim*.

[31]   Maiden and Webster, 'Political Protestantism', *passim*.

A 1958 report had proposed radical change according to a principle with which Ramsey had considerable sympathy: that the right to collective action lay with the whole body of the Church, clerical and lay.[32] Ramsey was less personally involved than in other matters in the protracted process by which the proposals of the 1958 report culminated in the General Synod and its inauguration in 1970. That said, he was clear that an effective system of government that fully included bishops, clergy and laity, at national and local levels, was essential to the project of winning greater freedom from the State and the task of mission to the nation.

In February 1963, with the plans bogged down in the Church Assembly, Ramsey and the archbishop of York, Donald Coggan, intervened to move the process on, reminding the Convocations that delay cemented an impression that the clergy were reluctant to accept the view of the House of Laity that greater lay involvement was key.[33] When the legislation effecting the change, the Synodical Government Measure, finally came to Parliament in 1969, Ramsey himself moved the Measure in the Lords, and left the House in no doubt as to its significance. The Measure was 'one of the most important for the Church of England' since 1919, removing much of the 'complexity and slowness' of the existing system, and the injurious separation of clergy and laity into separate houses.[34] Some of the agitation over Church measures in Parliament in previous years had centred on a perceived lack of representativeness in the Church Assembly, which the lay synod of Parliament could and was bound to try to redress if it thought it necessary. Here for Ramsey was a system that would ensure that that consensus was really achieved in the Church before it approached Parliament.

The House of Lords

As Owen Chadwick has pointed out, even though Ramsey described the bishops' work in Parliament as 'bearing the burden of history in Christ's name', he for his own part greatly enjoyed the life of the House.[35] He attended regularly,

---

[32]   *The Convocations and the Laity. Being the report of the commission set up by the Church Assembly to consider how the clergy and laity can best be joined together in the synodical government of the Church* (London, 1958). A useful account of the process leading to the formation of the General Synod may be found in Welsby, *Church of England* pp.146–50.

[33]   Draft report by the Archbishops to the Convocations, February 1963, Ramsey Papers 49, ff.12–14.

[34]   H.L. Deb. 16 June 1969, vol. 302 cols. 842–46, at 842.

[35]   Chadwick, *Ramsey*, pp.188–90, at 188.

spoke in debates and could expect to be listened to; and the correspondence speaks of warm relationships with many peers.

However, the project to reform the powers and composition of the Lords, begun with the Parliament Act of 1911, was about to enter a new phase. The Queen's Speech for the 1967–68 Parliamentary session included legislation to 'reduce the powers of the House of Lords and to eliminate its present hereditary basis'; this had been a commitment in the Labour party manifesto at the 1966 general election.[36] There then ensued a period of extensive consultation on what a reformed House might look like. Not surprisingly, the position of the bishops came into view. Occupants of the five sees of Canterbury, York, London, Winchester and Durham sat in the House by right; 21 other bishops entered the House in order of seniority and inclination; all could vote.

Amongst peers themselves, the bishops had a reputation as a progressive force within the House; for one peer, they were 'the spearhead of reform.'[37] However, despite considerable personal warmth towards them, there were doubts, mirroring those outside the House, as to whether such religious representation had any place in a 'modern legislative assembly', and to the exclusion of other churches and other faiths.[38] At the same time, the grounds on which their presence might be justified were also shifting. Once, the bishops had been viewed in much the same way as the hereditary peers: representatives of the immutable order of society; the establishment of the Church just as inevitable and right as the class system. Some bishops were now coming to see themselves as, as it were, Life Peers Spiritual: in the House not simply, or even mostly, by virtue of their historic office but on grounds of religious expertise. Part of this altered role was to hold open a space for viewing public affairs in a religious mode.

Ramsey had warmly welcomed the appointment of churchmen from other denominations as life peers under the provisions of the 1958 Life Peerages Act. The Methodist Donald Soper (1965) and George Macleod of the Church of Scotland (1967) had both distinguished themselves in the House, although there was some regret at Lambeth that they had been appointed by Prime Minister Wilson by dint of their politics, rather than as representatives of their respective churches in any formal way.[39] However, Ramsey knew well that the argument

36 On the reforms attempted by Richard Crossman, see Peter Dorey and Alexandra Kelso, *House of Lords Reform since 1911. Must the Lords go?* (Basingstoke, 2011), pp.135–70.

37 The words of Baroness Asquith of Yarnbury, H.L. Deb. 12 April 1967, vol. 281, cols. 1332–33.

38 Lord Silkin, H.L. Deb. 12 April 1967, vol. 281, col.1328.

39 Ronald Ferguson, *George Macleod. Founder of the Iona Community,* (London, 1990), pp.351–54; William Purcell, *Portrait of Soper,* (London, 1972), pp.162–65. Robert

that if the bishops sat in the Lords, representatives of other denominations ought to also, was weak. There was certainly some pressure in this direction: Cyril Black, Conservative MP, prominent Baptist and regular correspondent with Ramsey, tabled an amendment to the Bill to institute parallel representation for other denominations in the reformed House.[40] But the private correspondence between Lambeth and leaders of the Free and Roman Catholic churches shows no significant appetite for such a change; most were quite content for all the churches to be represented vicariously by the Church of England. However, Ramsey was sensible of the political delicacy of the position of the bishops, who by convention did not vote on political issues, but often did on issues in which the moral and political were intertwined, such as the imposition of sanctions on Southern Rhodesia or the Kenyan Asians Bill of February 1968 (see Chapter 5).[41]

As the deliberations that were to issue in the ill-fated Parliament (No. 2) Bill of 1969 proceeded, there was much discussion of the appropriate number of bishops and the expectations that ought to be placed upon them. Whilst Ramsey was open to adjustment in the numbers, he made the point on more than one occasion in private and in the House that reform of the Lords had to be seen in the totality of the Church-State relationship. So long as Parliament had a role in the government of the Church, and appointed its bishops, the place of the bishops in the Lords could not easily be reduced or removed.[42] Even if the number of bishops with the right to vote were to be reduced (with others able to speak but not vote, in a two-tier House), the numbers ought not to be so low as to make it impossible to sustain representation, given the other commitments of the bishops. Even if by and large the bishops rarely voted, there would be at least some occasions where a vote was at least symbolically, if not materially, important.

Beloe's view, as expressed at a meeting between Ramsey and Lords Carrington and Jellicoe (Conservative), 15 November 1967, Ramsey Papers 115, ff.308–10.

[40]   Robert Beloe memo on conversation with Black, dated 27 February 1969, at RP 159, f.22.

[41]   Chadwick, *Ramsey*, pp.184–85.

[42]   Ramsey to R.H.S. Crossman, 7 November 1967, at Ramsey Papers 115, f.301; Draft statement, probably from February 1968, at Ramsey Papers 134, ff.56. See also Ramsey's speech at H.L. Deb. *21 November 1968 vol. 297, cols. 1041–5, at 1044.*

The Church and State Commission

After the publication of the Howick report, and the passing of the Prayer Book Measure, the Church Assembly in November 1965 elected to set Howick aside in favour of a much broader re-examination of the whole matter of Church and State. Canon Max Warren of Westminster Abbey accepted the job of chairing the Commission, only to resign before the work began due to ill health.[43] His replacement was Owen Chadwick, then Dixie Professor of Ecclesiastical History in the University of Cambridge.[44] Much depended on this task, since Ramsey was well aware of mounting pressure within the Church for radical reform, and that conservative conclusions could only be acceptable if the hard questions had been squarely faced.[45] Beginning work in the autumn of 1966, the Commission made slow progress, and its report appeared in 1970.

The Commission concluded that there was 'widespread and basic agreement' that the Church of England ought to stand further apart from the State. At the same time, it found little agreement amongst those it interviewed on which elements of the establishment ought to change, and why. It thought a complete severing of the ties impracticable in the present state of opinion, since 'the people of England still want to feel that religion has a place in the land to which they can turn on the too rare occasions when they think that they need it'.[46] Much of the perceived value of the establishment accrued to the nation rather than to the Church.

Even if it stopped short of disestablishment, the Commission nonetheless recommended radical change. All matters of worship and doctrine should be 'subject to the final authority of the General Synod', along with the interpretation of doctrine by canon. When there were bishops to appoint, a board should be created to represent views of diocese and wider church. Other Christians should be invited to join the House of Lords. In general terms, the Commission thought it right that action by Measure in Parliament be restricted 'to fundamental changes of constitution or laws of property which affect secular rights'.[47]

Not all the commissioners agreed, and three members contributed memoranda of dissent from the report. The fullest was from Valerie Pitt, a prominent figure on the radical wing of the Church. For Pitt, nothing less than a complete severing of the ties would do, and it was part of the native complacency

[43]   Max Warren to Ramsey, 30 December 1965, Ramsey Papers 94, f.136.
[44]   Chadwick to Ramsey, 21 August 1966, Ramsey Papers 94, f.285.
[45]   Ramsey to Chadwick, 2 November 1967, at Ramsey Papers 112, ff.23–24.
[46]   *Church and State*, p.65.
[47]   *Church and State*, p.65.

of a national church not to feel the need. A church in which the majority of its nominal members never joined in the central act of its worshipping life had 'surely, a divided mind and a divided will. We need to discover our identity in Christ, our coherence in him and we cannot do this, we are not doing it, in the conditions of historical establishment.'[48]

The Worship and Doctrine Measure (1974)

Ramsey had stressed in his enthronement address in 1961 the need for 'a greater freedom in the ordering and in the urgent revising of our forms of worship.'[49] This work had to wait until the very last day of his time in office to be completed. The Worship and Doctrine Measure put into effect some of the recommendations of the Commission of 1970. It completed the process that some had thought had been accomplished by the Enabling Act of 1919 and the establishment of the Church Assembly, but had been shown to be incomplete by the Prayer Book Crisis of 1927–28.[50] Building on the experience with time-limited liturgical experimentation enabled by the Prayer Book measure of 1965, it gave the Church the freedom to determine its own liturgy and to revise its formularies of doctrine without recourse to Parliament. Ramsey himself moved the Measure in the House of Lords on 14 November 1974.

Ramsey was very sure of what the Measure did *not* provide for. It was 'not a Measure for the disestablishment of the Church of England, nor a step towards separating the Church of England from the Crown.' It was instead 'a chance for a partnership between the Church and the State in which the role of each will be better expressed and more effective.' The question could be put very simply: ought a church to be free, with pastors, ministers and laity working in concert, to order its own worship? Ramsey answered his own question thus: 'I do not believe that there is a single Church in Christendom which would not answer, "Yes." Certainly the Church of Scotland, established as it is, would say this. Certainly every province of the world-wide Anglican Communion would say this.'[51] The link between citizenship and membership of the established Church,

---

[48] *Church and State*, p.78. On Pitt, see Mark Chapman, '"A free church in a free state": Anglo-Catholicism and establishment', in Chapman, Maltby and Whyte, *Established Church*, pp.56–74, at 70–73.

[49] 'Whose hearts God has touched', in Ramsey, *Canterbury Essays and Addresses*, p.167.

[50] Matthew Grimley, 'The dog that didn't bark: the failure of disestablishment since 1927' in Chapman, Maltby and Whyte, *Established Church*, pp.39–55, at 49–52.

[51] H.L. Deb. 14 November 1974, vol. 354, cols. 868, 874, 869.

integral to the historic settlement between Church and State, would plainly be weakened: could a Church have this sort of autonomy and remain linked to the State in the way establishment implied? Ramsey thought so, and the example of the Church of Scotland showed it to be so.

But Ramsey knew that some of the Lords had received written protests about the Measure, mainly on the grounds that it had insufficient support from the laity, and that traditionalists, particularly those attached to the Book of Common Prayer, were not adequately protected against unwelcome change. On the future of the Book of Common Prayer, Ramsey thought that the Measure, far from putting its future in jeopardy, in fact put its status as one liturgical option and as a statement of historic doctrine on a firmer footing than during the preceding period of experimentation. As for the threat of the Church running away with strange and erroneous doctrine, Ramsey wryly noted the length and complexity of the decision-making processes involved: 'Is it likely that the Synod will be rash or hasty or unreliable in the use of this power? Its constitutional procedure would seem to make this somewhat unlikely'.[52]

The concern about the representativeness of the Synod was a more substantial one, and which went to the heart of the changed relationship between Church and State. How, it was asked, could a synod of a few hundred, elected by only 36,000, represent the two million people recorded on the Church's electoral rolls? Ramsey acknowledged that 'the desire for greater self-government for the Church was long vitiated by the failure to introduce the role of the laity effectively into a traditionally episcopal Church.' Ramsey thought that in the Measure there was now a means for the transmission of the voice of the laity in the localities, through the network of deanery synods to the General Synod. The advent of the Synod brought 'the partnership of the laity at every level of the Church's government'.[53]

So the Worship and Doctrine Measure completed the work that had been a central burden of Ramsey's programme on his enthronement. As we have seen, Ramsey set no particular store by establishment in principle, knowing that Anglican churches elsewhere and sister churches at home could survive, and had survived and indeed thrived without it. But in England in the 1960s, there were advantages to both Church and nation, as Ramsey saw it, in establishment. Ramsey's time saw no great disturbance in the symbolic link between Church and Crown. Despite the work of two Commissions, reform of the appointment of the Church's chief pastors by a politician had not come. The bishops retained

[52] H.L. Deb. 14 November 1974, vol. 354, col.872.
[53] H.L. Deb. 14 November 1974, vol. 354, col.869.

precisely the same position in the House of Lords, and thus as legislators for the nation, as had been the case in 1911 after the passing of the Parliament Act.

Despite these outward signs remaining the same, there had, however, been profound change in the relationship between the Church of England as a church for all the English, whether they desired it or not, and Parliament as the guarantor of their interests in it. The events of 1963–64 had shown that parliamentarians no longer had any confidence in their ability to adjudicate matters of doctrine within the Church; and even those traditionally most concerned about popish infiltration accepted that the lay synod of Parliament was no longer their best defence. The Chadwick Report had taken that reticence in Parliament as a signal that the time was right to bring forward proposals for greater freedoms.[54] By approving those proposals in the Worship and Doctrine Measure, the State had recognised that establishment no longer entailed the retention of a controlling veto over Church by State in these matters.

There was in this change a quiet recognition of a profound shift in what it meant to be a national church. Ramsey quite rightly argued that the General Synod now represented the laity far more effectively than the House of Laity in the Church Assembly ever had. But the line that circumscribed the body of the laity had been drawn much more tightly. The Synod of hundreds did indeed represent the thousands of members of deanery synods, who in turn were connected with the will of the 2 million on the Church of England's electoral rolls. But the representation by Parliament of the remaining tens of millions who took no part in their local church had been rendered considerably less potent in fact. Even if the outward trappings of the establishment were undisturbed, the shape of the Church had changed, to something much nearer Ramsey's conception.

---

[54]   *Church and State*, pp.19–20.

Chapter 3
Church and Nation

Introduction

An issue that became live in Ramsey's time as never before was the relationship between crime and sin. For centuries before the twentieth, there had been few useful means by which to think about moral behaviour and its regulation without authority exercised by or on behalf of the State. There had been no means by which to distinguish in principle between a private morality (the business of the individual alone), and a public morality in which society was an interested party. And as there had been near-universal consensus on the existence of such a public morality, there was also agreement on its sources: England was a Christian country, and its moral law was in large part based on Christian principles.

By the mid-twentieth century, things were changing, and quickly. Legislators had begun to ask fundamental questions about the imposition of Christian standards of behaviour on those who were ceasing to adhere to Christian doctrine or practice. And indeed about both the feasibility and necessity of a 'moral law' at all.[1] And this put all the churches in a new situation, and the established Church in particular, with its bishops legislating as peers in Parliament.

The Church of England and its leaders were pulled in many directions.[2] The seminal Wolfenden Report of 1957 (of which more below) sought to distinguish just such a private morality in the abstract, the concern only of private persons, unless their behaviour tended to disturb public order or decency, or to exploit or corrupt the vulnerable. There were Christians who welcomed the distinction, although on slightly different grounds. For these, the law needed reform as a simple recognition of the changed reality of the churches' relationship with the people. It also needed reform because certain behaviours, which they saw as morally disordered regardless of the law, could most easily be met, and their victims helped, if those people were not made criminals. It was only a minority

---

[1]　On the broader 'legislative revolution' in international context, see McLeod, *Religious Crisis of the 1960s*, pp.217–39.

[2]　On the response of the churches to this cluster of issues in general, see G.I.T. Machin, *Churches and Social Issues in Twentieth-Century Britain* (Oxford, 1998), in particular pp.175–210.

in the churches, albeit a visible one associated with John A.T. Robinson and the 'New Morality', which argued that the Church should support the reform of the law because it also needed to abandon its own strictures about the inherent immorality of this or that type of behaviour.[3] Instead, the churches should regard the moral status of an act as dependent on whether it was carried out in love; what the philosopher Alasdair Macintyre called a 'morality of intention.'[4]

There were also several strands of conservative thinking on the issue. Not all within the legal establishment were convinced by Wolfenden's attempt to carve out areas of behaviour that *a priori* were no concern of the State. The eminent lawyer and judge Patrick (later Baron) Devlin, a Roman Catholic, argued in 1959 that there were no solid logical grounds on which to do so, if indeed such a distinction were desirable. For a system of commonly held moral beliefs to function, and to command acceptance, mere enforcement by the law was not enough; and almost all accepted the need for such common belief. A society which willed the ends must also will the means; and 'no society has yet solved the problem of how to teach morality without religion.' The law had to base itself on Christian moral principles, and enforce them, not simply because they were widely held, or because it was the established Church that taught them 'but for the compelling reason that without the help of Christian teaching the law will fail.'[5]

There were those within the Church who held both that there was still a positive content to Christian morality beyond the Robinsonian emphasis on intention, and that it was the business of the law to enforce it. Christians with a relatively positive view of human nature and the prospects of perfecting it were sometimes inclined to view the law as a means of positively promoting greater virtue. Anglican evangelicals had long held a more negative view. Fallen man was prone always to vice, and the only means of altering that was renewed mission, and the conversion of souls to a godly life. However, even if the law could not promote virtuous living, it was at least valuable for many evangelicals as a means of restraint; of preventing even greater degradation. Although concerted evangelical campaigning on morality was relatively limited in the 1950s and 1960s (being more associated with the campaigns of the Festival of Light in

---

[3]   Robinson, *Honest to God*, pp.105–21.
[4]   Alasdair Macintyre, *Secularization and Moral Change* (London, 1967), p.71.
[5]   Patrick Devlin, 'Morals and the Criminal Law' in *The Enforcement of Morals* (London, 1965), p.25; a lecture first given in 1959.

the 1970s), the default evangelical response to relaxation of the law tended to be negative.[6]

There was also of course a close connection between the moral content of the law and notions of respectability at large. There has been much recent scholarship on the notion of the agreed public standard of behaviour and its complex relation with what was acceptable in private.[7] It is sufficient to note here that by no means all of the voices calling on Ramsey to oppose relaxation of the law belonged to those who were active members of the churches. For many, respectability entailed the observance of a largely Christian moral code, and it was part of the function of the established Church to resist anything that might weaken it.

Ramsey was thus hearing many voices, pressing him either to oppose or to support the changes in the law as they came forward. Ramsey's own academic career had been relatively little taken up with moral theology *per se*. In addition, although as a bishop he produced writings, sermons and speeches concerned with particular moral issues, he rarely addressed the relationship between public morality and the Church's own discipline in the abstract. However, something of his view can be seen in his *Image Old and New*, the pamphlet published in 1963 in reaction to John Robinson's *Honest to God*. Robinson's chapter on 'The New Morality' had for Ramsey taken some sensible premises from which much could be learned, and applied them to produce unwarranted conclusions. Yes, it was important that legalism in morals be avoided, and it was certainly more pastorally useful to show that this or that moral failing was 'to betray the obligations of love for the other person' than merely to point out that it was 'on the list of things forbidden without really showing "why"'.[8] For Ramsey, it was also true that Christ had not laid down a code of law, but had dealt with moral questions in their context, and with individual people.

Robinson had, however, gone much further than this, to argue that not only was context important, it was in fact all-important. For Robinson, no action could have intrinsic moral value; *Honest to God* suggested that almost any action could be justified if the intention of one was of love towards the other. Not all had been convinced. Alasdair Macintyre thought that Robinson had so emptied Christian morality of all substantial content as to render it meaningless in practical terms,

---

[6]   See Matthew Grimley, 'Anglican evangelicals and anti-permissiveness: the Nationwide Festival of Light, 1971–1983', in *Evangelicalism,* ed. Atherstone and Maiden, pp.183–205.

[7]   For a useful summary, see Ian Jones, *The local church and generational change in Birmingham 1945–2000* (Woodbridge, 2012), pp.155–59.

[8]   Ramsey, *Image Old and New*, p.13.

particularly once applied outside familial relationships.[9] Ramsey did not go quite that far; but Robinson, the eminent biblical scholar, had for Ramsey wrenched elements of Christ's teaching from the meaning of his whole ministry. Christ had not abolished the law but fulfilled it, and only an examination of Christ's pattern in its Hebraic context and Pauline elaboration could make sense of it. It was also too much to dismiss, as Robinson did, any meaning in the elemental institutions of the created order, including marriage and the family. For Ramsey, the whole revelation of God in scripture and in creation demanded that at least some acts and omissions remained intrinsically wrong.[10]

Capital Punishment

No-one, even amongst those on the furthest reaches of moral philosophy, thought that murder was anything other than intrinsically wrong, always and everywhere. Since it involved the most radical of harm to others, it was a matter for the law for Benthamite liberals as well as for the most staunch advocate of the moral law. The consensus ended over what the penalties ought to be, and the purpose of punishment more generally. As early as 1948 the House of Commons had supported abolition of the death penalty only for it to be overturned by the Lords. The Homicide Act of 1957 had not abolished the penalty, but greatly reduced the offences for which it could be applied. In the early years of Ramsey's time at Lambeth the impetus continued to grow for further legislation for either complete abolition or at least reform of an unworkable Act.[11]

The historic Christian position had for a long time been supportive of the ultimate penalty. When the House of Lords debated it in 1948, only George Bell of Chichester among the bishops had favoured abolition.[12] Geoffrey Fisher, speaking in the Lords in 1956, had disagreed with those 'sincere but mistaken people' in the churches who thought that the penalty was always and everywhere wrong. 'Society may use it in defence of society itself', he argued, to 'repair the

[9]   Macintyre, *Secularization*, pp.71–72; see also Rowan Williams, 'John A.T. Robinson (1919–1983). *Honest to God* and the 1960s' in *Anglican Identities* (London, 2004), pp.103–20.
[10]   Ramsey, *Image Old and New*, p.14.
[11]   Neville Twitchell, *The Politics of the Rope: the Campaign to Abolish Capital Punishment in Britain, 1955–1969* (Bury St Edmunds, 2012), pp.128–37.
[12]   Chandler and Hein, *Fisher*, p.125.

damage done by murder to its own integrity, and to bear witness to the majesty of its own first principles ... That is Christian doctrine'.[13]

Christian feeling was shifting, however, and already by 1956 Fisher was looking 'beleaguered and isolated'.[14] In October 1961 the Convocations of Canterbury and York passed a motion calling for abolition or at least suspension of the penalty.[15] The bishops of the southern province voted unanimously in favour of abolition on the issue in January 1962, as did those in the Convocation of York in May, opposed only by Maurice Harland of Durham.[16] The correspondent of *The Economist* noted the speed with which the bishops' views had changed since Joseph Hunkin, Bishop of Truro, had argued in 1948 for the *extension* of the penalty, and thought it likely to sway the views of Conservatives in Parliament when the time came.[17]

Within the churches at large, the matter was one over which there was genuine conscientious disagreement. For each who pressed the sovereignty of God in giving and taking life, there was the retort of an eye for an eye. Ramsey gave reassurances that the opinion of the Convocation was just that – an opinion – and not binding on the consciences of individual Anglicans.[18] There was thus a risk that by campaigning too prominently in favour of one opinion, those consciences would be troubled.

At the same time, the moral sense of public opinion – a sense shaped by custom, practice, and the historic position of the churches – was a good way away from the near consensus amongst the bishops for abolition.[19] As Patrick Devlin had argued, the moral law could only hold if it more or less reflected what 12 reasonable jurors, after deliberation, believed and felt; and all the evidence showed that those jurors favoured the retention of the ultimate punishment by

---

[13]   In the Lords on 10 July 1956, as given at Chandler and Hein, *Fisher*, p.213; *Spectator*, 30 April 1948, p.1.

[14]   Chandler and Hein, *Fisher*, p.125. See also the summary of the background and the shift in Anglican opinion in Harry Potter, *Hanging in Judgment. Religion and the Death Penalty in England* (New York, 1993), pp.191–99. Hugh McLeod, 'God and the gallows: Christianity and capital punishment in the nineteenth and twentieth centuries', in *Retribution, Repentance and Reconciliation*, ed. K. Cooper and J. Gregory (Studies in Church History 40, Woodbridge, 2004), pp.330–56.

[15]   See the papers at Ramsey Papers 4, ff.261–65; Riley and Graham, *Acts of the Convocations*, p.153.

[16]   Chadwick, *Ramsey*, p.159.

[17]   *The Economist*, 20 January 1962; *The Times*, 16 May 1962.

[18]   Ramsey to Sir Stephen Holmes, 16 February 1962, Ramsey Papers 16, f.152.

[19]   Potter, *Hanging in Judgment*, p.202.

a large majority.[20] So there was also a risk for the established Church if it were seen to be too far ahead of public opinion, even if as a result it were to lead it, over time, in a particular direction.

As with most things, Ramsey was called upon to act by both sides. The archbishop had often been regarded by at least some of the people as a moral arbiter: as an honest broker in the cause of peace or justice at the heart of the establishment. And so it was that Ramsey was approached three times in 1963 alone about impending or recent executions, asking him to intervene as 'spiritual leader of the Establishment' or chiding him for not having done so. The answer to each was the same: that the bishops had shown themselves in favour of abolition; that Ramsey had himself voted for abolition in the House of Lords; and that in the meantime, it was for the Home Secretary alone to make dispensation in this or that case.[21]

Ramsey's own view had been settled for some time before he was confronted with Sydney Silverman's bill in 1965, although his expression of it had an element of provisionality. Speaking in the House of Lords, his argument was one of moral principle and pragmatic accommodation. By means of the death penalty, the State said to a murderer that in return for the taking of one life it would take another: '[t]his does not enhance the sacredness of human life. I believe that it devalues it further.' Ramsey spoke strikingly of the necessity of retribution, but without emotion: its purpose was not vengeance, but moral reformation, and needed a 'retributive moral seriousness.' The life term showed the offender that he or she could have no claim to a normal life as part of society until such a time that society could know that 'you are on the way to being a different sort of person from what you are now.'[22]

Ramsey also noted the difficulties with the 1957 Homicide Act. Its attempt to distinguish classes of murder, some meriting death and some not, had been found by senior legal figures to be largely unworkable. Whatever the justification for the penalty in principle, the absurdities that the Act had produced, and their manifest injustice, presented a moral case for reform of the law, even if (as Ramsey admitted) it might be argued that the solution was to return to the state of affairs as it was *before* the Act. In addition, had advocates of the penalty been able to show that it was a uniquely effective deterrent, then that 'might throw an overwhelming weight if it were an argument that had real validity.'[23]

[20]   Devlin, *The Enforcement of Morals*, p.15.
[21]   The three exchanges from November and December 1963, are collected together at Ramsey Papers 33, ff.292–99. The phrase is quoted from f.294.
[22]   The speech was reproduced in Ramsey, *Canterbury Pilgrim*, pp.139–43; p.140.
[23]   Ramsey, *Canterbury Pilgrim*, p.142.

But ultimately that evidence had not been forthcoming, and so the punishment failed on its key pragmatic ground.

At the request of two fellow peers whom he respected, Ramsey then took a risk, which he had not taken before and was not to repeat: to consent to pilot Sydney Silverman's Bill when it came to the Lords in 1965. After some deliberation, Ramsey thought the task a 'duty and a privilege', even with the great expenditure of time involved, and the roughness of the exchanges into which he would necessarily be drawn.[24] As a result of his decision, back to the surface came the same tensions already evident in his postbag. For Ramsey to pilot this Bill, above all others, was to say very clearly that the abolitionist position had the weight of Christian authority on its side. When it came to it, ten bishops voted for the Bill and none against; Ramsey's view was clearly that of the bishops. However, his fellow peers told him very clearly, as did the press, that the public were not with them, and that to pilot the Bill would be 'both shocking and unwise' and was 'bound to impair your position and that of our Church.'[25] As another peer later put it, 'I firmly believe that the State has a right to take life in a proper case', something Ramsey himself had acknowledged, in general terms, when making his own maiden speech as Archbishop of York in 1956, and it had not been forgotten. 'In our previous debates', Lord Conesford continued, 'that was the view of both Archbishops, and I can scarcely believe, therefore, that it is a view which it is improper for a Christian to hold.'[26] And so, with reluctance, Ramsey bowed to the pressure and stepped aside, persuaded that his moving the Bill would hinder rather than help it. He had to content himself with speaking and voting in its favour at the successful second reading; and again in 1969 when Parliament reaffirmed its earlier mind.[27]

The Family

In his exposition of the 'New Morality', John Robinson had ruled out the two sources of authority from which fixed moral principles had traditionally been derived: Scripture when understood as normative, easy to interpret and fixed in meaning; and the witness of creation, often known as natural law. Such supranaturalist thinking was no longer tenable for "modern man". For Robinson,

---

[24]   Chadwick, *Ramsey*, p.160.

[25]   The view of Lord Dilhorne, as quoted at Chadwick, *Ramsey*, pp.160–61.

[26]   H.L. Deb., 20 July 1965 vol. 268, col.673; Ramsey's maiden speech as Archbishop of York is at H.L. Deb. 9 July 1956, vol. 198, cols.595–98.

[27]   Potter, *Hanging in Judgment*, p.203.

the indissolubility of marriage was not a matter of divine command 'delivered to Moses on the mountain top, graven on tablets' and transmitted by the written Scriptures. Neither was dissolution an ontological impossibility: marriage was not 'a physical or metaphysical union ... which cannot be abrogated any more than two persons can cease to be brother and sister.'[28]

Ramsey's own view, and his view of what the Church's position ought to be, was some way removed from that of Robinson. His address to an audience in Westminster Central Hall in November 1972 was an entirely traditional statement of traditional Christian doctrine. Marriage was a 'covenant to a lifelong union' of man and woman, 'a union in which they give themselves to one another until death parts them.' Within this union, men and women could share in the divine action of creation through the procreation of children, and within the stability of the married union children learned 'the freedom and discipline of mutual love and care for one another.' The family was not simply one contingent and local form of social relations that might be exchanged for another: 'the family has its own unique role within a society based on justice, brotherhood, and the true freedom found in the service of God.'[29]

Ramsey's interventions in the matters of family law described below must be read in the context of this understanding of the family and its social role. There were many and powerful social forces in play that affected its shape and character. Ramsey noted the change in gender roles in relation to employment and domestic work, pressure on the national housing stock, and growing physical distance between work and home, which had an impact on the time that fathers (and it was mostly fathers) spent with their families. Social change of this sort was the concern of the Church by reason of its impact on the family, and the obstacles it thus placed in the way of human flourishing in relation to the Creator.[30]

There was also the much-discussed 'sexual revolution', and it is crucial to understand the extent and limits of Ramsey's undoubted concern about its impact, since satirists at the time (and the Church itself more recently) have done well in suggesting that the churches were disproportionately concerned with sexual sin, to the point of obsession. Ramsey saw the danger of being seen to be obsessed with symptoms whilst missing the cause. 'If we are wise', he told his audience at Westminster Central Hall, 'we shall not concentrate on denunciations of evil in the sexual sphere but shall try to cope at every point with

[28]   Robinson, *Honest to God*, pp.106–7.
[29]   'The Family', in Ramsey, *Canterbury Pilgrim*, pp.168–70.
[30]   Ramsey, *Canterbury Pilgrim*, pp.168–69.

the sickness in society that leads to such evil.'[31] As Owen Chadwick observed, Ramsey was for several reasons reluctant to be too closely associated with the campaign for moral reform known as the Nationwide Festival of Light.[32] Whilst evil in the sexual sphere was important, there were dangers in making it central.

Ramsey's view of sex was very positive, in its right context. It was right, he thought, to have broken the Victorian silence on the subject. But sex was by God's design 'a bond of a union between two persons in their totality as persons', and so there was a need to resist 'those influences which separate sex from human personality and treat it as an excitement on a sub-human plane'.[33] It was this reason that he recoiled from 'horrible' commercial exploitation of sex, and this explains his public interventions in the matter of pornography.

Should the law be concerned with pornographic publication, and should the Church be pressing for such a change? For Ramsey and others in the churches, pornography was both harmful to the individual, and a solvent of important ties that bound wider society together. For the Benthamite liberal, however, the former effect on the individual was no-one's business but their own; and there was little consensus on the latter effect, and certainly not as articulated in Christian terms.

Ramsey did at one stage contact the Home Office to see if anything could be done about the receipt of unsolicited material by post, but the matter went no further.[34] In law, the matter had in fact been decisively altered before Ramsey's time, by the 1959 Obscene Publications Act (with minor amendment in 1964). In any case, there would not have been sufficient weight within the Church behind an *increase* in State intervention in moral affairs, as the current of liberal opinion flowed decisively in the opposite direction.

For Ramsey, the target at which Christian action should be directed was different, and more fundamental. People could most effectively be brought to see the deepest meaning of the family and of sex within marriage if they were first brought to the 'knowledge and love of God'.[35] So to counter increased sexualisation of culture, the need for Ramsey was for renewed mission. Within the Church, Christian families could be living models of the kind of freedom realised by means of Christian service to each other that Christ had himself modelled. For those who were not Christians, the Church needed to proclaim the same, but on the basis of what Ramsey called 'the natural law of morality'.

[31] Ramsey, *Canterbury Pilgrim*, p.170.
[32] Chadwick, *Ramsey*, pp.162–63.
[33] Chadwick, *Ramsey*, p.169.
[34] Chadwick, *Ramsey*, p.164.
[35] Ramsey, *Canterbury Pilgrim*, p.170.

Unlike John Robinson, Ramsey believed that certain moral principles could be read off from creation, and were to a degree part of human nature if brought to its highest pitch. It was a case of following the Maker's instructions for best results.

Theatre Censorship

There was, however, one important change in the law in relation to issues of freedom of expression with which Ramsey had to deal: the ending of theatre censorship under the Theatres Act of 1968. This particular matter was complicated by the longstanding involvement of the Archbishop himself in the very workings of the system. Entirely informally, the staff of the Lord Chamberlain had routinely consulted Lambeth in certain cases, usually where plays involved direct dealing with religious themes, but also where they touched on matters of moral conduct. By the end of the Second World War the rate of such consultations had dwindled to a trickle, and the only remaining rule of any fixity was a ban on the personation of any person of the Trinity, the last advice on which Ramsey gave in 1961.[36]

A great deal has been written on the disrepute into which the system of censorship had fallen by the mid-1960s, to which this account shall not add.[37] But within the Church there was an added pressure, since those who saw a relaxation of the law as a weakening of the bulwark against corruption were not the only voices to be heard. Christian secularists argued that the law could no longer seek to control the free expression of the artist, no matter how vulgar, trivial or shocking that expression was.[38] Within the Church there were also dramatists and players who found the censorship of the treatment of religious themes an almost insuperable barrier to the use of drama as a means of mission.[39]

---

[36]   Peter Webster, 'The archbishop of Canterbury, the Lord Chamberlain and the censorship of the theatre, 1909–49', *Studies in Church History* 48 (2012), pp.437–48.

[37]   *Inter alia*, see Steve Nicholson, *The Censorship of British Drama, 1900–68* (3 vols, Exeter, 2003–2009).

[38]   On the working out of these arguments in the context of the Lady Chatterley trial of 1960, see Stuart Mews, 'The trials of Lady Chatterley, the modernist bishop and the Victorian archbishop: clashes of class, culture and generations', *Studies in Church History* 48 (2012), pp.449–64; Mark Roodhouse, 'Lady Chatterley and the Monk: Anglican radicals and the Lady Chatterley trial of 1960', *Journal of Ecclesiastical History* 59 (2008), 475–500.

[39]   On the possibilities offered by greater Christian engagement with the theatre in general, see Kay M. Baxter, *Speak what we feel. A Christian looks at the contemporary theatre* (London, 1964), *passim*.

There was one play in particular, the treatment of which by the censor crystallised these tensions. *The Green Pastures* by the American playwright Marc Connelly was widely regarded by dramatists within the churches as a highly effective presentation of the Christian faith, and a film version had met with acclaim. But God the Father appeared in the play as an elderly man with cigar and gaiters and as such it was refused a licence several times between 1930 and 1961.[40] Approached in 1961 for his advice, Ramsey thought the play as good a case as any for an exception, but also that if the rule were to be relaxed, it ought to be on the basis of a more general relaxation of the rule; and so the play was refused a licence once more (although this was to be the last time).[41]

By 1966, pressure was building within the churches for change. Ramsey was approached by Martin Browne, a guiding spirit in English religious drama, for Ramsey's support for a deputation from the Religious Drama Society to the Lord Chamberlain.[42] Drama was now increasingly valued as a means of teaching, particularly the young; but the fact that modern drama could not portray Christ as a man, but only as a figure in a medieval mystery play, gave the impression that 'the belief in the incarnate Son of God, true God and true Man, is either irrelevant or a fable in need of artificial protection.'[43] Ramsey thought it best that he himself were not directly associated with the RDS's campaign, since he would most likely be consulted directly; but there was momentum towards the taking of a 'fresh look' at the issues, and Ramsey's own mind on the matter was moving. Although he could not immediately see an easy alternative to the blanket ban, 'I am aware that there are thoughtful and reverent people who think that one might be found.'[44]

There followed an example of a consultation amongst the leaders of all the denominations; an occasion on which the established Church acted as mouthpiece for all the others, channelling a consensus view to Parliament through its own unique connections. Noel, Lord Annan, had in the Lords called for a new Joint Select Committee to examine the system of censorship.[45] Ramsey's office thus canvassed opinion amongst the leaders of the Free Churches

[40] Webster, 'Censorship of the theatre', p.440.
[41] Ramsey to the Lord Chamberlain (the Earl of Scarborough), 29 October 1961, at Ramsey Papers 8, f.17.
[42] Browne to Ramsey, 3 January 1966, at Ramsey Papers 93, f.36.
[43] Religious Drama Society memo 'The visual representation of Jesus Christ on the stage', dated January 1965, at Ramsey Papers 93, f.37.
[44] Ramsey to Martin Browne, 6 January 1966, at Ramsey Papers 93, f.38; Ramsey to the Lord Chamberlain (Lord Cobbold), 11 February 1966, at Ramsey Papers 93, f.59.
[45] H.L. Deb. 17 February 1966 vol. 272 cols. 1151

on the specific point of the representation of God, whilst the Lord Chamberlain himself made enquiries of the Church of Scotland and of Cardinal Heenan. Some of the churches had considered the matter more than others, but there was general agreement that the rule as applied was too rigid, although not quite on how it might otherwise work in practice.[46] In reply, the Lord Chamberlain expressed himself willing to discontinue the absolute rule, but to continue to consult Ramsey and others on difficult cases.[47]

At the same time most of the leaders Ramsey consulted felt that there was yet a need for some form of censorship in general in relation to 'personal values and reverence for God', since (as Ramsey summed it up) the current system 'does not really achieve the object that censorship should have, namely of presenting the right things and forbidding the wrong ones.'[48] In its reflexive acceptance of the general need for the censor, this snapshot of general ecclesiastical opinion was clearly some way distant from the drift of wider public and expert opinion that would eventually issue in the 1968 Act.

The view expressed had been mostly concerned with the narrower issue of the churches' own use of drama, and the keenly felt restrictions the censorship placed on it. Events were now moving on a wider plane, and Ramsey was soon asked to make representations to the Joint Committee on the matter of the censorship as a whole. As such, a wider view was needed, which Ramsey's office set about obtaining from experts from within the Church. The resulting memorandum, over Ramsey's signature, was presented to the Joint Committee in December 1966, along with statements from Roman Catholic representatives and from the Free Church Federal Council.[49] In this statement Ramsey's view had moved in a more liberal direction. It was time that the current system was relaxed, so long as it was not at the cost of 'encouraging lower moral standards or a lessened sensitivity to other people's feelings on what is seemly and reverent in matters of religion'. How these provisos might be achieved was not clear; but, importantly, they were now a matter for the theatrical world to deal with, rather than the law, although the Church stood ready to advise if required. On the specific matter of representing God on the stage, religious susceptibilities had changed, in a new environment of greater openness to discussion of the nature of God, and theology in general. In this changed environment 'encouragement fearlessly to face unfamiliar and temporarily distressing images of Him is probably more help

---

[46] Ramsey to the Lord Chamberlain, 18 April 1966, at Ramsey Papers 93, f.76
[47] The Lord Chamberlain to Ramsey, 9 May 1966, at Ramsey Papers 93, f.79.
[48] Ramsey to the Lord Chamberlain, 18 April 1966, at Ramsey Papers 93, f.76.
[49] Ramsey's statement forms Appendix 6 to *Joint Committee on Censorship of the Theatre. Report etc.* (London, 1967), pp.130-33.

today than censorship designed to protect from the confrontation.'[50] This was the end of Ramsey's active involvement in the process, although his office did ensure, as it usually did, that there was at least one bishop available when the Bill came to the Lords in June 1968, which they did not oppose.

The Law on Divorce

Putting Asunder. A Divorce Law for Contemporary Society has a fair claim to be the most influential report produced by the Church of England in Ramsey's time.[51] It was commissioned in January 1964 with a brief that showed the key characteristics of Ramsey's approach to the law. It recognised at the outset that there was already a visible and persistent difference between the attitude of the State and that of the Church as to the permanence of marriage, since the State was prepared to recognise the second marriage of one with a living first spouse when the Church was not. The group was thus charged to see whether there was any new principle that might be added to the law that would see it operate more justly, but that would 'do nothing to undermine the approach of couples to marriage as a lifelong covenant.'[52] It was a clear recognition that those Christians who would see a closer alignment of the law with Christian doctrine were whistling in the wind.[53] The report's principal recommendation was that there ought to be a new ground for divorce: when a marital relationship had broken down and was beyond repair. This was in many ways preferable to the single available ground hitherto, that of the matrimonial offence, and rather than one being added to the other, there should be a substitution.[54]

The preliminary sections of *Putting Asunder* set out the distance between the theology of marriage and the legitimate and realistic concern of the Church with the secular law. The 'rational proofs' of the essential rightness of marriage could no longer easily be commended to secular listeners. The Church should now seek to emphasise the distinctness of two aspects of the marital state. On the one hand, there was a cluster of rights and obligations in law that constituted a marriage, and in which the State must have the right to intervene in its own

---

[50] Ibid., pp.132-3.

[51] *Putting Asunder. A Divorce Law for Contemporary Society* (London, 1966).

[52] *Putting Asunder,* p.ix.

[53] For much valuable background to the pre-history and effects of *Putting Asunder,* see Jane Lewis and Patrick Wallis, 'Fault, breakdown and the Church of England's involvement in the 1969 divorce reform', *Twentieth Century British History,* 11 (2000), 308–32.

[54] *Putting Asunder,* pp.33–62.

interests. On the other hand, there was the Christian understanding of the spiritual significance of the marriage relationship, as sacrament, as incarnation of the created order, and as such as an indissoluble bond with its own ontological reality. Difficult though it was, the authors thought it still possible for the Church to hold to the latter conception in spiritual terms, and its own discipline, yet speak intelligibly to the debate over the former more limited concept in law. Christians would still believe that general principles of justice were consonant with the created order, but it was possible to join the debate on the basis of those principles alone, rather than on the understanding of God that animated them.[55]

Before debate was joined in earnest over the proposals that were to become law in 1969, in early 1964 there was proposed by the Lord Chancellor an apparently minor procedural change, which was to bring to the surface an important difference in thought and feeling in relation to marriage. Legal aid was expensive, and the fact that divorce cases were all tried at the High Court added considerably to that particular bill. The vast majority of divorce cases were not contested by either spouse, and passed through on average in seven minutes. These, it was thought, should not require the full panoply of the High Court, and should be transferred to county courts, saving a considerable amount in the process.

It was a pragmatic move, achievable quickly, in pursuit of the most efficient and cost-effective means of administering the law. However, Ramsey was sure from the outset that a considerable portion of Christian opinion would oppose the move, and let first the Douglas-Home and then the Wilson governments know it.[56] In the eyes of God, divorce was a grave and solemn matter, contested or otherwise, and society needed to reflect that in the manner in which it was granted. To move it to lesser courts, mixed in with cases of hire purchase default and other mundanities, was symbolically important, and unwelcome.

There then followed an episode which neatly encapsulated the ambiguities and complexities of the position of the Archbishop. After the publication of *Putting Asunder*, members of that group met in June 1967 with representatives of the Law Commission, to see whether any compromise could be reached between the report and the thinking of the Commission.[57] A memorandum from Ramsey's office states that when asked by Hume Boggis-Rolfe, secretary of the Law Commission, it had been made clear that Ramsey had not approved all

---

[55]   *Putting Asunder,* pp.6–16.

[56]   Ramsey to Bishop of Carlisle, 21 February 1964, at Ramsey Papers 57, f.191.

[57]   Final TS of document 'Reform of Grounds of Divorce. Result of Discussions between Archbishop's Group on Divorce and Law Commission.' 2 June 1967, at Ramsey Papers 117, ff.328–36.

the elements of the compromise reached, and wished to stand far enough apart from it to allow him to criticise the Bill if necessary.[58]

Thus had Ramsey and his staff made the status of *Putting Asunder* and the subsequent discussions clear, or at least so they thought. As far as they were concerned, a view had been taken by a group of experts assembled by the Church, but not officially endorsed by it. Early in 1968 the Divorce Reform Bill appeared, and almost immediately criticism of it began to appear in Ramsey's postbag. Soon Ramsey made public his unhappiness with elements of the Bill. He regretted that the Bill differed from *Putting Asunder* in its enlargement of existing grounds for divorce, rather than the substitution of breakdown as the sole ground. 'I specially deplore the proposal for divorce by consent and the shortening of the period for desertion as a ground, and I think that it is not clear that the Bill would give enough protection to the interests of a faithful party and his or her children.'[59]

That an Archbishop should publicly disagree with proposed legislation was not in itself unusual. But several amongst the legal and political establishment had some difficulty in accepting that the discussions between the Law Commission and the *Putting Asunder* group should not be binding on Ramsey as events unfolded. The Labour MP Leo Abse accused Ramsey of a breach of faith, which Ramsey emphatically denied, stating that he had been clear with the Law Commission that there were elements of the compromise that he could not support.[60] More seriously, there was talk of a public breach between Ramsey and the Commission. Bryan Bentley, canon of Windsor, moral theologian and member of the *Putting Asunder* group, reported that even that group had been unaware that Ramsey had not agreed with their compromise, and Lord Scarman, chairman of the Commission, was reportedly incensed by some phrases in a newspaper article that Ramsey had issued.[61]

For a short while, this private discontent threatened to emerge into public view. It was, however, smoothed over by a letter to *The Times* by Norman Anderson, a member of the *Putting Asunder* group, and by a private visit from Robert Beloe, Ramsey's lay chief of staff, to Scarman and colleagues. In this,

---

[58] Memo dated 26 July 1967, at Ramsey Papers 117, f.337.

[59] TS of Ramsey's statement, at Ramsey Papers 138, f.14.

[60] See variously the reports in *The Times*, the *Daily Telegraph*, the *Daily Mirror* and *The Sun* from 19 January 1968, copies at Ramsey Papers 138, ff.11–13; transcript of remarks by Ramsey to the press in Manchester on 19 January 1968, at Ramsey Papers 138, f.15.

[61] Bentley to Ramsey, 13 February 1968, at Ramsey Papers 138, ff.196–97; memorandum of meeting at Lambeth Palace, 15 February 1968, at Ramsey Papers 138, f.201–2.

as in many other matters in relation to Parliament and the law, Beloe was highly effective in Ramsey's absences and his omissions.[62] Ramsey saw that his article in the *Sunday Times* had been susceptible to misinterpretation; and he wrote to Scarman to apologise for the misunderstanding.[63] Privately, however, he remained convinced that the Bill could rightly be criticised on grounds contained within *Putting Asunder*. He was also sure that it had been right to speak out, since the impression was given in the wider discussion that he and the Church supported the compromise simply because some members of the *Putting Asunder* group had been involved in its formulation: 'That fallacy had to be broken up.'[64] Bentley agreed that the public at large were apt to suppose that any Christian who expressed a view in public necessarily represented the Church, which seemed to make it impossible for Christians to act independently as citizens.[65] Eventually the Divorce Reform Bill passed into law in 1969, with Ramsey abstaining at the Second Reading, and the bishops dividing.[66]

Abortion

A second major plank of the moral law that saw decisive change on Ramsey's watch was the law on the termination of pregnancy.[67] As with the law on divorce, those churches that engaged sympathetically with the process of reform have later been indicted by conservative commentators with colluding with ostensibly limited reform which in fact opened the door to a more wholesale permission.[68] From the first, the effects of the change in the law were monitored, discussed and disputed; the numbers of legal abortions rose, although the statistics were disputed, since the law was designed to legitimise and thus control those abortions that already occurred illegally and went unrecorded. There

[62]   Chadwick, *Ramsey*, pp.116, 190, 248.
[63]   Ramsey to Scarman, 19 February 1968, at Ramsey Papers 138, f.222.
[64]   Ramsey to Bentley, 15 February 1968, at Ramsey Papers 138, ff.203–4.
[65]   Bentley to Ramsey, 16 February 1968, at Ramsey Papers 138, f.210.
[66]   Chadwick, *Ramsey*, p.153.
[67]   See the outline of the issue in Machin, *Churches and Social Issues*, pp.199–201.
[68]   See, for instance, the analysis of Raymond Johnston of the Nationwide Festival of Light; Andrew Atherstone, 'Christian family, Christian nation: Raymond Johnston and the Nationwide Festival of Light in defence of the family' in *Religion and the Household*, ed. John Doran, Charlotte Methuen and Alexandra Walsham (*Studies in Church History* 50, Woodbridge, 2014), 456–68, at p.464.

were difficult and indeed horrific cases, and sensational reporting in the press.[69] Abortion became a plot line in larger stories that were told of the nation's moral decay. Some thought there ought to be a national day of prayer on the matter, for 'true guidance to our leaders and for the awakening of Christian conscience.'[70] In 1973 Ramsey was petitioned by the Society for the Protection of the Unborn Child, that the Church of England should do more to stem the inexorable rise in the numbers, and to support doctors who conscientiously objected.[71] There was also criticism of the bishops' supposed collusion in the passing of the 1967 Act, and their quiescence since.[72] And so, it is necessary to peel away the contested later history of abortion in the UK to examine the reactions of Ramsey and the Church to the tightly constrained terms of debate on the issue in the mid-1960s.

In the early stages of that debate, there had been a consciousness that the present law was both ambiguous in part, and socially harmful where it was clear. The prevailing boundaries of legitimate abortion rested on statute law, significantly modified by a single case, never tested on appeal: the 'Bourne judgment' of 1938. The case of Aleck Bourne had left open the possibility that abortion might be permissible where there was significant risk to the health of the mother, and not to her life alone as the statute law required; a provision that was interpreted increasingly liberally as time went on. But access to abortion under this provision was in practical terms limited to those who could pay, and the numbers of terminations obtained illegally each year suggested that there was considerable demand for that which the law could not supply. When abortion was obtained illegally, the consequences for the mother were often dire.[73]

As was the case with the reform of the law on divorce, the Church of England had in progress a group examining the issue. As with *Putting Asunder*, the group was composed of experts: physicians, social workers, moral philosophers, and clergy specialising in issues of ethics. Its report *Abortion: an ethical discussion* was drawn into wider debates, and misrepresented, as *Putting Asunder* was to be.[74]

---

[69]   A particularly notorious case occurred in Glasgow in January 1969. See Scottish Office memorandum, undated, at Ramsey Papers 151, f.110; 'Are aborted babies being burned alive', *Catholic Herald*, 18 July 1969.

[70]   Mrs U.M Fuchter (Society for the Protection of the Unborn Child, Kent branch) to Ramsey, 7 November 1973, at Ramsey Papers 246, ff.62–65.

[71]   Nicholas Fogg to Ramsey, 27 June 1973, at Ramsey Papers 246, ff.9–11a.

[72]   Hugh Whitworth to Margaret White, 27 June 1973, at Ramsey Papers 246, f.13.

[73]   Nigel Yates, *Love Now, Pay Later? Sex and Religion in the Fifties and Sixties* (London, 2010), pp.93–95; Sheila Rowbotham, *A Century of Women. The History of Women in Britain and the United States* (London, 1999) pp.194, 306, 360–61.

[74]   *Abortion. An Ethical Discussion* (London, 1965).

It concluded that abortion was ethically acceptable under certain limited circumstances, being when there was a threat to the life or health of the mother, which included both physical and mental health. Crucially, the authors thought that this calculation should include aspects of the situation of the family, if the arrival of a new child into that situation would threaten the mother's well-being. The decision ought to rest with medical professionals, after due consultation with other experts in social welfare. The report therefore allowed room for the abortion of foetuses with physical deformity, or which had been conceived as a result of rape or incest. However, these were not in themselves to be the ground; they were significant only insofar as they affected the mental health of the mother. The authors acknowledged the fear of the traditional moralist 'of a steady increase ... so that abortion came to be demanded, and allowed, for minor inconveniences which fell far short of the seriousness which alone would make termination licit.' However, they were confident that 'such safeguards as are necessary can be devised.'[75]

It is worth noting that which the report did *not* propose. While it attributed a moral status to the foetus, as having the potential for life, it asserted that if the interests of foetus and mother were irreconcilable, then those of the mother should win out. In this, it was close to the present law as it was customarily read off from the Bourne case. It was also some distance from the more absolutist position that characterised Roman Catholic thought on the subject, which if pursued to its logical conclusion would, the authors thought, lead in some cases to the death of both mother and foetus, and which avoided such untenable conclusions only by casuistry. The authors were however confident that the solution proposed upheld the general right to life of the foetus, and thus recognised the sanctity of human life, whilst sufficiently recognising the realities.[76]

As it happened, the report was in its final draft in late 1965 when the Labour peer Lewis Silkin brought forward a Bill to amend the law. The events of the following year until David Steel's Bill became law again demonstrated the ambiguities of the positions of both the Church and the Archbishop. As word of Silkin's Bill spread around Westminster, Ramsey arranged for draft copies of the report to be sent to Silkin, the Lord Chancellor and various others, but stressed that he himself had not yet reached a firm conclusion on the matter.[77] He also stressed that the report did not commit the Church to any particular view; Silkin in reply acknowledged the state of play, and undertook not to use

---

[75]   *Abortion. An Ethical Discussion* p.34.
[76]   *Abortion. An Ethical Discussion*, pp.28–32.
[77]   Ramsey to Silkin, Earl Longford, the Lord Chancellor and other peers, 15 November 1965, at Ramsey Papers 70, ff.186–88.

the report in debate.[78] Ramsey shortly afterwards left the country for a visit to Africa, but left the matter in the hands of Robert Beloe.

According to his own records, Beloe continued to meet privately with Silkin, the government Chief Whip, the Roman Catholic peer Lord Longford and others, gauging the tenor of opinion, exploring where the Bill might be brought into line with the Church's report, and imparting useful information. Implicit throughout, but not stated, was Beloe's role (on Ramsey's behalf) as critical friend of the proposals: supportive of reform of the law, but not on any terms.[79] Some of the bishops were equally closely involved, both in the Lords and privately: Robert Mortimer, Bishop of Exeter, was in direct correspondence with Silkin in 1965 over detailed revisions to the proposed Bill.[80] However, there were dangers in this approach since, as with the case of divorce reform, press and parliamentarians alike appeared to struggle to distinguish between co-operation with the process and outright support for each and every proposal. Before long it appeared that Silkin had let it be known amongst Labour peers that the Bill had the support of the Church of England as it stood, in an undefined but important way.[81] A year later, Ramsey's office was alerted that Steel was suggesting the same, and that a public statement was needed.[82]

By this time, a year after the publication of the Church's report and the production of two Bills, Ramsey's own view had solidified. Cardinal Heenan had reinforced the Roman Catholic view from the outset, coming out in opposition to the abortion report at its publication.[83] Ramsey had always thought this absolutist position unworkable, and that Heenan's position was an evasion: an attempt to opt out of facing difficult issues.[84] It necessitated deciding when life began: was it at conception, at the implantation of the embryo, at the 'quickening' (an older understanding), or at birth? Ramsey knew that this could not be known. And even if it could be known with any security, an absolute insistence on the life of the foetus led to the moral absurdity of making no intervention when the lives of both mother and child were at risk.

---

[78]   Silkin to Ramsey, 17 November 1965, at Ramsey Papers 70, f.192.

[79]   See, *inter alia*, a memorandum on conversations with Longford, Silkin, the government chief whip, and the secretary to the leader of the House of Lords, dated 25 November 1965, at Ramsey Papers 70, ff.217–19.

[80]   Exeter to Silkin, 29 December 1965, at Ramsey Papers 91, f.93.

[81]   Beloe memo of conversation with Longford, dated 26 November 1965, at Ramsey Papers 70, f.222.

[82]   Bentley to Ramsey, 8 December 1966, at Ramsey Papers 91, f.212; Bentley to David Steel, 17 December 1966, at Ramsey Papers 91, f.216.

[83]   'Church leaders disagree', *Catholic Herald*, 11 January 1966, p.1.

[84]   Ramsey to Shirley Bragg, 12 February 1966, at Ramsey Papers 91, f.170.

In a statement to Convocation in early 1967, Ramsey laid out his position, coming out against those who would wish to see abortion available 'virtually at will.'[85] In a clear rebuke to the absolutist camp, he drew a distinction between abortion and infanticide, arguing that it was 'wrong to stir emotion by identifying them'. Nonetheless, the foetus had a unique status in the eyes of God. It was to 'to be reverenced as the embryo of a life capable of coming to reflect the glory of God'.[86] And once life on earth was over, it mattered that there was an 'eternal destiny with God in heaven, possible to every child conceived in the mother's womb'.[87] Ramsey had no sense that anything of the moral status of the foetus was being lost; but there was a messiness at the margins of decision-making that could not be avoided.

It was in the light of this that Ramsey thought that Steel's Bill went too far in two respects. It allowed for eugenic termination of a foetus with physical deformities on the basis of the interest of the foetus, rather than because it threatened the well-being of the mother. Opposition to this within the Church had been constant, since it involved a determination that it was better not to be born. 'While we must strive to remove suffering' Ramsey argued, 'we do not foreclose the ways in which in the midst of frustrations and handicaps some of the glories of human lives may be seen.'[88]

Steel's Bill also contained what became known as the 'social clause', that widened the relevant factors to include the interests of other children, and the strain on the capacity of the woman as a mother (as distinct from her health). Such situations 'draw out the sympathy of our hearts.' However, Ramsey at base felt that despite this, no-one (and certainly not medical professionals) was in a position to judge the matter with any safety, since it was 'amidst the utmost difficulties that some of the most splendid things in human nature have been seen'. 'Ought we to legislate', he asked, 'as though the grace and power of God in human lives did not exist?'[89]

It was on these points that Ramsey, in concert with other peers, tried to have Steel's Bill amended, and also signed a letter to *The Times* opposing the widening of the Bill's scope.[90] The Medical Termination of Pregnancy Act was eventually

[85]   The statement is reproduced in Ramsey, *Canterbury Pilgrim*, pp.163–67; p.164.
[86]   Ramsey, *Canterbury Pilgrim*, p.165.
[87]   Ramsey, *Canterbury Pilgrim*, p.167.
[88]   Ramsey, *Canterbury Pilgrim*, p.167.
[89]   Ramsey, *Canterbury Pilgrim*, p.166.
[90]   Letter from Ramsey, the Archbishop of York (Donald Coggan), the Bishop of London (Robert Stopford) and the Bishop of Durham (Ian Ramsey); 'Amending the Abortion Bill', *The Times*, 24 May 1967, p.11.

passed by Parliament in the autumn of 1967, amid talk of constitutional crisis as the Lords sought once more to block the social clause that had been re-inserted by the Commons, after having already been removed once by the Lords. Ramsey acknowledged Baroness Summerskill's evocation of the 'terrible conditions in certain homes, which has certainly evoked the compassion and concern of all of us' but this was a case not for abortion on social grounds, but for 'education in, and the practice of, methods of birth control and family planning.'[91] Ramsey again voted against the amendment, along with several of the bishops, but it was to pass into law.[92]

And thus the contested history of the effects of the reform began. To what extent can the Church of England be said to be responsible for a change that was to have consequences that were quite unforeseen, even by its proponents? To put the question differently, could Ramsey and the bishops have chosen to stand apart from the process, keeping themselves and the Church unsullied by what was messy and ambiguous business? Even the most implacable Roman Catholic opponents had recognised the need to reform the law in some limited ways, and the bishops had little option than to engage with the process and to make the best of embodying solutions to complex and disputed moral conundra in workable law.

As well as this positive engagement, Ramsey and the bishops had also attempted to amend the Bill in the places where it needed to be amended. Whilst doing so, he had written to Prime Minister Wilson explaining that whilst there were elements of the Bill which he would oppose, he should not like to see it fail. An imperfect Bill was better than no Bill at all.[93] Reform of the law was necessary, and so Ramsey did all that was possible to influence its formation; it could not be in either the interests of the Church or the nation that he should attempt to bring the whole Bill down. It was for the nation to legislate for itself. To this degree at least, Ramsey and his colleagues made the best of a difficult job; and later events should not be allowed to cloud necessary judgements about earlier ones.

---

[91] H.L. Deb. 23 October 1967 vol. 285, cols. 1457–58.
[92] Chadwick, *Ramsey*, p.155; H.L. Deb. 23 October 1967 vol. 285, cols. 1470.
[93] Ramsey to Wilson, 5 July 1967, at Ramsey Papers 110, f.67

The Sexual Offences Act 1967

Hugh McLeod has made the salutary point that, despite their chronological closeness, the several amendments of the moral law under examination here ought not to be seen as the result of a concerted campaign, but rather as a series of related but distinct movements. There was some overlap in personnel and organisations pressing for change, including such figures as Leo Abse; but the constellation was in each case different.[94] Different patterns of support and of opposition were to be found in different churches, and within those churches. At large, if the public were broadly in favour of liberalisation in the cases of divorce and abortion law, this was less the case when it came to homosexuality.[95] The law criminalised sexual activity between men of any age in public or private, and a significant section of public opinion wished it to remain that way. As with capital punishment, the support of the institution of the Church of England for reform put it at odds with considerable sections of the public, both affiliated with the Church and not.[96]

It was during Geoffrey Fisher's time at Lambeth that the issue had pressed itself into public consciousness with the publication of the Wolfenden Report in 1957. If Fisher was mostly supportive of reform, but with some ambivalence, Ramsey had made his support for a change in the law clear: change that was to come in 1967, with the passing of the Sexual Offences Act.[97] The Homosexual Law Reform Association numbered several bishops amongst its members, including Ramsey, who had joined before coming to Lambeth. Nearer the centre of the group still was John Robinson, who sat on its Executive Committee.[98]

Late in 1961 the Association had written to Home Secretary R.A. Butler warning of a growing demoralisation amongst gay men, and a cynicism concerning the delay in implementing the Wolfenden proposals. The Association's secretary enquired whether Ramsey wanted to remain a member of the Honorary Committee now he was Archbishop, and whether he would be prepared to sign the letter.[99] Ramsey, as Archbishop, was a member of a great many such

[94]   McLeod, 'Homosexual law reform, 1953–67' in *From the Reformation to the Permissive Society,* ed. Melanie Barber, Stephen Taylor and Gabriel Sewell (Church of England Record Society, volume 18, Woodbridge, 2010), pp.657–78, at p.667.
[95]   On the contradictory nature of the evidence regarding public opinion, see Yates, *Love Now, Pay Later?,* pp.102–5.
[96]   Yates, *Love Now, Pay Later?,* p.103.
[97]   On Fisher, see McLeod, 'Homosexual law reform', pp.660–61, 664–65.
[98]   Eric James, *A Life of John A.T. Robinson. Scholar, Pastor, Prophet* (London, 1987), p.253.
[99]   John Newall to Ramsey, 2 November 1961, at Ramsey Papers 8, ff.132–33.

committees, often little more than a useful name on a letterhead. Such was part and parcel of the role, and the connection was often very loose. In the case of the HLRA, Ramsey's interest was rather closer, as we shall see. But at the same time, there was a need to stand far enough apart from controversial causes so as not to be seen to commit the Church to every detail of a campaign. Ramsey replied, professing himself 'still as anxious as ever to see reform', but unable to sign the particular letter on grounds of some of the detail. 'I have no doubt' he continued 'that there will be a representative number of people, including churchmen, who may not feel the same difficulties and will sign it.'[100]

The law on homosexuality is a paradigm case of the central theme of this chapter: the proper relation between crime and sin in a post-Christian society. The Christian churches were united in regarding homosexual practice as sinful, and this had been in alignment for centuries with the general moral sense of the public. But there were many things which the Church thought were sins but which were not crimes, including adultery; and there were other matters which were both sins and crimes but which the public regarded as neither. Ramsey knew that the connection between crime and sin that many of the public felt very keenly, and which they expected the Church to preserve, was not sustainable.

As with the issues of abortion and divorce, the Church of England had recent resources on which to draw, in the shape of the extensive inquiries of its own Moral Welfare Council, and of Derrick Sherwin Bailey in particular: work which had begun in earnest well before Wolfenden began his investigations.[101] It is worth pausing over what it was that Anglican campaigners for reform in the law were arguing, and its limits. Almost all the churches were united in regarding the condition of homosexuality as intrinsically disordered, a state at odds with nature, and homosexual intercourse as the sinful outworking of that state. Some thought that as a condition it might be cured; others were less sure. But most knew that there was no possibility of help for unfortunate and unhappy men while their condition was the object of the criminal law. There were also the first signs of a reassessment of homosexual relationships as having

---

[100] Ramsey to Newall, 6 November 1961, at Ramsey Papers 8, f.134.

[101] On this, and the subject in general, see Matthew Grimley, 'Law, Morality and Secularisation: The Church of England and the Wolfenden Report, 1954–1967', *Journal of Ecclesiastical History* 60;4 (2009), 725–41. See also Timothy W. Jones, 'Moral welfare and social well-being: the Church of England and the emergence of modern homosexuality', in *Men, Masculinities and Religious Change in Twentieth-Century Britain,* ed. Lucy Delap and Sue Morgan (Basingstoke, 2013), pp.197–217.

a positive, indeed even equivalent moral status as heterosexual ones, particularly among the Quakers, but it was in no way the mainstream of Christian thought.[102]

In this, Ramsey's own thought was in line with the more advanced in his and the other churches in relation to the law; but not with regard to the moral status of the act. As he told the Lords, 'homosexual acts are always wrong in the sense that they use in a wrong way human organs for which the right use is intercourse between men and women within marriage.'[103] As such, despite talk of the 'new morality' there could be no wavering in the Church's own discipline: as he told the wife of the peer Lord Brocket, 'As to the wrongness of the sins in question and all other serious sins, we have to be perfectly plain in our teaching.'[104]

Some wondered, though, whether that moral teaching could remain plain if a change in the law opened the door to openly homosexual clergy. The former Lord Chancellor Viscount Dilhorne, famously abrasive and one of Ramsey's chief antagonists in the House of Lords, considered tabling an amendment to the Bill excluding clergy (of the established Church) from its provisions.[105] 'I can imagine nothing more damaging to the prestige of our Church', Dilhorne argued, 'than for it to be thought that parsons and other clergy of the Church of England will be free to engage in homosexual activities.' Did the public support from the bishops for the Bill not foster such an impression?[106] In this case, Ramsey was able to reassure his noble colleague, since the recent Ecclesiastical Jurisdiction Measure (1963) contained powers with statutory force to discipline clergy for moral offences that were not criminal.[107]

Insofar as it is possible to recover Ramsey's own feelings, they would seem to have been mixed. In private he was able to describe homosexual sex as 'disgusting', but this, when coupled to his concern with the law, issued in a desire to help; to provide for the rescue of the homosexual from his wretched state, and to set him on the right path.[108] As to the causes of the homosexual state, he was agnostic. He wondered in the Lords whether it was possible in some cases 'to change the direction of the sexual impulses from the homosexual to the normal'. In other cases, there was the need, as there was for all Christians in one regard or another,

[102] See Grimley, 'Law, morality and secularisation', *passim*; McLeod, 'Homosexual law reform', p.667.

[103] H.L. Deb 12 May 1965 vol. 266, col.80.

[104] Ramsey to Lady Brocket, 10 June 1965, Ramsey Papers 78, f.149.

[105] Chadwick, *Ramsey*, pp.147–48.

[106] Dilhorne to Ramsey, 28 May 1965, Ramsey Papers 78, ff.73–74.

[107] Ramsey to Dilhorne, 31 May 1965 Ramsey Papers 78, ff.76–77.

[108] Ramsey to Lambton, 24 June 1965, Ramsey Papers 78, ff.166–67.

for 'greater conscience or self-control'; this was important for 'those who believe seriously in the means of Divine Grace'.[109]

What was certain was that neither this help, nor the open and unhindered medical and psychological investigation that Ramsey thought necessary, were possible under the law as it stood. Those laws 'do not help morality, and give a good deal of hindrance to the promotion of what is right' and fostered nothing more than a 'sense of injustice and bitterness.' The case for change was on grounds of 'reason and justice, and on considerations of the good of the community'.[110] Ramsey spoke and voted in 1965 in favour of the Bill introduced by Lord Arran, and again in 1966 for the later Bill that was later to issue in the Act of 1967.[111]

Conclusion

The letters that Ramsey received were often expressive of strong feelings, whether it be on abortion, or on relations with Rome, or about race relations in England (as we shall see); but those which he received about homosexuality were in no few cases indicative of visceral feeling: of homophobia in its literal sense. One thought it a 'filthy business' and Ramsey 'a damned disgrace';[112] another asked 'Is there no longer such a thing as sin?'[113]

For many, the fact of the changes in the law was less shocking than the apparent abdication of responsibility by the established Church in failing to oppose them. As Hera Cook has argued, that a previously uniform standard of sexual behaviour was openly debated amongst the elite was itself instrumental in promoting change.[114] In the eyes of some observers the Church, however carefully it tried to distinguish between the law and its own discipline, was culpable. Lady Brocket, the daughter of a clergyman, declared herself and her husband 'truly and genuinely shattered by your support of the Bill, as are our many friends in every walk of life.' For her and for 'many good Church people' it simply passed understanding that Ramsey should collaborate in the passing of

---

[109] H.L. Deb, 12 May 1965, vol. 266, col.81.
[110] Ramsey to Lady Brocket, 10 June 1965, Ramsey Papers 78, f.149; H.L. Deb 12 May 1965 vol. 266, col.82.
[111] H.L. Deb, 16 Jun 1966, vol. 275, cols 154–55.
[112] Cyril Taylor to Ramsey, 14 May 1965, Ramsey Papers 78, f.41.
[113] Brig. T.W.R Hill to Ramsey, 14 May 1965, Ramsey Papers 78, f.40.
[114] Hera Cook, *The Long Sexual Revolution. English Women, Sex and Contraception 1800–1975* (Oxford, 2004), pp.285–87.

laws that both contradicted Christian morality, and threatened to undermine some of the basic building blocks of a stable society.[115]

But there was an opening up of a gap between crime and sin, which Ramsey knew was both inevitable and right, even if many of his correspondents could not begin to tolerate or even understand it. For Ramsey, Wolfenden had been right to argue that 'not all sins are properly given the status of crimes, ... To say this is not to condone the wrongness of the acts, but to put them in the realm of private moral responsibility.'[116] To address that was the task of the Church on its own account, and not of the law. Ramsey knew that the relationship between the established Church and the British people was changing. There were great tasks of re-evangelising the nation; of pastoral ministry to the divorcing or to men forced to work out their sexuality in fear. These were no longer aided, and indeed were hindered, by the law as it stood.

[115] Lady Brocket to Ramsey, 19 June 1965, at Ramsey Papers 78, ff.154–55.
[116] H.L. Deb 12 May 1965 vol. 266, col.82.

Chapter 4

The Church in a Time of Crisis

The 'long sixties' which for Arthur Marwick began in 1958 and ended in 1974 coincided almost exactly with Ramsey's time as Archbishop in first the northern and then the southern province.[1] It was during this most disputed of periods that recent historians have located the death of Christian Britain: the point at which the discursive frame of British life decisively lost its Christian shape. Churchmen had long agonised over the traditional indicators of church vitality, the headline numbers of communicants and baptisms; but Callum Brown's work, aspects of which have most recently been reinforced by Hugh McLeod's examination of Western Christendom more widely, has shown the more crucial shift to have been one of language and self-definition, both individually and as a nation.[2] And so this chapter is concerned with the Church of England as it was forced to address itself to the challenge of mission not in foreign fields but in England.

The need for such a re-evangelisation of ground previously taken for granted was not new in 1961. A Commission under the chairmanship of Christopher Chavasse, Bishop of Rochester, had in 1945 produced a report with the starkly realistic title *Towards the Conversion of England*. But some scholars have detected a complacency within the Church of England in the years after 1945.[3] In the words of the most recent biographer of Cosmo Gordon Lang, the Church had had a 'good war': it had played a more important part in stiffening the sinews of the nation that might have been expected, and (it was thought) had recovered something of its place in the national imagination.[4] The years after the war had thus seen renewed optimism about the Church as an institution: its mission in the parishes (when judged by the numbers) seemed to be working,[5] and amongst

---

[1]   Marwick, *The Sixties*, pp.3–20.

[2]   Brown, *The Death of Christian Britain*, pp.170–92; McLeod, *The Religious Crisis of the 1960s*, in particular chapters 1, 9, 10 and 11.

[3]   Welsby, *Church of England*, pp.44–50, 94.

[4]   Robert Beaken, *Cosmo Lang. Archbishop in War and Crisis* (London, 2012), pp.237–38.

[5]   Alister Chapman, 'Anglican evangelicals and revival, 1945–59', *Studies in Church History* 44 (2008), 307–17; Mark Smith, 'The roots of resurgence: evangelical parish

theologians, the awareness of crisis that had been acute in the 1930s and during the war had largely dissipated. And so, as Rowan Williams has suggested, the shock of the 1960s was much the greater for the unpreparedness of the Church of England to deal with it.[6]

This chapter attempts to place Ramsey's work in this context of religious crisis. The crisis was not only one of allegiance to the churches and of the simple habit of churchgoing, although the problems were acute, and worsening. It was also a wider crisis of communication, in which the churches' collective nerve failed when it came to their ability to articulate the faith in terms that remained meaningful and compelling. It examines Ramsey's role in the process of revising the Church's language, and in particular the Book of Common Prayer, unrevised in three centuries. The affair of *Honest to God*, by John Robinson, Bishop of Woolwich, shows the depths of the crisis in theology, the language in which the Church understood itself.

The early 1970s also saw a confluence of events, political, economic and moral, which gave some a sense of a wider crisis in the nation at large.[7] Chapters 2 and 3 showed the growing separation between the Church of England and the life of the nation, in law and in constitutional terms. Yet in a time of crisis, there were things which significant sections of the public still expected the Archbishop to address, even if the means by which to 'Do Something' were obscure both to him and to those doing the asking. One of these was the situation in Northern Ireland; but the chapter begins with the notion of the national day of prayer.

National Crisis and Days of Prayer

The late 1960s saw a cluster of specific national and international circumstances which were experienced by many as a more general crisis. Internationally, there was continuing war in Vietnam. At home, between August 1971 and March 1972, Ulster saw the introduction of internment, the Bloody Sunday massacre in Derry/Londonderry and the imposition of direct rule from Westminster. The period also saw inflation, a deteriorating balance of payments, increasing budget deficits and strike action by the National Union of Mineworkers from January 1972. December 1973 brought another strike, the imposition of the three-day

ministry in the mid-twentieth century', *Studies in Church History* 44 (2008), 318–28.

    6   Williams, '*Honest to God* and the 1960s', in *Anglican Identities*, pp.110–11.
    7   On the growing unease in the churches about 'permissiveness', see Lewis and Wallis, 'Church of England and Divorce Reform', pp.329–30.

week and soon afterwards the collapse of the government of Edward Heath. What could the churches do?

The early decades of the twentieth century had seen the emergence of a new form of national worship in the United Kingdom: the 'national day of prayer', which had reached a peak during the Second World War.[8] By Ramsey's time, however, there was little appetite within government or the wider establishment for occasions of national worship, and a similar reluctance amongst the bishops to call such occasions on their own initiative.

Nonetheless, just as Randall Davidson had been inundated with requests for days of prayer on 'the Japanese War, or Macedonia, or Armenia, or Chinese Labour, or Welsh Education, or the Revival Movement', the requests to Lambeth to call such days continued to arrive in a steady trickle.[9] As John Wolffe has noted, the felt need for national intercession was most acute in times of war and national emergency;[10] and the trickle became a steady stream in Ramsey's last years.

Ramsey's personal view had long been that calls for prayers for specific ends 'lend themselves to a rather mechanical view of what prayer means.'[11] It was better instead to call for constant personal prayer as a profitable habit among the body of lay Christians. There was greater benefit in 'constantly teaching Christian people about the meaning of prayer so that we are all the time building up in the world a community of praying people.'[12]

Quite apart from the problematic theology of prayer that national days implied, there were practical difficulties as well. There was a reluctance to arrange days of prayer on everything from the 1966 earthquake in Turkey to British entry into the Common Market, since by doing so serious inroads would

---

[8]   Williamson, 'State prayers, fasts and thanksgivings: public worship in Britain 1830–1897', *Past and Present* 200 (2008), 121–74; at 167; Williamson, 'National days of prayer: the churches, the state and public worship in Britain 1899–1957', *English Historical Review* 128 (2013), 323–66, at 363.

[9]   In a letter of 24 Jan 1905, as quoted in Bell, *Randall Davidson. Archbishop of Canterbury* (London, 1935), i.483.

[10]   Wolffe, 'Judging the Nation: Early Nineteenth-Century British Evangelicals and Divine Retribution' in *Retribution, Repentance and Reconciliation*, ed. Kate Cooper and Jeremy Gregory (Studies in Church History 40, 2004), 299; Williamson, 'State prayers', p.166.

[11]   Ramsey to R.E. Woods, 3 August 1961, at Ramsey Papers 10, f.153.

[12]   Ramsey to R.E. Woods, 3 August 1961, at Ramsey Papers 10, f.153. For Coggan's view, see Coggan to John Barton (vicar of Whitfield, Dover), 13 March 1973, at Ramsey Papers 251, f.63.

be made into the liturgical year. In addition, Ramsey's staff found it by no means straightforward to secure the media coverage necessary to effect the call.[13]

Even more pertinently, the issues around which public pressure for days of prayer crystallised in the early 1970s, such as the Troubles in Ulster or the miners' strike, were not ones that commanded any sort of national unanimity. The standard reply template being used by Ramsey's staff in December 1973 argued that the judgement was a fine one since 'it might be that a call to the nation of this kind would not have the same result in the country as in the days of the War, when we were all pretty solidly united.'[14]

So there were several reasons why Ramsey and his episcopal colleagues were reluctant to call days of prayer, and there were as a result only four such occasions during Ramsey's time at Canterbury. The first was in relation to Northern Ireland in September 1971, and a second on St Patrick's Day in the following March. The call on St Patrick's Day was repeated the following year, and the fourth was the final Sunday of 1973, called in relation to the economic situation. In December 1973 the call was for a 'day of prayer for the nation and its leaders that God may guide us in facing the present crisis with wisdom, justice and self-sacrifice'.[15] Even then, special care was taken that it was not described as a 'National Day of Prayer', since to do so 'could be severely criticised in the present climate of divisiveness and agnosticism.'[16]

In this, Ramsey was responding to a clear and growing sense of crisis both within the Church and in the nation at large, and to the expectations of at least some of the public that he ought to respond in this particular way. Ramsey and his colleagues were, however, neither silent nor inactive at other times. Ramsey used speeches to the Church Assembly and the Convocation of Canterbury to address issues of concern.[17] He spoke about Ireland in a BBC radio broadcast of 'Lift up Your Hearts' in September 1971, and on two separate occasions in the House of Lords.[18] Despite all this, the day of prayer was, for some, a weapon in the armoury which it was perverse not to employ more frequently. An examination

---

[13]   Geoffrey Maidstone to Mrs Mary Lowe, 15 January 1974, at Ramsey Papers 271, f.10.

[14]   Geoffrey Maidstone to Mrs Langley, 12 December 1973, at Ramsey Papers 251, f.67.

[15]   Memorandum dated 17 December 1973, at Ramsey Papers 249, f.1.

[16]   Memorandum dated 19 December 1973 at Ramsey Papers 249, f.2.

[17]   See draft statement to Church Assembly on Vietnam, dated July 1966, at Ramsey Papers 109, fols.169–70; his address to Convocation in relation to Ulster was reported in *The Times* on 13 October 1971: 'Dr Ramsey praises lead given to Christians in Ulster'.

[18]   See letters of protest about the broadcast at Ramsey Papers 205, ff.123–25; for Ramsey's interventions in the Lords, see H.L. Deb., 22 September 1971, vol. 324 cols 28–30; H.L. Deb., 5 December 1972 vol. 337, cols 161–63.

of the reasons advanced sheds valuable light on the understandings of the role of the archbishop and the providential history of the nation that were current among at least some sections of the British laity at this time.

One reason commonly advanced for such days of prayer was the symbolic effect of joint action between the denominations. Cyril Black, prominent Baptist layman and Conservative MP, advocated a joint call from Canterbury, Westminster and the Free Churches for prayer for Ulster, to demonstrate 'the united determination of Christians to seek increasingly a way to restore peace and goodwill, and to pray to Almighty God to direct, guide and bless all such efforts.'[19] For others, these were merely side-effects, since the primary purpose of such petitionary prayer was its direct and identifiable effect on events. In such times of crisis, it was for the nation as a whole to turn to prayer, and not simply those in the church: 'it is the people of the Land as a whole who must seek God together for deliverance in a time of extreme National Crisis (2 Chron: 7.14.)'[20]

For many, the time was one with marked parallels with recent British history. Occasional parallels were drawn with events during the First World War, not least the National Mission of Repentance and Hope in 1917.[21] However, for the majority the only benchmark against which the times could be measured was the most prominent historic crisis still in living memory; that of the Second World War. Of particular symbolic power for some was the great national delivery at Dunkirk, apparently in response to just such a day of prayer. One elderly woman with decades of missionary service remembered the day of prayer 'and the marvellous answer' at Dunkirk; another recalled it as 'a modern miracle performed because the whole country was praying together'. In 1973 another was needed 'to save us from ourselves.'[22]

These calls reveal a good deal about the role Ramsey was thought to play in the religious life of the nation. His correspondents included members of several other denominations, all quite sure that he held a position of peculiar importance amongst religious leaders. One member of the United Reformed Church wrote in February 1974 to assure him that her own congregation had

---

[19] Cyril Black to Ramsey, 6 September 1971, at Ramsey Papers 205, f.76.

[20] Norman Green (Chichester) to Hugh Whitworth, 24 August 1972, at Ramsey Papers 224, f.26.

[21] Wilfred Dillistone (Brighton) to Ramsey, 18 December 1973, at Ramsey Papers, 251, f.72. Mr Dillistone also wrote to the Prime Minister and the National Union of Mineworkers.

[22] Miss Grace Ponsford-Selby (London) to Ramsey, telegram, 3 January 1974, at Ramsey Papers 271, ff.4–5; Mrs McKeag (a Methodist) to Ramsey, 12 December 1973, at Ramsey Papers 251, f.68.

that morning prayed for him, and called on him to take a lead, as the '*national religious leader.*'[23]

Petitions for days of prayer could also function negatively, as implicit criticism of the direction of travel in the nation's moral and religious life, and of perceived neglect on the part of the Archbishop. One Lincolnshire rector criticised the recent deputation of bishops to the Prime Minister concerning the supply of arms to South Africa. 'Would it not have been far better,' he continued, if the bishops had paid more attention to the situation at home, and instead asked the Prime Minister 'to call the people of our own country to a national day of prayer?'[24] 'This country has been sliding from crisis to crisis', thought one group of correspondents, and 'the moral trends have been ever more permissive and ever less Christian.' Why then had Ramsey 'not felt the desire, and indeed the necessity, to call the Church of England and all devout Christians to a special day or week of prayer.'[25] For this correspondent at least, there was indeed a general crisis, in morality as in economics and politics; and it was clear what the nation expected of its Archbishop.

However, Ramsey was becoming more and more one leader amongst many, and less and less the religious leader of the nation that many of his correspondents supposed him to be. By the early 1970s it had long been the case that the calling of such occasions of concerted prayer was co-ordinated between the various denominations.[26] The octave of prayer for Ulster of September 1971 was arranged jointly with Cardinal Heenan and the moderator of the Free Church Federal Council.[27] The role of the British Council of Churches was expanding to include the calling of joint days of prayer, as was the case for St Patrick's Day 1973.[28] There was also increasingly an international context. In June 1973 there was a joint appeal for worldwide prayer for Northern Ireland from the World Council of Churches and the Secretariat for Promoting Christian Unity, the Vatican's

---

[23]   Miss Jones (Tunbridge Wells) to Ramsey, 10 February 1974, at Ramsey Papers 271, f.22; see also letters from a Baptist, one Mrs Langley of Hove, 7 December 1973, at Ramsey Papers 251, ff.65–66; from an Elim Pentecostal minister, the Revd. F. Lavender, District Superintendent of the South London Presbytery, 14 December 1973, at Ramsey Papers 271, f.70.

[24]   The Revd. David Scott, as reported in *The Times* 15 February 1971, 'Rector says bishops give no leadership', p.3.

[25]   Mrs Elizabeth Breton et al, Cirencester to Ramsey [no date, probably late 1973/early 1974], at Ramsey Papers 271, f.3.

[26]   Williamson, 'State prayers', p.168.

[27]   See Ramsey Papers 205, ff.77, 81–82, 84–85.

[28]   *The Times* 16 March 1973.

department for ecumenical endeavour.[29] The Pope additionally instituted an annual Sunday in January dedicated to prayer for peace for Catholics, beginning in 1968, which Ramsey was later to commend to his own bishops.[30]

It may well be the case that the cluster of days of prayer called by Ramsey in 1971–73 were the last such significant group. These occasions, and the public correspondence concerning them, reveal much about perceptions, both within his own church and without, of the Archbishop's own peculiar role at the interface of the British Church, State and nation. In times of national crisis, many felt they knew what an Archbishop was for. And he bore particular historic responsibility for one aspect of the crisis especially: the situation in Northern Ireland.

Ireland

Central to Ramsey's concern was the growing together of the churches in holiness and truth, locally, nationally and internationally. This, for Ramsey, required that all of the churches, whilst acknowledging their respective pasts and the record of struggle and martyrdom, chose collectively to move beyond those pasts into uncharted territory, trusting that the Holy Spirit could and would honour that step of faith.

Chapters 2 and 3 sought to show that this very growing together of the churches implied, not to say required, a reconsideration of the relationship of the Anglican Church established in England and the idea of Britishness. Within the island of Great Britain, Ramsey's time saw the completion of the process by which 'political Protestantism' moved from the mainstream of political opinion to the margins. In England, at least, it had become less important that the established Church was a Protestant one.

For many unionists on both sides of the Irish Sea, however, Ramsey's office still embodied important facts about the distinctively Protestant settlement between Church, Crown and people, even though the Anglican Church in Ireland had been disestablished for a century. At the same time, for some nationalists in Ireland, the position of the archbishop made him a part of the British religio-political complex of which they wished to be independent: an agent, indeed, of an occupying power.

---

[29]   *The Times* 11 June 1973.
[30]   Council for Foreign Relations memorandum, dated 11 December 1968, at Ramsey Papers 140, f.212.

As figurative head and leader of the worldwide Anglican Communion, Ramsey was pastor and confidant of the Anglican archbishops in Ireland north and south. Ramsey's personal standing in relation to Ireland was more complex still, since while he was closely identified with Protestant ecumenism, he was at the same time associated with the Catholic wing of the Church of England more strongly than any of his immediate predecessors. As Chapter 3 showed, he was also closely associated with the liberalisation of the moral law, much of which had not been applied to Northern Ireland in deference to the relative conservatism of the province.

Such were the symbolic complexities of Ramsey's position in Protestant-Catholic relations in Ulster. This section examines his public pronouncements and private diplomacy from the late 1960s. It considers the delicate balancing act which Ramsey needed to perform between his multiple roles, and the conflicting expectations that many had of him. It will be shown that Ramsey's position in relation to Ireland is a microcosm of the complexity and even impossibility of his task at large. While at heart Ramsey knew which were the things that were not shaken, much of the experience of being Archbishop was one of pressure: of irreconcilable conflict, impossible expectation and of powerlessness in the face of circumstance and the weight of history. Such was Ramsey's experience of the Troubles.

The particular story of the Troubles begins in 1968; but for some Protestants both in Ulster and in England, Ramsey already had form with regard to Rome. For Ian Paisley, Ramsey's meeting with the Pope in Rome in 1966 was but another step in the process of conditioning Ulster for 'Roman take-over' in a united Ireland. Ramsey was 'a traitor to the Constitution': he was 'like Terence O'Neill – he is a modern bridge-builder. A bridge and a traitor are alike in one thing – they both take you to the other side.'[31]

Neither was Ramsey merely a dupe; one columnist in the *Protestant Telegraph* thought him one of a group of Jesuit infiltrators within the ecumenical movement in the Protestant churches, as well as an idolater, a liar, and probably a cardinal in secret.[32] Though far removed from reality these perceptions were, some elements of the Paisleyite worldview were more widely held among mainline Presbyterians

[31] As cited by Eric Gallagher and Stanley Worrall, *Christians in Ulster 1968–1980* (Oxford, 1982), p.26.
[32] An article dated 10 January 1970, as cited by Gallagher and Worrall, *Christians in Ulster*, p.55.

in Ulster, if less strongly expressed.[33] Ecumenical contact with Rome was suspect to many Protestants, and Ramsey bore its taint.

This suspicion was of course not limited to Ulster. Anti-Catholic Protestantism in England was by no means spent, and showed itself in relation to Ulster. In 1971 Ramsey spoke in the House of Lords of the work of the North of Ireland Ecumenical Youth Service. 'How much better', he argued, 'for boys and girls to grow up learning to enjoy the friendship of boys and girls of the other sort, rather than learning to take part in marches and counter-marches and to live and think in the seventeenth century!' In time, he asked, was it not too much to hope that 'there might be a generation of boys and girls who know the word "orange" only as the name of a delectable fruit ... ?'[34] The Revd W. B. Makin of the Loyal Orange Institution of England strongly disagreed. 'When', he asked, 'will we have Abps and Bps who abide by [their] Consecration Vow to drive away strange and erroneous doctrine – when we do, we shall have work in common to do.'[35] For Makin, the work of the Orange order would only be complete when there were no longer archbishops prepared to dally with Roman corruption. This variety of English Protestantism, whilst losing ground in the early 1970s, was not yet so marginal that Ramsey could safely ignore it.

Ramsey and his staff were well aware of such views, and this awareness in part conditioned their general policy in relation to intervention in Ulster, which was one of caution. Contrary to the assumption made by many of his correspondents, Ramsey had no power to direct the archbishops of Dublin or Armagh to act in any particular way, although his views would have weighed heavily. Neither was this a power that he would have exercised had he been able. This was partly due to a clear sense of how well the intervention would most likely be received. Lambeth made every effort to respond to Irish church initiatives but without giving 'the impression of dictating to the Irish churches from London, which would in fact be likely to do more harm than good.'[36]

It was a measure of Ramsey's exasperation (with no small element of despair) that a visit to Ulster planned for May 1973 almost did not take place. Ramsey wrote at length to George Simms, Archbishop of Armagh, to cancel the trip, which had been planned nearly three years before as a visit to lecture the Anglican clergy in private at a retreat. In the current climate, he thought, it would be impossible to prevent the visit becoming a public event, fraught with

[33] See, *inter alia*, Steve Bruce, *God save Ulster! The Religion and Politics of Paisleyism* (Oxford, 1986), *passim*.

[34] H.L. Deb., 22 September 1971 vol. 324, col.30.

[35] Makin to Ramsey, 23 September 1971, at Ramsey Papers 205, f.121.

[36] Whitworth to a Mrs Robinson, 9 April 1973, Ramsey Papers 255, ff.50–51

danger both physical and in terms of public relations. It would be impossible, Ramsey felt, to avoid either being drawn into public discussion of controverted issues or (perhaps worse) 'there would be a suspicion that something secret was going on or that I was showing indifference to the great issues.' Ramsey was thus on a hiding to nothing, as well as 'being a worry to those who look after security in the country.'[37] Ramsey was later to reverse his decision, after receiving reassurances concerning security from the Northern Ireland Office; but his letter shows just how hemmed in Ramsey felt by the situation in Ulster.

As well as facing pressures within the UK, the Archbishop and his staff had always to reckon with the international ecumenical context. As time went on and the situation worsened, concern amongst the worldwide churches grew. In 1971 the Pope, through the representation of the Duchess of Westminster, expressed his distress and his readiness to join with Ramsey in some joint action.[38] By early 1973, the duration and apparent intractability of the situation had led to a highly unusual joint venture between the World Council of Churches and the Vatican Secretariat for the Promoting of Christian Unity, being a joint worldwide campaign of prayer at Pentecost 1973. This Ramsey could put his name to, along with leaders of the all the main denominations in Ireland north and south, with the exception of Ian Paisley.[39]

Ramsey's direct interventions in the relations between the churches in Ireland were few. He and Simms stayed in very close contact, but whilst doing what was possible to amplify and support those moves, he would instigate little, if anything. There were occasions where it was necessary to smooth ruffled feathers in England on behalf of the Church of Ireland. The National Council for Civil Liberties had been concerned by comments on a violent confrontation in Armagh in November 1968 by Simms' predecessor, James McCann.[40] Conscious that McCann was 'liable to impulsive things without apprising himself of immediate circumstances', Ramsey sought out a later, more measured, statement for the Council's consumption: 'I should be sorry if [the Council]

---

[37]   Ramsey to Simms, 9 February 1973, Ramsey Papers 255, ff.223–24.
[38]   Note of meeting with the Duchess of Westminster, dated 20 September 1971, at Ramsey Papers 205, f.127.
[39]   Joint memorandum from the Secretariat and the World Council of Churches to WCC members, 19 April 1973, Ramsey Papers 255, ff.55–60.
[40]   Tony Smythe (general secretary) to Ramsey, 23 December 1968, at Ramsey Papers 159, f.218.

were led to conclude that the Church of Ireland was unenlightened about these goings on.'[41]

In England, however, Ramsey could feel relatively free to act; and there were happenings of considerable symbolic significance in English inter-church relations. Chief among these were the three national days of prayer for Ulster described above. It is an indication of the gravity of the situation in Ulster that these three days were among only four in total in Ramsey's 13-year tenure.

There were also demands made for public acts of joint intercession and worship. In February 1972 Lord Stamp called for a memorial service for British soldiers killed in Ulster, to be held at Westminster Abbey, the symbolic centre of the relationship between Church and Crown. Ramsey and Eric Abbott, Dean of Westminster, were agreed that the time was not right, partly because of the delicacies of precisely who should be remembered and how, but mostly because they suspected (rightly, as it turned out) that the armed forces had not seen their last casualty and so such a service was premature.[42] As it happened, there was at that point in the offing a joint service of intercession at Westminster Cathedral, at which Cardinal Heenan was to lead intercessions, Ramsey to preach and the moderator of the Free Church Federal Council to give a blessing. Both the Prime Minister and the leader of the Opposition were present at the service on 14 March.[43] When we consider that this was only four years since Ramsey had been the first archbishop to set foot in Westminster Cathedral, it may be seen that in some ways the Troubles in Ulster acted as a catalyst to greater ecumenical contact in England, as was the case in Ireland, despite the belief amongst Paisleyite unionists that such ecumenism was the problem, not the solution.

As Archbishop, Ramsey was never short of opportunities for public comment, in the House of Lords and in the media, which he often took, but with particular pains to confine those comments to uncontroversial themes. Whilst avoiding any comment on the politics of Ulster and the successive attempts at a settlement, he regularly urged all sides to peaceful accommodation and an end to violence. He wrote in the *Belfast Newsletter* at Christmas 1972 in support of 'the united Christmas message of Protestant and Catholic church leaders in Northern Ireland, knowing how many there are, both Protestants and Catholics,

[41]   Ramsey to Kenneth Sansbury (British Council of Churches), 30 December 1968, at Ramsey Papers 159, f.222.

[42]   Abbott to Maidstone, 28 February 1972, at Ramsey Papers 228, f.180; Ramsey to Stamp, 7 March 1972, at Ramsey Papers 228, f.184. The *Daily Telegraph* had published a letter from Stamp on 15 February 1972; copy at Ramsey Papers 228, f.170.

[43]   'Leaders pray for Ulster', *Guardian* 15 March 1972; see also the preparatory papers at Ramsey Papers 228, ff.172–91.

who long for the end of violence and the coming of peace. May their prayers and ours be answered.'[44] He told a congregation in Belfast Cathedral (in a 1974 service disrupted by a Paisleyite demonstration) of those on both sides 'who are ready to pray together and to seek reconciliation. The future lies with those who have such thoughts in their hearts.'[45]

On occasion, he could be more robust. The day after the IRA bomb attack at Aldershot in February 1972, he happened to be lecturing students in Cambridge on the problem of the use of political violence. In an addition to his prepared text, he noted this use of violence that 'lies right outside the kinds which we are discussing in relation to justice [and] which is neither just war nor just rebellion, but cruel killing in order to injure or to frighten or to advertise a point of view.' ... This kind of violence was 'odious and deplorable.'[46] In a June 1974 speech to the Lords which Owen Chadwick thought his most respected amongst peers, he urged Westminster politicians to a greater moderation in language in relation to Ulster, and chided both Edward Heath and Harold Wilson for their errors in both action and public statement. Such language as Wilson's televised reference to 'spongers' in the province was 'just not the way to talk about Irish affairs' and needed to cease.[47]

Despite all of this action, the calls for Ramsey to 'do something' continued. Ramsey was lectured by two teenage girls about his duty to 'make some positive contribution' – the pair had also written to the Pope in the same vein.[48] Another correspondent suggested that Ramsey and the Pope should visit Ulster and walk arm in arm in the streets.[49] As well as from members of the public in England, and in Ireland north and south, these calls came from individuals within the churches, Catholic and Protestant, as far apart as Lincolnshire and South Australia. Ramsey's position as part of the political establishment led some to regard him as a potential broker of a settlement to the conflict, or at least as one of several allies whose support for such a settlement would be necessary. Such was the hope of the delegation to Lambeth from the New Ulster Movement in

---

[44]   Draft (undated) at Ramsey Papers 228, f.353–54.

[45]   Chadwick, *Ramsey*, p.203.

[46]   See the addition to a lecture script dated 23 February 1972, at Ramsey Papers 228, f.175.

[47]   H.L. Deb., 3 June 1974, vol. 352, col.31.

[48]   Catherine Skillings and Janet Stimson to Ramsey, 24 February 1973, at Ramsey Papers 255, f.32.

[49]   Mrs Robinson to Ramsey, 10 March 1973, at Ramsey Papers 255, f.37.

1973: a meeting brokered by Bruce Kent, then Roman Catholic chaplain to the University of London, and later prominent as an anti-nuclear campaigner.[50]

This perception of the Archbishop went beyond a residual understanding of the office, but was attached to Ramsey personally, due in no small part to his public comments about race relations at home, or on apartheid South Africa (see Chapter 5). This perception extended even to civil rights figures amongst the nationalist community. Some approaches to Ramsey were clearly engineered as publicity, such as the invitation in April 1973 from a group of prisoners to visit the Long Kesh Detention Centre, addressed to Ramsey 'as an Englishman, a Christian, and one who has involved himself in the human rights struggle of the World'.[51] The number of other approaches from nationalist civil rights groups would, however, suggest that Ramsey was seen as the conscience of the British establishment, a channel through which an appeal on ethical grounds could be made directly to London. The Archbishop was petitioned by the Irish Civil Rights Association in 1973 to press the Westminster government for the release of prisoners, and shortly afterwards by Irish Republican Prisoners Welfare (Belfast) in relation to prison conditions.[52] As in other cases, Ramsey's staff thought better of making any formal reply, but Lambeth did however act behind the scenes in one case. Following contact with the Association for Legal Justice about a recent suicide at Long Kesh, the information was passed to the Northern Ireland Office, and enquiries made about conditions in the prison; but after civil servants replied at length, the matter was allowed to rest.[53]

The complexities of the Archbishop of Canterbury's position in relation to Ulster is a microcosm of his wider predicament. In Protestant eyes, there was an inescapable contradiction between Ramsey's constitutional role as head of a Protestant church born at the Reformation, and his own fervent commitment to the ecumenical movement and to closer relations with Rome in particular. In this, Ramsey was caught between genuine ecumenical enthusiasm within his own Church and within the Irish churches, and residual anti-Catholic sentiment in the nation at large.

Amongst moderate elements, he was seen as an honest broker at the centre of power, able to create a neutral space in which political schemes to end the

---

[50]   Memorandum, dated 3 Feb 1972, at Ramsey Papers 228, f.160; memorandum dated 7 Feb 1972, at Ramsey Papers 228, f.165.

[51]   Phil McCullough, to Ramsey 19 April 1973, at Ramsey Papers 255, f.262; reply from Kirkham at Ramsey Papers 255, f.271.

[52]   See the petition, dated 6 November 1973, and related papers at Ramsey Papers 255, ff.166–68; telegram dated 8 December 1973, Ramsey Papers 255, f.174.

[53]   See the exchanges from June 1973 at Ramsey Papers 255, ff.94–97, 100–105.

Troubles might flourish. His own public interventions in relation of issues of human rights abroad caused others to see him as a friend of victims of perceived injustice. But many of the calls upon him to intervene were based on either naivety or a misunderstanding of the real powers of Canterbury over the government or over the independent Church of Ireland. In a time of crisis, the Archbishop still counted for something, even if it was not always clear what that something was.

Reforming the Language of the Church: Prayer Book Revision

This chapter has so far examined Ramsey's reactions to perceptions of a general social and economic crisis in the nation at large. These issues might have been easier to handle had the Church of England been robust and confident within itself; but this was far from the case. By the late 1960s the shocks of declining attendances, the kind of rapid cultural change examined in Chapter 3 and the shaking of older certainties about the identity of the Church in relation to other churches (Chapter 1) all contributed to a growing sense of unease. This should be seen as part of what several scholars have identified as a period of religious crisis in the UK and across the West.[54]

Part of this crisis was a collapse in confidence in the capacity of the Church's worship to be meaningful to the public. Were it possible to frame the question in sufficiently abstract a way, almost all within the Church of England could have agreed that its worshipping life was in need of reform. However, the Book of Common Prayer, which reached its three-hundredth year in 1962, was too freighted with accumulated historical meaning, too emblematic of other things, for it to be possible to deal with it so dispassionately.

Frustrated by the failure of the last attempt at reform in 1927–28, many Anglo-Catholics had continued to make use of variations that were (strictly speaking) illegal, some of which canon law reform was designed to regularise; unexploded bombs from a previous conflict which (it was thought) could now safely be defused.[55] Both evangelicals and Protestants, whilst deeply attached to

---

[54] See, *inter alia*, Welsby, *A History of the Church of England*, pp.189–92; Adrian Hastings, *A History of English Christianity 1920–1990* (London, SCM, third edition, 1991), pp.585, 590; McLeod, *The Religious Crisis of the 1960s*, pp.188–214. See also Sam Brewitt-Taylor, 'The invention of a "Secular Society"? Christianity and the sudden appearance of secularization discourses in the British national media, 1961-4', *Twentieth Century British History* 24:3 (2013), 327-50.

[55] For the immediate aftermath of 1927–28, see Beaken, *Cosmo Lang*, pp.143–81.

Prayer Book and Authorised Version as symbols of the Protestant basis of the national Church, were more and more feeling the need for re-evangelisation of the people as if *tabula rasa*.[56] And amongst an increasingly self-conscious radical movement, the Prayer Book itself and all the paraphernalia of an earlier age that surrounded it were the problem. The Church spoke a dead language; no wonder fewer and fewer people wished to hear what it had to say.[57]

Ramsey himself felt deeply the value of the Prayer Book, as key to the visible stability and continuity of the Church. Preaching on the occasion of its 1962 tercentenary, he argued that it had been part of the 'rule of faith' and a 'bond of unity' both in England and throughout the Anglican Communion. The Prayer Book had also been the 'moulding influence of a Christianity able to reach out to the ancient Churches of East and West and to the Reformation Churches too', and embodied key aspects of the mixed nature of the Anglican Church that made such an interface possible. Finally, its very words had become part of English speech, and as such its real influence was incalculable: 'its subconscious influence has perhaps been deeper even than the conscious loyalties it has evoked'.[58]

However, inestimable though its influence and value had been, the Prayer Book had never been revised in those three centuries, and things had changed. Part of the change was in the Church, Ramsey argued: thinking about the nature of worship had so developed as a result of the liturgical movement that liturgists across the churches argued for a much more active role for congregations in their liturgy. But the change was also amongst the public; patterns of speech had shifted, and worshippers were now much less accustomed to the 'sustained literary periods' of the Prayer Book, and more likely to respond to shorter biddings and responses: to prayers that were less 'intellectual' and which played more on the affections.[59] 'We give not dishonour, but honour, to the authors of our Prayer Book by trying to meet the needs of our time.'[60]

Although it was too much to expect another Cranmer, however, the task still demanded writers who 'with pen in hand can be like men inspired'. There was yet a need to retain 'undiminished, the note of mystery. Christians go to church not

---

[56] Maiden and Webster, 'Political protestantism', pp.376–77.

[57] Mark Chapman, 'Theology in the public arena: the case of South Bank Religion', in Jane Garnett et al, *Redefining Christian Britain. Post 1945 perspectives* (London, 2007), pp.98–99.

[58] 'The Tercentenary of the Prayer Book' in *The English Prayer Book 1549–1662* (London, 1963), pp.1–5, at pp.2–3. The sermon was preached in St Paul's Cathedral on 29 May 1962.

[59] 'Why the Prayer Book needs revision', *Observer*, 20 May 1962, p.10.

[60] Ramsey, 'The Tercentenary of the Prayer Book', p.4.

only to lay their immediate needs and those of the world before Almighty God, but also to be lifted out of things contemporary into a communion of saints reaching across the centuries and into the timeless mystery of the divine.'[61] Later commentators have argued that none of Cranmer's successors were able so to balance freshness and directness with durability and simple beauty; and indeed the Book and the Authorised Version shortly became standards raised in a more general reaction against the modernising trends of Ramsey's time.[62] However, the task of at least some sort of revision was necessary and urgent.

There were, however, already processes in train that made the task more difficult. As was noted in Chapter 2, Ramsey was impatient that the protracted process of reforming the canon law be concluded with all possible speed, since (in his view) it connected liturgy with other matters of discipline so as to obscure their right relation. Important though it was to have a secure legal basis for the qualifications of godparents or the material out of which the communion table was made, these were ancillary to the main task of the worship of God. As he told Convocation in June 1962 'as the worship of Almighty God has a primacy amongst the privileges of his creatures and children so ... it will be the worshipping life of the Church that has the first place in our concerns. Law and order are necessary elements in our worship, and we shall rejoice at the recovery of law and order with a good conscience. But these are the servants of worship, and not its master.'[63]

This disentanglement of worship from other issues was urgent because the church's mission to the people appeared to be failing. Ramsey had for many years been conscious of the disconnection between what the Church did and the people it was intended to serve. In *The Gospel and the Catholic Church*, Ramsey noted a mood of 'apathy and bewilderment' towards the church's hierarchy, its dogmas and its services with their 'archaic and beautiful language'. The question was asked: '"What is this strange thing, the Christian Church?"'; what relation did it have with the 'things that matter supremely.'[64] And it really mattered to Ramsey that there was such a disconnection, since 'the chaos of the world has beneath it the deep estrangement of the world from its Creator.' The world had 'lost the desire to have that communion with its Creator for which the world was made'. There was thus a renewed call to Christians to greater depth in their

---

[61] 'Why the Prayer Book needs revision', p.10.

[62] See several of the essays in Brian Morris (ed.), *Ritual Murder. Essays on Liturgical Reform* (Manchester, 1980).

[63] Draft text of Presidential Address to Convocation, 15 May 1962, at Ramsey Papers 23, ff.240–45, at f.245.

[64] Ramsey, *The Gospel and the Catholic Church*, p.3.

worship because 'in so doing they are serving the world, they are helping to keep the soul of the world alive'.[65]

By the early 1960s Anglican awareness of such a disconnection was growing quickly.[66] The urgency was evident in Ramsey's enthronement address in 1961 in which he stressed the need for 'greater freedom in the ordering and in the urgent revising of our forms of worship'.[67] By 1964, legislation allowing the Church to experiment with revised liturgies was before the Church Assembly. Ramsey exhorted the Assembly to 'Pass this Measure: that is my plea; ... and then use it with unity of purpose, with mutual tolerance within our Anglican comprehensiveness, and with sole inspiring motive of being a Church which worships God as well as it can worship, and brings the meaning of worship home to the people of the country'.[68] For Ramsey, the urgency was a matter of eschatology. The Christians of 1962 were called, no less than those of 1662, to worship as had Archbishop William Laud 'who said on the day of his execution, "Lord, I am coming to thee as fast as I can."'[69]

The process also had a further purpose: to demonstrate to the State that the freedom that was desired in the longer term was something with which the Church could be trusted. Once a measure could be steered through Parliament allowing the Church to introduce experimental liturgies, there would be an opportunity, which would need to grasped, for the Church through the new services to 'discover its unity and its wishes'. Only after several years of such self-discovery could any wider autonomy be sought from the State: 'only a Church that is really united and knowing its own aims can ask for such autonomy with any hope of success'.[70] As Ramsey put it to Donald Coggan, it was necessary to show that 'we all desire a greater Order and mean to have it'.[71]

Part of that greater order was to stay within the law even if that law was likely to be revised. It was also important not to alienate traditionalists who would need to be brought along if the changes were to stand any chance of success. Ramsey thus needed to act to dampen down enthusiasm which threatened to

---

[65]   Ramsey, 'The Tercentenary of the Prayer Book', p.5.

[66]   Harold Loukes, *Teenage Religion* (London, 1961), pp.74–77; Peter Webster and Ian Jones, 'Anglican "Establishment" Reactions to "Pop" Church Music in England, *c*.1956–1991', in Kate Cooper and Jeremy Gregory (eds), *Elite and Popular Religion* (Studies in Church History 42, *Woodbridge,* 2006), pp.429–41.

[67]   Ramsey, *Canterbury Essays*, p.167.

[68]   Text of speech on 6 July 1964, at Ramsey Papers 63, ff.287–98, at f.298.

[69]   Ramsey, 'The Tercentenary of the Prayer Book', pp.5, 3.

[70]   Confidential memorandum for the Bishops' Meeting, October 1961. 'Church Reform in Relation to the State', at Ramsey Papers 9, ff.244–46.

[71]   Ramsey to Coggan 11 July 1963, Ramsey Papers 42, ff.139–40.

overstep the mark. The staff of Coventry Cathedral petitioned their bishop in 1961 to be allowed to use the recently published New English Bible in services, who in turn sought Ramsey's advice. For the new cathedral the new translation was an 'instrument of unmatched power for the communication of the Word of God and the proclamation of the gospel to our contemporaries'. The effect of the Authorised Version was by contrast to 'reinforce the conviction, widely prevalent today, that what goes on in church is mere mumbo-jumbo, utterly unrelated to life in the world.'[72] Ramsey had a great deal of sympathy with this feeling, but could not agree that the legal and disciplinary problems created by such anticipatory use should be secondary to immediate evangelistic and pastoral need. Despite the urgency which he acknowledged, Coventry would need to wait until the law was changed.[73]

The law was changed by means of the Prayer Book (Alternative and Other Services) Measure of 1965, which allowed experimental use of new liturgies, and which was in turn cemented by the Worship and Doctrine Measure of 1974. Whilst the rights of traditionalist parishes were protected by the 1974 measure, there was now a free market in liturgical practice: parishes could experiment with and settle on the service patterns that best fitted their communal life and aided their witness. Change in the worship of local churches was, in the following years, to become one of the most particular points of contention, and Ramsey in later life regretted the insensitivity with which some of those changes were handled by enthusiasts for the new.[74] Despite these reservations, he knew the changes had been necessary, and right.

Theology in Crisis and Authority in the Church: *Honest to God*

The public furore over John Robinson's *Honest to God* is the single most well-known public theological event of the 1960s, and perhaps even of the twentieth century.[75] The book appeared in 1963, in the now iconic series of

---

72   Memo from the staff of Coventry Cathedral to the Bishop of Coventry, 1 November 1961, at Ramsey Papers 14, f.334.

73   Ramsey to the Bishop of Coventry, 20 January 1962, at Ramsey Papers 14, f.338.

74   Chadwick, *Ramsey*, p.195.

75   The events and their immediate context are examined from close up in David L. Edwards (ed.), *The Honest to God Debate* (London, 1963), pp.7–44, which should be read alongside the account in Eric James, *A Life of Bishop John A.T. Robinson*, pp.110–34. Later reflections include two by later archbishops: Rowan Williams, 'John A.T. Robinson (1919–83): *Honest to God* and the 1960s' in his *Anglican Identities*, pp.103–20; George Carey, *Development and Change: an examination of Michael Ramsey's response to Honest to*

slim pocket paperbacks from the SCM Press, with a modern sculpture of an earnest young man in thought on its cover: Modern Man grappling with the challenges of 'religionless' Christianity in a time of crisis. Already well known for his intervention in the Lady Chatterley trial, the Bishop of Woolwich had published his experiment in recasting the traditional language of faith in the hope of reconnecting with the people it was felt had been lost to the church.[76] Its arrival was announced in an article in the *Observer* entitled (against Robinson's better judgment) 'Our image of God must go.'

To focus too closely on whether Robinson was right or wrong – a prophet of a credible young church or a destroyer from within – is to miss important wider questions. The central issue for Ramsey was the limits of doctrine in the Church of England, and the means of setting them. Recent commentators have divided over the subject. For Edward Norman, the Church was, and is, bound to repeat such incidents, since it is without any central means of defining doctrine and accommodating its development.[77] For others, George Carey amongst them, such episodes rather show the elasticity of the Anglican polity, in which the very absence of a rigid central curia holds open a safe space for such theological adventure.[78]

Ramsey knew early on from his postbag that feelings were running high; and there was in the air the threat of concrete and drastic action against Robinson. An aspect of the crisis often overlooked was the sensitivity at precisely this time concerning the Ecclesiastical Jurisdiction Measure, then passing through Parliament with no little difficulty. Designed to reform the Byzantine system of church courts, it vested greater power in the bishops to stay proceedings against errant clergy; and its opponents thought this a retrograde step, when the bishops themselves could apparently not be trusted to safeguard orthodox doctrine.[79]

It was against this background that Ramsey learned of an intention to have the book and its orthodoxy debated in the Convocation of Canterbury.[80] Mervyn

---

God and its implications today (Durham 1993), reprinted as 'Michael Ramsey's response to *Honest to God*' in Robin Gill and Lorna Kendall (eds), *Michael Ramsey as Theologian*, pp.159–75 (the version here cited). For the wider context of 'South Bank religion', see also Mark Chapman, 'Theology in the Public Arena: The Case of South Bank Religion' in Jane Garnett et al (eds), *Redefining Christian Britain*, pp.92–105.

[76] Robinson, *Honest to God*, pp.7–10.

[77] Edward Norman, *Anglican Difficulties. A new syllabus of errors* (London, 2004), pp.101–11.

[78] Carey, 'Ramsey's response to *Honest to God*', pp.171–72.

[79] See Maiden and Webster, 'Last gasp of political Protestantism', p.367.

[80] G.F.Hilder, prolocutor of Convocation, to Ramsey, 10 April 1963, Ramsey Papers 50, f.124.

Stockwood, Bishop of Southwark, was also preparing himself for a petition for proceedings against Robinson in Stockwood's own court.[81] There appeared to be a real threat of what would be widely viewed in the media as a heresy hunt, and in two forums, neither of which were well constituted to do the job. Ramsey thought this to be avoided at all costs.

Yet he needed to do something. Stockwood, genuinely torn between his theological closeness with Ramsey and the evangelistic fervour of Robinson, offered parallels with earlier figures in Anglican history including William Temple who had similarly attracted suspicion but had gone on to be among the greatest.[82] None of these convinced Ramsey. Try as he might, he could not see how Robinson, despite his protestations, had stayed within the field of historic orthodoxy, even allowing for the obscurity of parts of the book. In a letter to all the diocesan bishops, he was sure that the book 'removes the conception of God known to us in the Bible and the Creed, and while some sort of doctrine about God and the Deity of Christ emerges, it is impossible to identify this doctrine with the doctrine of our Church which as Bishops we have promised to uphold.'[83] Conservatives were always ready to remind him of this consecration vow to 'drive away strange and erroneous doctrine', and so Ramsey needed to act, and quickly, using the only tool available to him: his own personal authority.

On 1 April Ramsey gave a television interview, stating that Robinson had been 'utterly wrong and misleading to denounce the imagery of God held by Christian men, women and children ... and to say that we can't have any new thought until it is swept away.'[84] The statement was short, and blunt, and provoked Robinson to protest; but Ramsey was at the time also writing the response that was to be published three weeks later. The pamphlet *Image Old and New* was an attempt not at debunking so much as to show at greater length that the Church was prepared to engage with the issues whilst at the same time emphasising the necessary limits.[85] Finally, there was still the matter of an impending heresy hunt in the meeting of Convocation on 7 May, and with no little reluctance Ramsey used part of his presidential address to meet the point. In the opinion of one involved in the management of Convocation business, Ramsey's intervention defused the tension and averted the danger of proceedings against Robinson.[86]

[81] Stockwood to Ramsey, 3 May 1963, Ramsey Papers 50, f.160.
[82] De-la-Noy, *Mervyn Stockwood*, p.167.
[83] Ramsey to Stockwood, 26 April 1963, at Ramsey Papers 50, f.137.
[84] As quoted in James, *Bishop John A.T. Robinson*, p.118.
[85] Ramsey, *Image Old and New* (London, 1963)
[86] G.F. Hilder, prolocutor of Convocation, to Ramsey, 1 May 1963, Ramsey Papers 50, f.152.

To what extent could Ramsey have handled the affair differently? More than one historian has noted his later regretting of his severity, citing Ramsey's later view that there had been 'in the background a widespread crisis of faith which cried out for another kind of spirit in meeting it.'[87] There may be an element of truth in the charge that Ramsey was not quite engaged with some of the theological currents with which Robinson's mind was flowing; they were certainly not those he found most congenial. Ramsey was to return to many of the same issues in *God, Christ and the World*, published in 1969, in which he tacitly acknowledged the slowness of some in the insular world of English theology to grasp what was happening.[88] That said, *Image Old and New* shows a quite sufficient grasp of the main issues for the needs of an archbishop, if not indeed of a professional theologian, and Ramsey had not come to them anew in 1963. While at Durham he had reviewed *Kerygma and Myth*,[89] the seminal 1954 collection of essays by Rudolf Bultmann and others, even then noting the need not only for demythologizing, but also both the need for new parables and symbols ('neo-mythologizing') and the re-discovery of imaginative power in apparently exhausted ones ('re-mythologizing'). 'How prosy is Bultmann's idea of presenting the Gospel! How limited is his existentialist philosophy!' For the Church to jettison all symbolic and parabolic language was voluntarily to relinquish a most effective teaching tool: the evocation of the poetical in a world of bland prose.[90]

Ramsey certainly regretted the pastoral damage that the episode did to his relationships with both Robinson and Stockwood, with whom tensions were at one stage so great that Max Warren had to act as a go-between.[91] The correspondence with Robinson is amongst the most painful in the Ramsey Papers, and his chaplain thought he had never seen Ramsey so upset in 10 years as over *Honest to God*.[92] And it was perhaps in the church's pastoral role that Ramsey was caught behind the pace. Ramsey was certainly alert to the estrangement of some of the public from the Church and its message. Since the war, he conceded, the Church had been too concerned with itself, 'perhaps assuming too easily that the faith may be taken for granted and needs only to

[87] See Carey, 'Ramsey's response to *Honest to God*', p.169, and De-la-Noy, *Michael Ramsey*, pp.187–88., both citing Ramsey, *Canterbury Pilgrim*, p.4.

[88] Ramsey, *God, Christ and the World. A study in Contemporary Theology* (London, 1969), pp.9–10.

[89] Published in English by SPCK in 1954.

[90] 'Demythologizing' in *Durham Essays and Addresses*, pp.29–34, at p.34.

[91] De-la-Noy, *Mervyn Stockwood*, p.170.

[92] John Andrew to George Carey, cited at Carey, *Development and Change*, pp.1–2.

be stated and commended.' Such commendation could only be possible so far as 'we go out and put ourselves with loving sympathy inside the doubts of the doubting, the questions of the questioners, and the loneliness of those who have lost their way.'[93] In the case of *Honest to God*, however, he was slow to grasp the depth of that estrangement. The testimonies brought together in the later *The Honest to God Debate* clearly show that Robinson had touched a great many people, and to the quick, and it was this that Ramsey was slow to appreciate; that the debate was an opportunity to be grasped, rather than a threat to be repelled.

Ultimately, however, Ramsey had no choice. For all the comfort and relief that the book had brought to some, it had also caused acute distress to many others within the Church: distress that went far beyond the recurrent and formulaic expressions of discontent with modernising currents in general, and with Robinson in particular after the Lady Chatterley trial.[94] A priest in Ramsey's former diocese of Durham felt that the ground had been cut from beneath the ordinary parish clergy, confronted with questions from their flock with which they could not deal: 'what are we poor priests to do?'[95] If there was a pastoral need to meet the doubts of the doubting, it was to be balanced with a responsibility to the existing faithful.

More fundamentally, Ramsey's hands were tied by his responsibility to the integrity of the Church of England as a whole. There had to be something, however small, that distinguished a church from a voluntary society for the discussion of religious opinions, and that something was fixity in doctrine at its core. The Church had a difficult double role, he told Convocation, of 'encouraging freedom of enquiry and adhering to a definite faith revealed in Holy Scripture and summarized in the historic creeds ... if heresy is a danger then so too is an obscurantist spirit in respect of the study of truth.' In a phrase of the bishop and historian Mandell Creighton, there was a need to balance '"the right of the individual to be free and the duty of the institution to be *something*."'[96] Paradoxically, it was only by being something, by holding some core conviction, that the churches could best serve the freedom of the individual. Once Ramsey had been convinced that Robinson, however unwittingly and however well intentioned, had subtracted from that essential something, then there was no option than to act with the means available.

---

[93]   *Image Old and New*, p.14. Ramsey also used the latter phrase in his address to Convocation.

[94]   Mews, 'The trials of Lady Chatterley', *passim*.

[95]   Raymond Hooper (Middlesborough, St Columba) to Ramsey, 25 March 1963, Ramsey Papers 50, f.74 and Ramsey's reply at f.77.

[96]   *The Chronicle of Convocation: 6–9 May 1963*, p.36.

Conclusion

To what extent is the title of this chapter justified: that is, how real was the crisis in church and in nation in the long 1960s? Historians have often traded in the language of crisis, and argument is from time to time joined as to how far-reaching or fundamental the tensions were in reality. By and large one's answer is conditioned by what one views as fundamental, but it seems clear that there was a widespread sense of rapid change, in the churches and in economic and social life, from the late 1960s onwards.

The Introduction to this study, along with Chapter 2, stressed how little importance Ramsey attached to the outward trappings of social success that had accreted to the Church of England. The established Church could not expect, and should not expect, to occupy the same place as it once had in the consciousness of the nation, nor to be the natural leader amongst the other churches. *The Gospel and the Catholic Church* had shown how the Church's message would, and must, always be 'difficult', a stumbling block and an offence to many. There was, then, in Ramsey's thought a preparedness for difficulty, indeed an expectation of it, in solidarity with the suffering church in other countries and with the martyrs of previous times.

How well did Ramsey as Archbishop manage the series of crises that presented themselves? As his handling of days of prayer and of Northern Ireland shows, he faced mutually incompatible demands: that he should continue to exercise an older role in calling the nation to book, when all other indicators showed that a large proportion of the public did not think the role was his to perform. It was a role that he would much rather not perform on his own. In this, a middle course was the only prudent one to steer, which Ramsey and his staff by and large achieved. In Northern Ireland, he was similarly caught between the symbolic complexities of his office when viewed from Belfast, his personal associations with the ecumenical movement, and the severe practical limitations on what he could actually achieve.

Within the Church, his own affection for the Book of Common Prayer did not blind him to the fact that the difficulties that many had with the Book were part of a more general crisis in communication. Because of his own personal centring in worship, Ramsey made reform of the liturgy a priority from the very beginning. This he achieved, even if in retrospect the result did not produce what had been hoped.

In the matter of *Honest to God*, in retrospect, Ramsey appears squarely in the theological centre ground. Although he disappointed many in appearing to come out against the 'New Look' in theology in which many hopes were placed, later commentators, and some at the time, have seen *Honest to God* for the flawed work that it is. Ultimately it was the fact of who had written the book that was decisive. As the Introduction showed, Ramsey overcame his reluctance to leave Cambridge to become Bishop of Durham because of his sense of the importance of the teaching role of a bishop. Robinson had communicated his thought in a way that a Cambridge don could, but a bishop could not.

Chapter 5

The Prophetic Church

Introduction

One yardstick by which Archbishops of Canterbury seem often to be judged is one that contradicts most of the others. This study has so far examined Ramsey's success in leading the Church of England in its role as the religious department of the State, and in overseeing the fundamental renegotiation of that relationship, both with regard to the State's powers in the internal affairs of the Church, and of the Christian element in the State's moral law. Yet the salient elements in the memory of at least some of Ramsey's predecessors are of the precise opposite: the degree to which they were prepared to kick over the traces; to challenge government policy or social consensus in the name of the gospel; to speak prophetically. If in Chapter 3 the institutional Church was often in line with, and indeed slightly ahead of the consensus among the ruling class, the matters in this chapter show Ramsey acting in an older prophetic mode, calling the mighty to account both at home and abroad.

There were precedents for such action, of which Ramsey the student of history was very aware. Anselm was known not only for the theology of the *Proslogion*, but as 'the heroic statesman of the Church against the intolerable claims of kings and princes.'[1] The example of Thomas Becket needed no glossing.[2] But there were dangers in being seen as a 'political parson'. There were strong Christian elements in each of the main political parties, but any attempt to claim conservatism or socialism as the more authentically Christian form of politics was doomed to failure. There was no shortage of clergy who had attracted notoriety, or at the very least criticism, for attempting to apply Christian principle to national and international affairs, outside the limited sphere of matters regarded by many as the proper province of 'religion'. Perhaps the paradigm case was that of Hewlett Johnson, the 'Red Dean' of Canterbury, still in post as dean of Ramsey's cathedral

---

[1]   Ramsey, 'Anselm' (an address given at Bec in 1967), in *Canterbury Pilgrim*, pp.88–89.
[2]   Ramsey spoke on Becket in Canterbury Cathedral on the eighth centenary of Becket's death, published as 'Becket', *Canterbury Pilgrim*, pp.185–88.

until his retirement in 1963, which he followed with a trip to Cuba to meet Che Guevara at the invitation of Fidel Castro.[3]

It was not only mavericks like Johnson who allowed themselves to be drawn onto this controverted ground. Each of Ramsey's three predecessors had form in this regard. Lang concerned himself publicly in wartime with the treatment of conscientious objectors, refugees and evacuees, as well as criticising the mores of the social circle around the outgoing Edward VIII.[4] In foreign affairs, Fisher was outspoken in relation to the Suez crisis, constitutional settlement in Uganda and apartheid South Africa.[5] Temple proposed nothing less than top-to-bottom social and economic renewal at home, but had not time to pursue it.[6]

The historian can gain a false impression of order from the archiepiscopal papers at Lambeth, arranged neatly in subject divisions, in chronological order. Most archbishops, like all senior managers, would in reality have experienced their times in office as a rapid succession of disconnected matters of greater or lesser urgency. The period from the mid-1960s into the early 1970s presented a more diverse and greater load of national and international crises than perhaps any other recent period of peacetime, some of which were examined in Chapter 4, and so the opportunities were there for Ramsey to be a very political parson indeed.

Partly in reaction to difficult times, the late 1960s saw a radicalisation of sections of Christian opinion with regard to questions of race and economic inequality. As we shall see, the World Council of Churches became clearly aligned, at least in public perception, with radical opinion on many of these questions. The 1968 Lambeth Conference had concerned itself with poverty and injustice to a degree not visible in the 1958 event,[7] but it was not always obvious in the polemical turmoil of 'The Sixties' what a distinctively Christian prophetic position might be. Some campaigned on issues of peace, liberation or justice, motivated by all manner of forces that might include both a Christian faith and an atheistic Marxism; and Hugh McLeod has noted the pathways by which some strands of Christian idealism carried people leftwards and out of the churches.[8] But in other things, some Christians felt the forces of the counter-culture acting against the gospel, and so a prophet was needed to call the nation back to older ways.

---

[3]   Robert Hughes, *The Red Dean* (Worthing, 1987), pp.197–98, and *passim*.
[4]   Beaken, *Lang*, pp.193–95, 203–7, 119–24.
[5]   Chandler and Hein, *Fisher*, pp.127–40.
[6]   John Kent, *William Temple*, (Cambridge, 1992), pp.115–67.
[7]   *Lambeth Conference 1968. Resolutions and Reports*, (London, 1968), pp.23, 35.
[8]   McLeod, *Religious Crisis*, pp.146–51.

14

As was seen in the Introduction, despite his outward appearance of otherworldliness, Ramsey was himself political to his core. Chapter 3 showed his morally conservative and socially liberal sides working in tandem. However, to understand Ramsey's small-l liberalism in political terms alone would be to see only half of the picture. Some strands of Christian liberalism had for Ramsey seemed too ready to sanctify progressive elements in contemporary society as bricks in the building of the Kingdom of God on earth. Ramsey's apprehension of the real prospects for human flourishing without dependence on God was much darker. Preaching at Canterbury at Easter 1970, he called on his hearers to join with him and 'proclaim that a country which rejects God's laws brings judgement upon itself.' There were three crosses, not simply the one on which Christ has died. There was a second, that of Christian suffering and martyrdom, and thirdly 'where there is in the world selfishness, hatred, violence, cruelty, lust, there comes a Cross of human suffering, dark and bitter, with none of the radiance of Calvary to lighten it.' On this world 'the judgement of God falls and Jesus weeps over the city that does not know the things that belong to its peace.'[9] The church in its witness had to be stirred to counter these things, and help in the world's deliverance from that third Cross.

Christianity and Pacifism

There was a durable and significant strand of Christian pacifism that had received new impetus in recent years with the advent of uniquely destructive and indiscriminate weapons. This was an ever-present note in denunciations of the war in Vietnam, but also of the heavy threat of the atomic bomb. Ramsey was no absolute pacifist, although he was dedicated to peace. Christ's injunction to turn the other cheek was best understood as concerning motive rather than action; and Christians had, under certain conditions, found it 'possible, however hazardous, to strike in defence of others without hatred, anger or self-concern'.[10] So it was necessary to take on the difficult task of applying much older Christian principles of the 'just war' to newly horrific and tragic situations as they presented themselves. There was always a danger 'that a war waged with idealistic motives may see those motives corrupted as the process goes on' and danger too in saying 'It will be a just war if we win it.' Even if, under modern

---

[9]   Ramsey, 'The Three Crosses', *Canterbury Pilgrim*, pp.160–62.
[10]   A lecture in the University of Cambridge in February 1972, published under the title 'Christianity and Violence' in Ramsey, *Canterbury Pilgrim*, pp.129–36; p.129.

conditions, the old tests were becoming harder to apply, the principles still had weight and usefulness. As we shall see, Ramsey knew that the war in Vietnam 'with its continuing destruction without winners' was not a war which could pass the tests.[11]

A Christian position on active belligerence had a further component for Ramsey, however. The Christian might counsel peace in one situation, and reluctantly urge war in another. But in both, Christians could not hope to be accepted if they were to commend a costly course of action to others without being prepared to share that cost themselves. It would be incredible to 'encourage people to belligerence while ourselves keeping out of the conflict' or to suggest to others in another situation that 'their Christian calling is to suffer patiently in the spirit of the Cross of Christ ... we can safely say anything at all only if we are ready to be at one with those who are suffering. It is this that is imperative; it is also this that is sometimes so hard as to be near-impossible. This is our tragic situation.'[12]

Ramsey did, however, leave open the door not only for just war, but for just rebellion against a tyrannical government. In South Africa, non-violent resistance had been long tried and had failed, and activists such as Nelson Mandela and his associates had been 'crushed by the regime's own use of violence. So they asked: "What then is left to us but violence?"' But Ramsey saw an inescapable tension in any honest Christian position on the matter. Inconsistency had to be avoided, since '[w]e cannot applaud Europeans who resisted the tyranny of a Hitler and then be shocked when Africans want to resist a tyrannical regime today.'[13] But to urge rebellion may have consequences which cannot be predicted, for all peoples in South Africa, for the churches, and internationally, and Christians would need to be prepared to share in those costs too.

This kind of principled pragmatism was evident in Ramsey when it came to the atomic bomb. The Lambeth Conference of 1958 had called for work 'as a matter of the utmost urgency' towards international agreement on abolition; a judgment reiterated in similarly strong terms in 1968.[14] As Matthew Grimley has shown, Ramsey viewed the very existence of such weapons as fearful, the sign of a civilisation in the gravest moral danger. But the Campaign for Nuclear Disarmament (CND) was, for Ramsey, guilty of sentimentality in advocating unilateral disarmament without any international agreement. Just as to oppose

[11] Ramsey, *Canterbury Pilgrim*, pp.130–32.
[12] Ramsey, *Canterbury Pilgrim*, p.134.
[13] Ramsey, *Canterbury Pilgrim*, pp.132–33.
[14] *The Lambeth Conference 1958* (London, 1958), resolution 106 at p.1.55; *The Lambeth Conference 1968* (London, 1968), resolution 8, at p.31.

abortion under any circumstances was an evasion (see Chapter 3), CND's position avoided facing the cost of figuring out the consequences. Ramsey thus arrived at a qualified defence of retention as a deterrent of something worse, although with 'some agony of mind' in concluding so.[15] Such agony of mind was the necessary price Ramsey sometimes paid to arrive at a view with which he could live.

South Africa

One tragic situation, intractable yet urgent, was apartheid South Africa. The South African state claimed to be a bastion of Christian civilization and to be a representative and promoter of that civilization on the continent. Within South Africa itself, Christians were ranged on both sides, with the South Africa Council of Churches being in part born out of the fight against apartheid, whilst the Dutch Reformed Church (not a member of the Council) gave solid support to the regime.[16] There were white Anglican clergy who had worked in South Africa, such as Trevor Huddleston or Ambrose Reeves, through whom Anglicans in England had learned of South Africa and its problems.

In the same year that the South Africa Council of Churches was formed, the bishops at the 1968 Lambeth Conference called for penitence for the Church's own failings of non-white brethren in the past.[17] Ramsey thought the apartheid regime the worst case of a phenomenon in which all white Westerners were implicated, 'the phenomenon of white supremacy in history.'[18] As the established Church of perhaps the premier white colonial power, the Church of England had a particular share in that phenomenon. Ramsey had also to reckon with his responsibilities to Anglicans in South Africa. But what to do? Ramsey was sure that it could not be enough to urge blacks to contain themselves, since this involved comfortable First World Christians asking their brethren elsewhere to accept their sufferings without being prepared to share in them. There were

---

[15] Matthew Grimley, 'The Church and the Bomb: Anglicans and the Campaign for Nuclear Disarmament, c.1958–1984', in *God and War: The Church of England and Armed Conflict in the Twentieth Century*, ed. Stephen G. Parker and Tom Lawson (Farnham, 2012), pp.147–64, at 155–57.
[16] On the worldwide Christian response to liberation struggles, see Morris, *The Church in the Modern Age*, pp.80–83.
[17] Resolution 16; *Lambeth Conference 1968*, pp.33–34.
[18] Ramsey, *Canterbury Pilgrim*, p.134.

moral risks involved, too, in maintaining economic, cultural or educational contacts with an evil regime, a complicity in 'the bolstering up of injustice.'[19]

At the very least, it was possible to deny the South African regime the means of repression: its arms. Shortly before visiting South Africa in 1970, Ramsey, with a very large group of bishops, wrote to Prime Minister Heath, asking for an end to the British export of weapons to South Africa: an act that, whilst rejected by Heath, did not go unnoticed in South Africa itself.[20] Another option was to urge rebellion, and indeed to foster it from without. As a result of its Assembly at Uppsala in 1968, the World Council of Churches began to grant monies to organisations within South Africa and Rhodesia that appeared to many in Europe to foster violent rebellion. Ramsey had been President of the WCC until 1968, and could hardly avoid comment. He could see no body in South Africa organised and responsible enough to receive such funds; Christian concern had here overrun itself.[21]

In November 1970 Ramsey had the opportunity to see all sides of the South African situation at first hand. *Canterbury Pilgrim* contains an address to which Ramsey gave the title 'Apartheid', which was preached to a large congregation in St Mary's Cathedral, Johannesburg. Despite the title, which indicates where Ramsey felt its burden to be, the address actually approached the subject obliquely, within a more general exposition of the apostolic vision of authentic Christian fellowship. The Johannesburg congregation was 'a picture of what the Church is meant to be' as 'people of black races and coloured people and Afrikaners and English-speaking people have been drawn to Christ lifted up on the Cross.'[22]

Ramsey rejoiced with his South African hearers in the ecumenical progress towards the full realisation of such fellowship, but there were still barriers. The same undermining of Christian morality that Ramsey saw in Europe likewise hindered the work in Africa, as did the system of migrant labour and its impact on families. As the apostle Paul had rebuked Peter at Antioch for restricting fellowship around the Lord's table on ethnic grounds, so Ramsey addressed the 'separation of races in churches and in homes and in social life [that] mars the character of Christian fellowship as the apostles understood it.'[23] Ramsey stopped short of condoning violent action to solve either this or the other worldwide

---

[19]   Ramsey, *Canterbury Pilgrim*, p.135.
[20]   Chadwick, *Ramsey*, p.257
[21]   Chadwick, *Ramsey*, pp.256–57; McLeod, *Religious crisis*, pp.155–56; Morris, *Church in the modern age*, pp.66–69.
[22]   Ramsey, 'Apartheid' in *Canterbury Pilgrim*, pp.144–47; pp.144–45.
[23]   Ramsey, 'Apartheid', p.146.

problems he described, but there was a clear warning nonetheless, since time was short. 'But the alternative to violence is the making of considerable changes by those who have the power to make those changes, while there is still time. That is the issue.'[24]

Ramsey's most difficult task while in South Africa was a visit to the head of the state that so restricted and marred Christian fellowship. Ramsey visited Prime Minister Vorster on 27 November, and a more complete mismatching of thought and feeling is hard to imagine, a dialogue in which one participant at least was deaf. Ramsey later described the day as 'the worst day of my life', and the photographs show Ramsey with a most uncharacteristically serious face, which he later admitted to have deliberately pulled.[25]

Vorster thought Ramsey's intervention over arms sales 'a most unfriendly act' and that Ramsey did not care about protecting Africa from the 'terrible danger' of communism. Ramsey replied that 'the policies of discrimination by Christian countries do put Africans off Christianity and therefore make them more vulnerable to Communist propaganda.' Ramsey expressed concern about the system of migratory labour and its 'strain on family life and marriages'. Vorster responded that the system had not been invented there, that it was not compulsory (as Ramsey thought) and that the British practised it elsewhere. Vorster thought that police methods of detention and interrogation resembled nothing so much as those in operation in Northern Ireland, as if Ramsey were responsible for them and were representing the British government rather than the Church.

Ramsey persevered, speaking of the work he had seen in the churches, amongst white, coloured and black, in bringing people to Christ; Vorster disagreed. 'The Anglicans meddle in politics and condemn our policy', he argued: 'the Church should preach the gospel and not pass judgements'. The ecumenical contact between Anglican and Reformed churches was for Vorster a mere pretext for criticism of apartheid. Those Anglican priests who were 'subversive' such as Trevor Huddleston and Ambrose Reeves would be shown the door, as indeed was Ramsey, rather abruptly.[26] The account does indeed read, as Ramsey later described it, as 'a meeting between heads of State of two nations at war.'[27]

If there was considerable delicacy in relations abroad, Ramsey's stock by and large rose on arriving back in London. Some in the churches had wished him to go further, and some that he had done rather less; but there were few who would

---

[24] Ramsey, 'Apartheid', p.147.
[25] Chadwick, *Ramsey*, pp.259, 262–63.
[26] Ramsey's full note is given in Chadwick, *Ramsey*, pp.260–62.
[27] Chadwick, *Ramsey*, p.260.

argue that apartheid should not have been opposed by at least some means. There was a private interview with Prime Minister Heath, but also support from less accustomed quarters. There had been in some parts of the Labour party a reflexive opposition to the established Church; but for his interventions concerning South Africa Ramsey was congratulated in the Commons from the Labour back benches.[28] One MP thought that '[b]oth Front Benches of the House could learn a great deal from what [Ramsey] has said on this subject.'[29] Another later quipped that if the 'Church of England carries on with its progressive pronouncements the Tories may very well have to find somewhere else to pray.'[30]

Vietnam

Perhaps the single issue that did most to polarise opinion in the West, particularly among the young, was America's war in Vietnam. From the very outset there were voices on the Christian left who saw few, if any, shades of moral grey: all the fault lay with the United States.[31] At the same time, the reflex position of many Christians was to support any action taken that would counter the threat of communism.[32]

Ramsey's dealings with the issue showed his characteristic principled pragmatism: there were Christian principles in play, but there was a cost in applying them realistically in complex and morally ambiguous circumstances. Ramsey's settled view was that given to the press whilst in the Canadian provincial capital of Fredericton in October 1966. He said (as summarised later) '[t]hat the United States had entered Vietnam with the sincere motive of resistance to Communist aggression, that the war was now achieving nothing, that it was urgently necessary to bring it to an end, that he agreed with Mr Wilson in deploring the American bombing of the North, that the American bombing of

---

[28]   Chadwick, *Ramsey*, p.264.

[29]   William Molloy (Labour, Ealing North), H.C. Deb., 9 December 1970, vol. 808, col. 528.

[30]   David Stoddart (Labour, Swindon) H.C. Deb. 26 January 1971, vol. 810, col. 487.

[31]   On the radicalisation of opinion as represented by the journal *New Christian*, see McLeod, *Religious Crisis of the Sixties*, pp.87–89; see also pp.144–45.

[32]   Dianne Kirby, 'The Church of England and the Cold War', in *God and War: The Church of England and armed conflict in the twentieth century*, ed. Stephen G. Parker and Tom Lawson (Farnham, 2013), at pp.129–35.

the North ought to cease, that American initiative was needed in bringing about a settlement, that both sides however must contribute to achieving a settlement.'[33]

Ramsey had initially been rather less sure of what ought to be done, and how it could be done most effectively. Statements from the British Council of Churches were necessarily associated with Ramsey, as its chairman. But without the wholehearted support of the chairman, the Council passed a resolution in April 1965 calling for the restoration of peace and order and for an end to attempts to 'alter international situations by armed force'. The Council called also for a re-examination in international law of the use of indiscriminate weaponry and, in the meantime, for Christians to press their governments for a rigorous observance of existing international law.[34] In a further statement in October, the Council expressed sorrow at the intensification of the war, but stressed that negotiations would need to include the National Liberation Front of North Vietnam, however unpalatable that might be.[35]

In May 1965 Launcelot Fleming, Bishop of Norwich, was considering joining the British Council for Peace in Vietnam, which counted amongst its leading lights the Labour peer Fenner Brockway. Ramsey, after taking advice, thought the group 'pacifist, fellow-travelling and left-wing', and that it went much further than the position of the BCC in calling for immediate US withdrawal and the unification of Vietnam, possibly by force. Ramsey hoped that Fleming would not cause the Church possible embarrassment and give support to 'anti-American propaganda' by joining the group.[36]

In these early stages Ramsey had tried to avoid too much in the way of public intervention. As the war dragged on, Ramsey's advisers became increasingly conscious of growing pressure for Ramsey to 'do something'. Some members of the public thought Ramsey had not condemned the violence often or forcefully enough, drawing contrast with the public position in favour of the war from Billy Graham. 'When will you, in the name of Jesus Christ, be brave and speak out against this murder of a nation?' asked one.[37] In the summer of 1966, the diplomats at the BCC were warning Lambeth of growing pressure from Anglicans internationally, particularly in the US and Australia.[38] There

---

[33] John Satterthwaite to the editor of the Journal of the Moscow Patriarchate, 20 February 1967, Ramsey Papers 123, f.123.

[34] Resolution passed at meeting of BCC on 27/28 April; text at Ramsey Papers 89, f.192.

[35] Text of resolution passed at meeting of 26/27 October, at Ramsey Papers 89, f.214.

[36] Ramsey to Fleming, 13 May 1965, at Ramsey Papers 89, f.191.

[37] Wilfred Abbs to Ramsey, 4 July 1966, Ramsey Papers 109, f.173.

[38] Paul Oestreicher (BCC) to Beloe, 16 June 1966, at Ramsey Papers 109, f.160.

were also signs that Christian youth was becoming increasingly radicalised. The Student Christian Movement had called on the British government to disassociate itself from the American administration and to support the United Nations. They expressed solidarity with those Americans jailed for refusing the draft on conscientious grounds, and advocated direct action by British members themselves in person in Vietnam.[39]

Not for the first time, public expectation ran ahead of what it was possible for the Archbishop effectively to do. Ramsey did take part in a special broadcast service of intercession at Westminster Abbey in July 1966, in which the congregation prayed for 'all who have leadership in Vietnam, North and South, that they may have restraint and wisdom', and that world governments 'may know what is right and may do it.'[40] Ramsey continued to make statements from time to time about the war, often at periods of particular intensity in the fighting, but these became shorter and more weary as the 1960s gave way to the 1970s and there was yet no end in sight.

As the conflict stretched on, there were signs of increased global co-operation amongst the religious to find ways of ending the war. When pressed in 1965 to act in concert with the other British churches, Ramsey's office had expressed some caution, lest an intervention from Western religious leaders should do more harm than good.[41] By 1968 much of this caution had dissipated. Ramsey supported initial moves in a WCC initiative for joint action worldwide between the Pope, Ramsey and (crucially) the Patriarch Alexei of Moscow, sending the Bishop of Chichester to a meeting in Zurich to begin work.[42] February 1968 saw a remarkable joint statement from several of the churches of the BCC including Ramsey and Cardinal Heenan, in conjunction with the Chief Rabbi Immanuel Jakobovits and the president of the Friends of the Western Buddhist Order. It called for an end to the 'intolerable suffering [of] the people of Vietnam ... We pray for peace and, as a nation, as religious communities and as individuals, we must seek to promote peace.' Until peace could be achieved, it continued, 'we can give aid' and made an appeal on behalf of aid charities, religious and not.[43]

The international context for Ramsey's action was not always straightforward. Shortly after Ramsey's comments in Fredericton, the Council for Foreign Relations spotted an article in the journal of the Moscow Patriarchate, to which Ramsey's office gave a guarded private reply. Bearing the title 'Regrettable

[39]   Resolution from meeting at New Year 1967, at Ramsey Papers 123, f.153.
[40]   Draft order of service at Ramsey Papers 109, ff.176–78.
[41]   Ramsey to John Collins, 10 August 1965, Ramsey Papers 89, f.207.
[42]   Ramsey to Eugene Blake (WCC), 5 March 1968, Ramsey Papers 148, f.175 et ff.
[43]   Appeal dated 13 February 1968, at Ramsey Papers 148, f.161.

speeches by the Archbishop of Canterbury', it showed the hand of the Soviet authorities intervening in international religious affairs. In it, the Archpriest Ivanov, whom Ramsey had met in Moscow in 1956, tried to point out an 'increasingly widening divergence of opinion' between Ramsey and 'the majority of the present-day Christian world', as Ramsey had attempted to defend the American position as 'justified in order to counteract communist aggression'. 'Shocking in its violence', this view was apparently held personally by Ramsey 'with full clarity' since he had often 'made declarations about his spiritual and moral independence from the line of state policy and its vacillations'.[44] As with many things, Canterbury could not intervene in international affairs with the same freedom as could the laity or even other bishops.

Southern Rhodesia

In the summer of 1965 the Rhodesian United Front, led by Ian Smith, seemed poised unilaterally to declare independence from Britain, setting up a permanent white minority government in power over a black majority along South African lines. The United Nations General Assembly was sure that Britain had the responsibility to prevent this, by the use of force if necessary. The Prime Ministers of the Commonwealth countries agreed; but the Wilson government was rather less sure.[45] The matter of Rhodesia showed up an apparent inconsistency in Ramsey's position on the use of force in a right cause. Owen Chadwick reproduced a cartoon from the *Daily Express* from February 1968, showing Ramsey bursting in on Prime Minister Harold Wilson wearing a CND-style badge that read 'Don't bomb Ho Chi Minh', but also a pendant in the form of a bomb inscribed 'Bomb Smith.'[46] Why one and not the other? Why, it asked, should foreign intervention be justified in the case of Southern Rhodesia, but not in Vietnam? For Chadwick, Ramsey's intervention in the autumn of 1965 over the future of the Ian Smith regime in Southern Rhodesia placed him at the 'centre of the windiest political storm endured by an Archbishop of Canterbury' since 1688, which saw Ramsey under police protection for a time.[47]

---

[44] The translation is dated January 1967, at Ramsey Papers 123, ff.118–19.

[45] See the general accounts of Peter Clarke, *Hope and Glory. Britain 1900–2000* (London, 2004), pp.297–98, and Dominic Sandbrook, *White Heat. A History of Britain in the Swinging Sixties* (London, 2006), pp.120-6.

[46] Chadwick, *Ramsey*, plate facing p.243.

[47] Chadwick, *Ramsey* gives a very full account of the chronology at pp.241–50; quotation at p.245.

In October, Ramsey wrote to Wilson to argue that there was a responsibility not to allow Britain's colonial story to end in such a way, and that force would be justified if all else failed. He also, in conjunction with the British Council of Churches, sent Smith a telegram urging him not to make a Unilateral Declaration of Independence (UDI).[48] But it was a speech made at a meeting of the British Council of Churches on 26 October, at which time Wilson was being treated with open contempt in the Rhodesian capital, Salisbury, that stirred up the press storm. It was not the business of the churches to give military advice to the government, he argued; but if Rhodesia were to 'go over the brink', and Wilson decided that military force was necessary 'then I think that as Christians we have to say that it will be right to use force to that end.'[49] Richard Crossman, one of Wilson's cabinet, noted the 'storm of indignation' that had ensued in the press, which showed that the British public would not countenance 'a war against fellow white men who are also British subjects.'[50]

As Ramsey told an emergency debate in the Lords after Smith had made the UDI on 11 November, the affair had 'brought to many people grief between friends, and grief between relatives, too.' Ramsey himself had found long-term friendships in the House of Lords and elsewhere damaged by his stance. But once Smith had made the UDI, the terms of the debate had shifted, even if the moral issues had not, and Ramsey believed that 'the people of this country, after some inevitable bewilderment, are grasping what these moral issues are.'[51] The precise system of democracy in Rhodesia was less important for Ramsey than education, civil rights and freedom from discrimination for the black majority. He thought that economic sanctions (Wilson's measure of choice) could be effective, if intended as an agent of change and not as a punishment, but that they must be effective in short order.

But Ramsey was speaking not merely as a pragmatist, but as archbishop, gentle but insistent prodder of the national conscience. The issue was now 'that our country should be seen to uphold law, order and justice with the same resolution everywhere, whatever be the race and colour of those in relation to whom law has to be upheld. Nothing could damage us more in the eyes of African countries – and, I would add, in the eyes of the God of justice and righteousness – than that we should even seem to falter in this duty and

---

[48]   Chadwick, *Ramsey*, p.245.

[49]   De-la-Noy, *Michael Ramsey*, pp.184–5; De-la-Noy and Chadwick give the quotation slightly differently, and the version here is as at Chadwick, *Ramsey*, p.245.

[50]   Richard Crossman, *The Diaries of a Cabinet Minister. Volume One: Minister of Housing 1964–66* (London, 1975), p.361.

[51]   H.L. Deb. 15 November 1965 vol. 270, cols 265–66.

obligation.'[52] In some circumstances Christians were compelled to approve the use of force to achieve necessary ends, and ultimately this might be the only acceptable course for Britain in the context of its historic obligations: 'I do not believe that the Government could, without dishonour, be acting differently.'[53]

Immigration

When talking about the countries of the Commonwealth, Ramsey was certain that the obligations of the UK to its former subject peoples had not ended with their independence. This legacy of affinities, familial ties, obligation and guilt touched daily life in Britain directly in the form of immigration from the Commonwealth. That immigration began, symbolically at least, with the arrival of the SS Windrush at Tilbury in 1948, but the temperature of debate about its effects and its limits reached a new height in Ramsey's time at Canterbury. The 1960s saw two related series of legislation, one of which dismayed liberal opinion, and a second that pleased it. Beginning with the Commonwealth Immigrants Act of 1962, Parliament limited for the first time the total number of immigrants to Britain, and subsequently introduced what amounted to a racial qualification for that entry. In parallel, mounting tension in local areas from west London to the west Midlands pointed towards legislation to protect the immigrant population from discrimination once they had reached and settled in the UK.[54]

In the midst of this, Prime Minister Wilson asked Ramsey to chair the new National Committee for Commonwealth Immigrants (NCCI), set up by the government to monitor the situation of immigrants in the UK. It was highly politicised work, which saw police protection officers shadowing Ramsey in 1968 after threats were made to his life, guards at Canterbury Cathedral to protect the fabric from possible damage, and National Front hecklers at a public meeting.[55] The NCCI was for some an unwarranted interference in the right of the English to discriminate against outsiders as they pleased. For others, including Ramsey, it was not half as powerful as it needed to be.

---

[52]   H.L. Deb. 15 November 1965 vol. 270, col. 266.

[53]   H.L. Deb. 15 November 1965 vol. 270, col. 267.

[54]   In general, see Zig Layton-Henry, *The Politics of Immigration* (Oxford, 1992); Matthew Grimley, 'The Church of England, race and multiculturalism, 1962–2012' in *Rescripting Religion in the City: Migration and Religious Identity in the Modern Metropolis* (Farnham, 2013), ed. Jane Garnett and Alana Harris, pp.207–21.

[55]   Chadwick, *Ramsey* pp.166–76.

Ramsey spoke out frequently on immigration and community relations, from the beginning of his time at Canterbury until the end. Two principles guided his speaking. As with Rhodesia, Britain had obligations to the Commonwealth. Ramsey had been in India as news of the 1962 Bill had spread, and it had 'been a great shock and in future years, very likely, history will note it as one of the shocks in the story of our country and Commonwealth.'[56] Ramsey spoke of 'this lamentable Bill, this Bill introduced with repugnance, this Bill which is indeed deplorable':[57] strong words in the context of his dealings with the House of Lords.

Just as there were residual obligations to protect black Rhodesians in Rhodesia, the nation had obligations to those who needed to flee their own country. March 1968 saw the rapid introduction of legislation to restrict the immigration of Kenyans of Asian extraction, many of whom had retained British passports, who had been forced out of Kenya by the government of Jomo Kenyatta. Ramsey stayed up late into the night to speak and vote against the Kenyan Asians Bill. The Bill left Kenyan Asians with a citizenship of paper without substance when it really mattered, and thus 'virtually involves this country in breaking its word.' The nation had during its colonial history 'by its total action, involved itself in a certain obligation, and ... this Bill abrogates that obligation.' Several years later Ramsey included this speech in *Canterbury Pilgrim*, an indication of its importance to him.[58]

Enoch Powell made what was an almost certainly conscious reference to Ramsey in the 1968 speech that has become known by a single phrase (which he did not quite in fact use), the 'rivers of blood'. Powell attacked newspaper leader writers guilty of a form of appeasement, and 'Archbishops who live in palaces, faring delicately, with the bedclothes pulled right up over their heads.' All of these had the matter 'exactly and diametrically wrong.'[59] Ramsey knew that even if Powell thought restricting the flow of migrants was a humane policy, in the best interests of the immigrant himself, it failed on pragmatic grounds. To pull up the drawbridge and to leave a rump of isolated people who felt unwelcome was to create a 'dangerous ghetto situation', the seeds of which he knew much about through his work with the NCCI. There was already real tension in local communities, and discrimination in housing, employment and other matters, both overt and covert. Ramsey knew that the new Community Relations Commission, set up in 1968, needed more staff and more money than

[56]   H.L. Deb. 12 March 1962, vol. 238, col. 25.
[57]   H.L. Deb. 12 March 1962, vol. 238, col. 26.
[58]   Ramsey, 'Kenya Asians' in *Canterbury Pilgrim*, pp.148–52; pp.150–51.
[59]   As quoted at Chadwick, *Ramsey*, p.174.

the NCCI had had, and that the Race Relations Board needed more teeth in enforcement of the law.[60]

There was a second and stronger ground on which to resist the direction of Powell's thinking, and work towards better relations between communities. There was a small but durable strand of thought amongst some Christians that connected national identity with racial purity, however defined. Ramsey would have none of this: the questions turned on 'basic Christian beliefs in the equality of man'.[61] Although it did not contain a racial qualification, Ramsey knew that the 1962 Bill would nonetheless be viewed that way: 'The news, put very crudely, has travelled about in the form, "Great Britain will admit Irish people without restriction but will restrict immigrants from the West Indies."'[62] The Kenyan Asians Bill contained what had become known as the 'grandfather clause', which although technically about geography, was for Ramsey bound to act as a racial distinction, such that white Kenyans would by and large not be restricted but Kenyan Asians would. The clause 'virtually distinguishes United Kingdom citizens on the score of race'.[63]

Not long after the threats made on his own life, Ramsey was still able to take a characteristically long view in the House of Lords: 'Centuries hence our successors may be astonished at this phase in human history, that there was so much trouble and discussion about the colour of human skin.' Ramsey was not naïve about the part which questions of race played. As well as the 'frank colour prejudice which certainly exists' trouble arose 'when colour becomes a symbol for things more complex than itself. That, I believe, is part of our contemporary tragedy in this country.'[64] But there was work to be done, and delicate balances to be struck between competing interests. In 1962, Ramsey had hoped that the passing of the Bill would 'arouse in the conscience of our country a new determination to attack again the conditions which have led to this reversal of one of our country's great traditions.'[65]

There was a further aspect to race relations at home, which Ramsey as traveller and confidant of Anglicans worldwide, saw more clearly than politicians in the UK. There was a worldwide crisis in race relations; it hung in the balance 'whether in the world as a whole there is to be racial conflict or racial harmony.' Not least in the Commonwealth, and in southern Africa, populations

---

[60] H.L. Deb. 15 July 1968 vol. 295, col. 61.
[61] Chadwick, *Ramsey*, pp.167–76.
[62] H.L. Deb. 12 March 1962, vol. 238, col. 25.
[63] Ramsey, *Canterbury Pilgrim*, p.150.
[64] H.L. Deb. 15 July 1968, vol. 295, col. 57.
[65] H.L. Deb. 12 March 1962 vol. 238, col. 26.

of different origins thrown together by force of colonial circumstance were faced with the task of working out new ways of living. Although racial and religious identity were often hard to separate, Ramsey's response to the other faiths as they sought to establish themselves in England also had always to keep in mind the often vulnerable position of Christians abroad .[66] The Race Relations Bill, through 'the help which this Bill gives to the building up of good community relations in this country will be a contribution which our country can make to racial harmony in the world at large.'[67] Ramsey had not lost faith in the role that the British could play on a world stage.

Conclusion

To what extent was Ramsey a 'political parson', and any more or less so than either his predecessors as archbishop or other senior Anglicans? Was the vision of justice he had any different to that of a figure such as George Bell, Bishop of Chichester? Bell was also prepared to oppose government policy in times of pressure, as in his opposition to the obliteration bombing of German cities by the Royal Air Force. Just as Ramsey had become known as a friend of the oppressed, so did Bell provide support to refugees from Nazi Germany, as did Cosmo Lang.[68] Viewed from this angle, Ramsey's vision of peace and mutual respect at home and the resolution of conflict abroad was not a radically new one.

There was responsibility on the Church on its own account, internationally and domestically. Ramsey knew that all white Western Christians were implicated in the sufferings of black majorities in southern Africa. Although the matter is not examined at length here, he also knew that the manner in which the UK treated its religious minorities had a direct effect on the position of Christian minorities around the world.[69]

And yet Ramsey's work appeared increasingly radical, as the context in which he operated changed. Pronouncements on government policy were heard differently when made by the leader of an established Church that was at the same time seeking greater autonomy from the State. As the Church was

---

[66]   Peter Webster, 'Race, religion and national identity in Sixties Britain: Michael Ramsey, archbishop of Canterbury and his encounter with other faiths' in *Studies in Church History*, vol. 51 (2015), 385–98.

[67]   H.L. Deb. 15 July 1968 vol. 295, col. 61.

[68]   On Bell, see Andrew Chandler, *Piety and provocation. A study of George Bell, Bishop of Chichester* (Chichester, 2008), pp.45–54; Beaken, *Lang*, pp.205–7.

[69]   See Peter Webster, 'Race, religion and national identity', *passim.*

seen voluntarily relinquishing the support of the State in the preservation of Christian morality, clear blue water could be seen opening up between the established Church and the State. Across this growing gap, the Church's voice began to sound more like prophetic utterance.

Yet this should not be overstressed. Ramsey's pulpit was still a bench in the House of Lords, and more people than just Ramsey thought it was still for the Archbishop to call the nation to remembrance of its duties. Intractable though the situation was, the British could not avoid the responsibilities of a decolonising power in Southern Rhodesia. Over successive pieces of immigration legislation, Ramsey stressed the point that the UK owed much to its former colonies, and could and should not lightly repudiate the rights it had previously given to colonial subjects. Even if the Church was becoming less obviously part of the Establishment, Ramsey continued to claim the right to speak to, and for, the nation.

Conclusion

How then should we judge Michael Ramsey? In general, later interpreters of Ramsey have judged him well. For Adrian Hastings, Ramsey was the greatest of the holders of the office in the twentieth century: a man of 'exceptional intelligence, openness of mind and depth of spirituality' offering 'an extended and convincing leadership which combined intellectual depth with practical decisiveness.'[1] However, much depends on the criteria one chooses, since the terms of reference under which successive archbishops have operated have rarely been explicit, and have varied greatly with circumstance.

The search for archetypes amongst Ramsey's predecessors is a temptation best avoided, since the choice of archetype is by no means a neutral act, but rather the assertion of a norm. The greatest temptation is to view Ramsey in relation to William Temple, not least because of the regard in which Ramsey himself held Temple, and for the many parallels between the two men. But the comparison is of limited use, since Temple operated in wartime and for only two years, as against Ramsey's 13 years.

Ramsey is, of course, often viewed in relation to his predecessor. The oft-quoted quip of Harold Macmillan that in 1960 there had been enough of Fisher's Martha, and it was time for some of Ramsey's Mary, caught an important aspect of the differences between the two men. The two together have themselves become the archetypes against which later archbishops have come to be judged: the question might be put, 'is he a Fisher or a Ramsey?'[2] Later archbishops have been assessed tacitly or otherwise against these two poles: of Fisher's pragmatic, efficient but godly worldliness, as against Ramsey's holy eccentricity. The tenures of Robert Runcie and Rowan Williams have come to be read in relation to Ramsey: differently from each other to be sure, but both in ways that those of Donald Coggan or George Carey could not.

Fisher's most recent interpreters have rescued him from the caricature of the 'headmasterly archbishop' disposed to deal with the Church of England as if

---

[1]   Edward Carpenter with Adrian Hastings, *Cantuar. The Archbishops in their Office* (3rd ed., London, 1997), pp.525, 527.

[2]   I am grateful to Andrew Chandler for discussions on this point.

it were 'some kind of elongated classroom.'[3] But there was work to be done in the reordering of the Church, in its canon law, in its finances, in bettering the lot of the parochial clergy; and Fisher set to it to great effect. Ramsey's interests lay not in the administrative routine of the Church. Andrew Chandler has recently opened up the importance of the work of the Church Commissioners in reforming the finances of the Church; but Ramsey by and large concerned himself little with the detail of their work.[4] Ramsey's time also saw the Paul Report (1964) and the Morley Report (1965) on the organisation and funding of the local ministry of the Church, followed by the Pastoral Measure of 1968.[5] Although Ramsey gave some encouragement to those within the Church who desired more radical reform, this kind of major administrative reform was never his prime concern, and has not been treated at length here.[6] In part, that lack of personal concern with the administration of the Church has become a component of the archetype that Ramsey has come to define. That said, there was little at the end of Ramsey's time that Coggan needed either to repair or to undo.

It may be, in fact, that Ramsey's greatest significance lies not in those things which he managed to achieve, but in what he came to symbolise, and the directions in which he pointed the Church. The Anglican Communion no longer needed an executive chairman, but it found in Ramsey one who modelled unity not through structures, but through a lively growing together of Christians, individually and corporately, through prayer, worship and mutual learning. Amongst the world churches, Ramsey's personal standing provided an anchor around which real but tentative understanding could grow between Anglicans, Roman Catholics and Orthodox. Within the Church of England, even the conservative evangelical constituency, the least integrated part of the church in the 1950s, came to recognise in Ramsey personally many of its own fundamental concerns.[7] Amongst the British churches, even if all but one of the

---

[3]   Chandler and Hein, *Archbishop Fisher*, p.149, and *passim*.

[4]   Chandler and Hein, *Archbishop Fisher*, pp.119–21; Chandler, *The Church of England in the Twentieth Century: the Church Commissioners and the Politics of Reform, 1948–1998* (Woodbridge, 2006), pp.150–51 and *passim*.

[5]   See the detailed account in Welsby, *A History of the Church of England 1945–1980*, pp.131–39.

[6]   Ramsey himself later regretted that more radical steps had not been taken: 'Church and State in England' in *Canterbury Pilgrim*, p.177; see also Edwards, *Great Christian Centuries*, p.23.

[7]   Webster, 'Archbishop Michael Ramsey and evangelicals in the Church of England', pp.180–84.

practical schemes for union between denominations came to nothing, Ramsey
continued to represent a continuing commitment to the task.

The task of assessing Ramsey in relation to the nation outside the churches is
made doubly difficult by the times through which he lived. Arguably, the pace of
change both within the Church and in the society around it leave the historian
and the theologian without clear criteria against which to judge. The legacy of
the 'long sixties' remains keenly contested in contemporary religious, political
and philosophical debate. In the words of Gerard de Groot, the decade 'has
been transformed into a morality play, an explanation of how the world went
astray or, conversely, how hope was squandered.'[8] As a result, one's assessment of
Ramsey depends upon into which of the competing narratives of the nature of
both Church and nation one has invested.

For some, most likely on the political and ideological left, the 1960s were
an age of liberation. The process of jettisoning the Empire was nearly complete;
deference to the 'powers-that-be' was weakened, and a new emphasis on personal
authenticity as the key criterion of good conduct was beginning to emerge.[9]
This renegotiation of the relationship between public and private included the
changes in the moral law, as we have seen, and so Ramsey's role in fostering that
process would put him, for some, firmly on the side of the angels.

Co-dependent with this narrative is another, about the Church's own moral
discipline and its broader relationship with society. For many liberals within
the Church of England, Ramsey and the Church's support for the recession
in the Christian content of the moral law was welcome; but the retention of
a conservative moral discipline for the Church's own purposes was not. In this
view, there was and is unfinished business for the Church in bringing itself 'up
to date', in its style and language as well as the demands it made on its people.[10]
Viewed from this perspective, Ramsey appears a more problematic figure: not
actively obstructive, but at least conservative.

A second pair of related stories told about the period places equal, if not
greater, emphasis on the 'long Sixties', but interprets them in polar opposite
terms. For a significant body of conservative opinion in the early twenty-
first century, the Sixties saw the insertion of the thin end of the wedge into
the nation's moral fibre.[11] The charge sheet is long: relaxation of the moral

---

[8]   Gerard DeGroot, *The Sixties Unplugged* (London, 2008), p.1.
[9]   DeGroot, *Sixties Unplugged*, pp.1–5, 445–50.
[10]   On the history of the continued debate about Anglican teaching on homosexuality,
see Stephen Bates, *A Church at War. Anglicans and Homosexuality* (London, 2004),
pp.85–108 and *passim*.
[11]   Peter Hitchens, *The Abolition of Britain* (London, 1999), pp.285–96.

law; a putative breakdown in law and order and respect for authority figures; diminished commitment to the institution of the family and indeed to common civility on a crowded island. In this, (runs the story) liberal-minded and muddle-headed clergy in the 1960s, in a misguided attempt to be 'go-ahead', sold the pass to moral decline by not resisting the changes strongly enough when still capable of influencing their course.[12] Insofar as Ramsey could be charged with such lack of fight, he is implicated in the decline that has been observed subsequently.

Held largely outside the churches, this view also has a counterpart within them. Hugh McLeod and others have noted a marked conservative reaction in the early 1970s against much of the reforming movement of the previous decade, and that reaction in opinion established within in itself a key narrative of those years as a time of failed experimentation: of the deliberate jettisoning of accumulated treasure, and of the adoption of alien currents of thought at the Church's heart.[13] In this view, the abandonment of the Book of Common Prayer and the Authorised Version was part of a cult of the shoddy and unworthy, and the accommodation of moral theology to the mores of wider society had come at the cost of abandoning the Church's soul.[14] In this view, the assessment of Ramsey is more mixed. While he resisted the weakening of the Church's own moral discipline, this point was lost on those who could not see beyond the change in the law. His censure of John Robinson, whilst much too strong for some, was too weak for others, and did nothing to limit the damage done by liberal theology.[15] For at least some on the Protestant wing, Ramsey's enthusiasm for Rome promised fatal compromise with key Reformation principles, but at the same time for some Anglo-Catholics his support for the Anglican-Methodist reunion scheme jeopardised the essential catholicity of the Church of England.

Such questions may not easily be answered without the kind of broader ideological consensus about the 1960s which is hard to obtain, but it is the central burden of this study that Ramsey's period as Archbishop saw a more subtle but no less profound shift in the shape, both in law and in feeling, of the Church of England. It may be that this shift may prove to have been more fundamental

---

[12]   See, amongst many, Melanie Phillips, *The World Turned Upside Down. The Global Battle over God, Truth and Power* (New York, 2010), pp.343, 346–48, 353–68.

[13]   McLeod, *Religious crisis of the 1960s*, pp.207–12; Brian Morris (ed.), *Ritual Murder*, *passim*.

[14]   Jones and Webster, 'Anglican "establishment" reactions to "pop" church music', pp.439–40; Atherstone, 'Christian family, Christian nation', *passim*.

[15]   On a supposed progressive decline of the Church of England into heresy, see David Holloway, *The Church of England. Where is it going?* (Eastbourne, 1985), pp.113–23 and *passim*.

for the religious life of the United Kingdom than the more spectacular cultural fracture of the 1960s.

Ramsey's time at Canterbury saw profound shifts in the relations between the churches in the United Kingdom that rendered the older settlement of Church, State and law no longer fit for purpose. The Second Vatican Council, against all expectations, seemed to signal a future in which co-operation on a level almost of equals was possible between the worldwide Roman church and Anglicans, at international, national and local level. Among the British churches, the process of ecumenical contact and indeed of concrete moves towards unity was forcing many in the Church of England to abandon any sense of superiority. Indeed, Ramsey felt that the eventual outcome of the Anglican–Methodist negotiations had placed the baton firmly in the hands of others; no longer could Anglicans assume to take the lead. As some involved in the making of the Scheme had noted, a genuinely national church would not be created simply by other churches merging themselves into the Church of England while the latter remained unchanged.

The questions of Church and State which then arose with fresh force had been visited and revisited over many years, but Ramsey was not alone in feeling that the need for change had become pressing. Aspects of the establishment hindered the building of a national church formed of the various churches. In addition, as Chapter Four showed, there was a consciousness of a crisis during the 'long Sixties', for which the apparent tranquillity of the immediate post-war period had not prepared the Church. The questioning revealed by the *Honest to God* affair, and the mounting evidence that the languages that the Church used in worship, in its buildings, and in its theology were failing to be understood: all these pointed to the need for radical change. Whilst Ramsey knew that all the elements of the establishment were finely balanced, he was sure that the Church had to be free in three key matters: the ordering of its worship, the settlement of its doctrine, and the appointment of its chief pastors. In 1974 many of the paper trappings of the establishment remained undisturbed, and Parliament still retained some powers, which it has most recently exercised in relation to the consecration of women as bishops. However, the Worship and Doctrine Measure had in large part secured the freedom that Ramsey desired in the first two cases.

However, the price (or achievement) of that freedom was a quiet but unmistakeable redrawing of the outer boundary of the Church, which changed its shape in a far-reaching way. The 1974 Measure was a consequence of the advent of synodical government, which had clarified the ways in which decisions were made, and had brought the laity into the heart of the process. In part, this was a completion of the work begun by the Enabling Act of 1919, and of the underlying logic of the Church Assembly. However, the definition of that laity had changed. Gone was the symbolic control of the established Church by the lay synod of Parliament on behalf of all those in England, whether or not they concerned themselves with the Church under their delegated control. The laity, insofar as the State was concerned, was now those active members of local churches who elected their parochial church councils. As Ramsey left office, there were of course obligations on the clergy to all in their parishes, not least in conducting the rites of passage. However, the idea of the national Church was now to a greater extent in the mind of the Church and not of the nation. Such a conception was a product of the Church's own sense of its mission, rather than due to any positive claim made upon it by the State.

This growing distance between the Church's internal life and that of the wider public was examined in Chapter 3. Although the sequence of changes to the moral law that occurred between 1960 and 1969 were no concerted effort, the direction of travel was clear and logically coherent. The moral law was based on an older moral consensus that had manifestly lost its force; and law that was not credible to a majority was bad law, and unenforceable. Ramsey was consistent throughout, in knowing there was no necessary inconsistency in the church at once reasserting traditional moral positions amongst its own people, and acknowledging the principle that Parliament could and ought to settle the moral law on a wider basis. Ramsey could and did support or oppose particular measures on traditional Christian grounds, but this was no longer with an expectation that the Church's view ought to be accepted by right. The Church's voice was becoming a prophetic one, calling on the nation to act in certain ways, but from a greater distance. The national Church could speak to the nation, and (still at this stage) expect to be heard; but no longer could it expect to command assent by right.

All this changed what it meant to be a political archbishop. At one level, there was little to remark in an Archbishop of Canterbury intervening in controverted issues of the day. Different archbishops had been by temperament disposed to different degrees towards intervention on matters of politics, economics and international relations. Ramsey's own political make-up perhaps made him more susceptible than some of his predecessors to this particular temptation. However, as the positive identification between established Church and the State receded, there came into sharper relief the prophetic dimension of the church, and of the Archbishop in particular: a dimension that had been there all along but less visible. Ramsey was prepared to challenge governments overseas on moral grounds, as in South Africa or Rhodesia, or the government of the United States in relation to Vietnam. And despite the propaganda of those at whom some of the criticism was aimed, his voice was by and large not heard as a mere extension of British diplomacy.

At home, he was prepared to challenge government policy in relation to Rhodesia or Northern Ireland. This was sometimes in conjunction with leaders of the other churches, and, less often, of other faith groups. But this cooperation was not at the expense of the uniqueness of his position. Here was the leader of a Church which was becoming less and less established in nature (even though the trappings remained), but still clearly retained within its sense of its mission a vocation to speak to the nation as a whole. By and large, this role was one which leaders of other churches were pleased to see Canterbury fulfil; and significant sections of the governing class, the media and the public expected it.

Ramsey thus established a model of the archbishop as figurehead of a church that viewed itself as *primus inter pares* in an embryonic national Church: the coming together of all the churches as they each grew towards God, in holiness and truth. As ecumenical advance pulled the Church of England towards other Christians, it moved away from its formal relationship with the State, just as the State lost confidence in its own ability to administer its powers over the Church, and as legislators acted to diminish its grip on the moral law, already loosely and somewhat reluctantly held. The Church of England was redefining itself, and being redefined, as an increasingly gathered body, learning to act prophetically, and to sing the Lord's song in an increasingly strange land.

PART II
The Texts

Editorial Conventions

Ramsey's occasional archaisms in spelling, such as 'shewn', are retained. When editing from a typescript original, obviously typographical errors (such as transpositions and missing characters or whitespace) are silently corrected. Manuscript emendations of typescript drafts intended for later verbal delivery or publication are accepted without note, unless the emendation alters the sense. In these cases the emendation is adopted but noted in a footnote.

The original formatting in matters of indentation and formatting of headings is not retained, but standardised with the rest of the current work. Words given all in CAPITALS are set down to Initial Capitals. Other than in these cases, the capitalisation of the original is retained, excepting where it was dictated solely by the page format and not the sense. These cases (such as the use of a new capital in mid-sentence at the top of a typed page), are silently amended.

When identifying correspondents and other named individuals in the footnotes, the information is gathered from standard biographical reference sources unless stated otherwise. These are principally the Oxford Dictionary of National Biography, and the several annual editions of Crockford's Clerical Directory.

1961

Speech to Congress on Public Morality, 18 July 1961, at Church House, Westminster

[Ramsey Papers, vol.10, ff.333–5]

It is my privilege to be one of those who say a word of welcome to this Congress. I hope that its members will enjoy their time in London, as well as use it to the great advantage of the cause which we have at heart.

That cause is the protection of public morality. But we all know that in this connection the word "protection" is inadequate. In matters of morality the only way of being protective is to be creative, and morality needs to be presented not as a fragile thing to be defended but as a creative thing powerful to demolish evils and to use for its good and glorious ends the things which might have evil uses.

When I look at the fascinatingly interesting Agenda of the Congress I see that it might well have the general title of "The Eye And the Ear", for it is cinema, television, radio, theatre, that are going to be under consideration. The eye and the ear have always been crucial for human morals. What does a person enjoy seeing and hearing? That is the crucial question for [f.334] the standard of taste in this is a large part of what makes the moral standard of a people.

The coming into existence of television has brought with it a whole new set of data for the moralist. The eye now sees far more things than it used to see; most citizens live in a visual world bigger, more complex, and more rapid. We need at this stage not dogmatism about the effects of this, but scientific enquiry. There is an immense field here for the scientific sociologist to investigate, and this Congress can point the way to some of the matters to be investigated. I mention now one matter which strikes me forcibly. People's moral condition is affected not only by the quality of what they see, but by its quantity and speed. When people are shewn so many things passing before the eye in rapid succession the mind goes in for snippety interests and excitements, and it is the "snippetiness" of so much that is read and seen which undermines mental effort and deeper appreciation. T.V. can of course avoid this, and often does. The recent presentation on T.V. of the Enthronement of an Archbishop is an instance of sustained visual concentration upon an event full of spiritual [f.335] meaning.[1]

It is a plain fact that our tradition of morality has come down to us from and through the faith of Christendom. That faith has inspired great and glorious creations of the eye and ear in painting, architecture, music and letters. It is for those who adhere to that faith not just to cling to its past victories but to use imagination and scientific method in defending and creating morality in the midst of all the new uses of the eye and ear which the modern world has brought. May this Congress give great service to that cause.

Confidential Memorandum for the Meeting of the Bishops, October 1961: 'Church Reform in Relation to the State. A Note for Discussion.'

[Ramsey Papers, vol. 9, ff. 244–46]

The Church is now in the midst of a series of tasks involving necessary reforms for itself as well as its relation to the State.

I am anxious that three things specially should be kept in mind.

1. The important objectives need to be held in view, so that we do not lose proportion or direction in a haphazard mass of detail.
2. The Bishops should collectively know their mind about important policy and share fully in its formulation.
3. In all that is done regard should be given to the impression of the Church upon the country, for the Church's own preoccupations are a part of its witness for God and the Gospel.

With each of these three things in mind I would comment on certain matters of policy.

I. Canon Law Revision

I think it is urgent that the process should be speeded up. The continued preoccupation with Canon Law has been producing a disproportion in the Church's mental energies. Furthermore, the process of revision has been allowed

---

[1] Ramsey was enthroned in Canterbury Cathedral on 27 June 1961. See the very full account in Simpson, *Hundredth Archbishop*, pp. 1–7.

to wander away from a sense of the proper limits of Canon Law which the Canon Law Commission had originally emphasised. The result has been the inclusion of several matters of detail which really need not be included within Canons at all and could be better left to time-to-time Regulations. There is still time to consider whether some of the matters need be included within Canon at all.

II. Canon 13 and Freedom for Liturgical Revision

It is a great pity that the outstandingly important matter of the obtaining of power for limited liturgical revision has come to be seen as one element within the field of Canon Law, with its many complexities and difficulties, so that the public does not grasp the distinctive importance of the issue. I think that it is important to show clearly what is at stake, and that this can be done if emphasis is placed upon the *Measure* to which the Canon is attached rather than upon the Canon itself. The phrase *Enabling Measure* would bring home what is involved: a measure which goes further than the Enabling Measure of 1919 in making it possible for liturgical reform to begin.[2]

[f.245] With the passing of the Measure and the enactment of the Canons I should hope there would begin a period of years in which liturgical reform would be the centre of interest. There would be a period of years in which the Church would devote itself to a united attempt to secure a substantial amount of liturgical revision. One of the proposals for drafting the measure is that the seven year period for the experimental use of a new service may be extended by a second seven year period. This would enable the Church to have about a decade and a half in which to discover its unity and its wishes in the realm of liturgical reform. It will be urgent to concentrate upon the wise use of this time.

III. Beyond the Next Phase

It will, however, be asked whether such a Measure and Canons would permanently suffice for the Church's needs. For one thing it would be unlawful to continue the use of a particular experimental service indefinitely; and to get permanent sanction for any such service it would be necessary to take a Measure to Parliament. For another thing, it is doubtful whether the proposed Measure and Canon can cover such a matter as Reservation.[3] It might therefore be

---

2   The Enabling Act of 1919 brought into being the National Assembly of the Church of England, known as the Church Assembly.

3   Reservation of the Sacrament, the Anglo-Catholic (and Roman Catholic) practice of setting aside the consecrated elements of bread and wine for administration outside the

found that a larger autonomy for the Church will be needed, and this might be a problem which the Episcopate of fifteen years hence would have to face. To those, however, who say that a larger autonomy on the lines of the Scottish Establishment is necessary my own answer would be that only a Church that is really united and knowing its own aims can ask for such autonomy with any hope of success. I would therefore think that the successful use in the coming decade, or decade or two, of the autonomy that I have described is the necessary prelude to anything more radical. We should however have to plan with the awareness that a set of difficult problems will be arising when the first phase of experimental variations runs out.

IV. Crown Appointments

The Church Assembly is likely to ask for a Commission about this. Rightly or wrongly it seemed to me better to have an Archbishops' Commission than a Committee of the House of Clergy perhaps supplemented by a Committee of the House of Laity.

I do not think that a radical alteration of the system is possible apart from a radical alteration of the Establishment itself; and the Church is not united in asking for the latter. Possibly the time will be more opportune for change when first autonomy for liturgical revision has been achieved and put to effective use. But the question of Crown appointments has now been pressed.[4]

I think there would be a lot of good will from the political side towards some important reforms, on the assumption that the Crown still nominates on the advice of the Prime Minister: e.g. the abolition of the congé d'élire[5] and the penalties of praemunire[6], and the establishing of the principle of consultation with Province and Diocese as a constitutional necessity, difficult though this will be to formulate.

[f.246] The Bishops will no doubt consider what advice they would give about the character of a Commission on the subject and the scale of its inquiry if it is to be profitable.

---

context of a communion service.

4   Shortly before Ramsey's appointment, the Church Assembly had formed a group to examine the issue.

5   The licence issued by the Crown to the dean and chapter of a cathedral, authorising the election of a new bishop or archbishop.

6   The medieval statute of *praemunire* outlawed the assertion of papal or any other foreign authority, which was thought to be applicable to cathedral chapters that did not ratify the Crown's appointment of a bishop.

V. Liturgical Revision: its content

There will not be time at the October Bishops' Meeting for more than a brief glance at this matter, but we should be preparing for the full consideration of it.

We need to achieve a proper relation in functions between the Bishops, the Convocations and the Liturgical Commission. Hitherto the Liturgical Commission has had little or no guidance as to what sort of services it is being asked to compile.

I think that before a new service is compiled there is a good deal of background work to be done, and in this the guidance of the Bishops and Convocations is needed. First, it has to be decided what kind of doctrine the service is to express, or what limits of doctrine it is to comprehend. This preliminary is most necessary in revising a service of Baptism or Holy Communion. Next, it has to be decided what sort of liturgical materials and what sort of language it is desired to use. Then, when the service is compiled it needs at an early stage to have criticism and comment from various standpoints including that of the parish priest. I think that the procedure for liturgical revision, and the role and character of a liturgical commission need new consideration.

Meanwhile there is the Schedule of Variations[7] to be put into effect when canonical authority has been obtained. This in due course will need the careful consideration of the Bishops.

---

[7] The Schedule of Permitted Variations laid out the circumstances in which an officiating minister could depart from the text and rubrics of the Book of Common Prayer.

1962

Speech to the House of Lords on the Commonwealth Immigrants Bill

[House of Lords Debates, 5th series, 12 March 1962, vol. 238, cols.24–26]

My Lords, I am sure it is unusual in your Lordships' House for a Bill introduced with such lucidity and skill as this Bill has been introduced to-day, also to be introduced with so little enthusiasm. The noble and learned Viscount the Lord Chancellor[1] used the word "repugnance". If I may add a word of my own, let it be the word [col. 25] "lamentable". It is, indeed, lamentable that this reversal of a great tradition of our country should have happened – whether we should say, "has happened" or, "has had to happen". There is no doubt that the introduction of the Bill caused something of a shock of feeling overseas. At the time the Bill was introduced I myself was in India, and I saw something of the pain caused by the news of the introduction of the Bill, especially as the news about the Bill was not always accompanied by explanation or complete information. The news, put very crudely, has travelled about in the form, "Great Britain will admit Irish people without restriction but will restrict immigrants from the West Indies."

In justice to Her Majesty's Government, I think it must be said that it is utterly unfair to ascribe to their motive any intention whatever of colour discrimination, and it is also fair to acknowledge the great desire on the part of Her Majesty's Government to avoid the growth of certain conditions in some of our towns, conditions as unacceptable to immigrants as to anyone else. None the less, the news of this Bill has been a great shock and in future years, very likely, history will note it as one of the shocks in the story of our country and Commonwealth. But I believe, my Lords, that if this shock has something of a moral, that moral is not that we should attack Her Majesty's Government; still less that we should allow the colour question to be a matter of Party politics – that would indeed be lamentable; but that, as a country, we should set about attacking with far greater vigour those conditions which have created any case

---

[1] David Patrick Maxwell Fyfe, 1st Earl of Kilmuir, was Lord Chancellor from 1954 until 1962.

whatever for this proposal of restriction. I think it is the ambition of all of us that our country should be one where the restrictions imposed by this Bill could not be conceivably necessary.

It is easy to say that because the ideal is not attained – and, indeed, is perhaps not attainable for quite a time – restrictions are necessary, and to leave it at that, but I think it is far more important to see what urgent effort can be made within our country to narrow the gap between the ideal and the actual. In that effort legislation has indeed its part, but so also have innumerable forms of action by the citizens of this country [col.26] in many places. In the first place, we are not, as a country, free from colour discrimination in feeling and behaviour. There has been in some of our towns prejudice in housing and lodging, which has resulted in excessive charges and in the hanging together of coloured people and overcrowding. Thus a vicious circle is created, and thereby are created some of those conditions which have made a case for the introduction of this Bill. Second, if as a country we had done more to overcome our own problems of housing – and we might indeed have done more – the colour problem would not have been so conspicuous, as, for instance, it is now in South London. Had the colour problem in housing not bulked so large, I do not believe that the demand for this Bill would have seemed nearly so insistent.

I therefore hope, my Lords, that the promotion of this Bill, by the very shock it gives, will lead to stirrings of action and conscience in many places, in tackling those long-term problems in our country which are the background of this whole matter. There are, for instance, some Christian congregations which set themselves vigorously to befriend and integrate coloured immigrants, but there ought to be far more of those – for, indeed, we have been woefully behind. I am thinking of the long-term attack on the background of circumstances which has created the arguments for this Bill. Given this Bill, I think that we should all welcome the instructions to immigration officers issued in the White Paper – instructions which could not show more care, consideration or liberality. For my part, I welcome also the inclusion in the Bill of the power to deport immigrants who behave as criminals. Besides people who slip into crime, there are from time to time people who enter the country for the express purpose of carrying out crime; and, indeed, it is time that their deporting was made easy. So, my Lords, I do most earnestly hope that the restrictions introduced by this lamentable Bill, this Bill introduced with repugnance, this Bill which is indeed deplorable, will be short-lived, and that the episode will arouse in the conscience of our country a new determination to attack again the conditions which have led to this reversal of one of our country's great traditions.

Letter from Archbishops Coggan and Ramsey to Members of both Houses of Parliament, July 1962[2]

[Ramsey Papers, vol.24, f.323]

Legislation Proposed by the Church of England

It is likely that within the next year or two some Measures of more than usual importance to the Church of England will come before Parliament. May we briefly give some account of the proposals and the reasons for them.

A Church, like other organizations, must have a code or framework of rules of conduct. Because the Church of England is an established Church, its rules are contained in the Common Law, in Statute Law, such as the Act of Uniformity, 1662, as well as in its own Canons. It has been felt that a thorough revision of these Canons is long overdue, a revision involving in some cases, as will be seen, alteration of the Law. The Convocations and the Church Assembly have, therefore, been engaged since 1947 in discussing both the rules themselves and the machinery for making any necessary alterations.

Revision of the Canons

Very few of the Canons of the Church of England have been made or altered since 1604.[3] Since that time much of the general Law relating to the Church has changed and some of the Canons have, therefore, become void or obsolete.

Canon 65 of the 1604 Canons, for instance, orders that all those who obstinately refuse to frequent Divine Service because of their allegiance to some other body than the Church of England shall be publicly denounced. Canon 112 orders the churchwardens to present to the bishop all who fail to receive the Holy Communion at Easter. Canon 74 lays down detailed rules for the dress of the clergy not only in the day-time but also at night. We are seeking to bring our Canons up to date as all the other Provinces of the Anglican Communion can do.

We, however, cannot make or alter a Canon without the approval of the Crown. If a new Canon or the revision of a Canon would alter the general Law,

---

[2]   The letter was sent to peers, and to MPs from all four home nations, and to leaders of the Free Churches.

[3]   On the 1604 Canons, see the edition in the series of the Church of England Record Society by Gerald Bray: *The Anglican Canons, 1529–1947* (London, 1998).

the change cannot take effect until either a Measure or a Bill has been passed by Parliament which alone can alter the general Law.

The Book of Common Prayer

By the Statute Law of the Realm the Church of England is bound strictly to the Book of Common Prayer, which is a schedule to the Act of Uniformity of 1662. We are with very good reason celebrating its tercentenary this year. It is greatly loved. Yet with very minor exceptions it has never been amended and there is no doubt that some reforms in public worship are needed. At present any use of amendments of the Book of Common Prayer or alternatives to its contents is contrary to the Act of Uniformity.

Thus, strictly, a layman may not read the Lessons from the Bible at Morning or Evening Prayer. In the Holy Communion Service no version of the Epistle or Gospel may be read but that of the Authorized Version of 1611. In the marriage service the bride must say 'obey'.

Authority to amend the Book is needed. Also needed are alternative services which are more suited to the needs of to-day.

The thought which is being given to these problems in our own Church is being matched in other parts of the Anglican Communion and, indeed, throughout Christendom. Practice is altering accordingly but in the Church of England alteration is still prohibited.

There is in the Church of England a widespread desire to obtain authority to make such variations and to provide for such alternatives as will bring our forms of worship up to date.

Experimental Period for Alternative Services

We shall not seek, as was done in 1927 and 1928 unsuccessfully, a complete alternative Prayer Book containing services largely untried and unknown.[4] Our main request will be in the Prayer Book (Alternative and Other Services) Measure for Parliamentary authority for the sanctioning in the first instance of experimental variations in public worship. In order to ensure that these represent genuine and properly considered demands they would have to receive two-thirds majorities in both Convocations and in the House of Laity. They would then be authorized for use, in each church only with the agreement of the Parochial Church Council, for a period of up to seven years, followed, if

---

4   On the events of 1927–28, see Maiden, *National Religion, passim.*

desired, by another period of up to seven years. After that, if it were proposed to make an alternative version permanent or to [f.323v] continue experimenting, further Parliamentary authority would have to be obtained. There would also be provision for preliminary trial periods of two years under certain conditions.

It is our hope that if the Measure comes forward with two-thirds majorities in the Convocations and the Church Assembly this will show how strong is the desire of the Church for it.

The Laity

Much attention is being given at the present time to the question of fuller participation of the laity in the synodical government, that is in the Convocations, of the Church. The proposals in the Canons to permit liturgical revision have been under discussion since 1947 and at each stage have been referred by the Convocations to the House of Laity. Further, as has been said above, in the important matters of public worship the proposed Measure requires the agreement of the laity as well as of the bishops and clergy to experimental changes.

Ecclesiastical Courts

If the Church can obtain services in accord with its prevailing needs, discipline and order should fall into their proper place. Yet a procedure may still be needed by which genuine cases concerning ritual and doctrine may be brought before Church Courts and appeals may be determined. Provision for this is included in the Ecclesiastical Jurisdiction Measure which after many years' preparation was brought before the Church Assembly in 1961.

Conclusion

Some of the legislation proposed will only reach the Church Assembly this summer. When it has passed the Assembly it must go before the Ecclesiastical Committee of Parliament before it can reach either House for approval.[5] The issue is not an immediate one so far as Parliament is concerned. Yet we have ventured to write to you at this moment, because this summer most, if not all, of the matters we have mentioned will be under public discussion.

---

[5]   The Ecclesiastical Committee, a group of peers and members of the House of Commons, was brought into being by the Church of England Assembly (Powers) Act of 1919, to review measures brought forward by the Church Assembly.

As our Church of England bodies are representative, varying opinions will be expressed. There may be differing points of view on one or other of the proposals. There will also be constructive criticism. Those of us, bishops, other clergy and lay men and women, who have introduced them, believe that these proposals have the steady support of the great majority in the Church. We also are convinced that there are adequate safeguards to protect the doctrine and historic mission of the Church of England.

We who sign this are very anxious to give any further information that may be asked for and we should be glad to come and address a meeting or meetings in the Houses of Parliament if this should be desired by Members of either House. The diocesan bishops, too, are very ready to answer questions and give further information. We hope you will not hesitate to write to either of us if you feel inclined to do so.

1963

Ramsey to a Parish Priest, Raymond Hooper, on *Honest to God*, 27 March 1963

[Ramsey Papers vol.50, f.77]

My dear Hooper,[1]

Thank you for your letter. I am glad that you wrote to me. I am, of course, deeply distressed by these matters about which you write, and you can be sure that I will continue to do my utmost to state and commend the Faith of the Church.

When you ask "What are we poor priests to do?", I would say first of all bear in mind that we know that our Church is a true part of the Catholic Church, not because it is free from some terrible sins and follies, but because it is able to overcome them by the strength of the Divine life which is present within it. There have at different times in our history been things as distressing as those about which you write, and you can recall some of the most distressing upsets in the last and in the present century, but God took care of His Church and went on enabling faithful Bishops and Priests to dispense God's heavenly gifts to the people, and to lead souls in the way of grace and to the reward in heaven.

I write as one who knows and feels the distress of wrong things as much and perhaps more even than yourself who, I know, feel these things greatly. I hope that these few words bring you some help and comfort.

I write to you with grateful memories of the days when I used to meet you as your Diocesan, and I pray that in your beautiful church of St. Columba you and your people may continue in the love and service of God.

With my affection and blessing,

Sincerely your Father in God,

---

[1]   Raymond Hooper was vicar of the church of St Columba, Middlesbrough, in Ramsey's old diocese of Durham. He had written to Ramsey on 25 March 1963; Ramsey Papers, vol.50, f.74.

Ramsey to Mervyn Stockwood, Bishop of Southwark, on *Honest to God*, 17 April 1963

[Ramsey Papers, vol.50, ff.125–7]

My dear Mervyn,

Thank you for sending me your article in the Evening Standard. I do, of course, applaud the quotation from Archbishop Temple with which the article starts, and I should always wish to encourage the spirit expressed in it. But I do deeply regret that you should have gone on to what is a sheer falsification of history in connection with Archbishop Temple. It is quite untrue that he at any time "received his measure of abuse as a heretic". With a pretty full knowledge of his life and writings, I know of nothing remotely resembling that, and I am very sorry indeed that you should give to the public such a travesty of fact.

I am not sure that you realise how very great is the distress with which I have had to deal about this matter, distress caused less perhaps by the book than by the article in the Observer,[2] and the irresponsible manner of presenting the issues to the public. Not the least part of the distress has been in the ecumenical region (both Roman Catholics and Methodists) where I have found the matter almost heartbreaking.

However, whether you and I agree or not about that, and possibly we do not, there is now the issue of orthodoxy pending. I have been trying to my utmost to avert the discussion of the matter on "orthodoxy v. heresy" ground. That is one of the reasons why I have written a pamphlet, to be published next week,[3] in which I try to help bewildered people to understand some of the questions and to avoid heresy hunts, while exposing things which I believe to be misleading. But anyone could have foreseen that the issue of orthodoxy would be raised, and when once it is raised neither you nor I can evade it.

Here the line followed in your article does not give me much help. The analogies which you quote go very little way. Temple was never accused of heresy. Gore was criticised by old fashioned churchmen of accepting Biblical criticism and a theory of the limitation of our Lord's human knowledge.[4] Henson was criticised for having appeared to interpret two clauses in the Creed symbolically rather than literally.[5] These episodes give no real parallel [f.126]

---

2   Robinson's book had been preceded by an article in the *Observer*, on 17 March 1963, bearing the title 'Our image of God must go'.
3   *Image Old and New* (London, 1963).
4   Charles Gore (1853–1932), theologian and Bishop of Oxford.
5   Herbert Hensley Henson (1863–1947), Bishop of Durham.

to the present issue which is that the Bishop of Woolwich appears to many to reject as unacceptable the conception of the Deity embodied in the Creeds and held both in popular Christianity and in responsible orthodox teaching, and to say that atheists and agnostics are right to reject it too. That, at least, is what the discussion will be about it if the matter of orthodoxy is raised.

What are my responsibilities, and indeed yours, in respect of this? With the utmost wish to approach the matter in as liberal a way as possible we are pledged to maintain a standard of orthodoxy. I expect you remember Bishop Creighton's saying that we must "combine the right of the individual to be free with the duty of the institution to be *something*."[6]

It is obvious that to have debates in Convocation might be very chaotic and achieve nothing but harm. Some statement from myself might well stave off debates: equally, if there are debates, some lead will be expected of me. On this I am asking your advice. Several courses might be suggested.

(1) I find it impossible to take the line of your article, which is to say in effect "this book may be Heretical: but in the long run that won't matter. Several great men have been held to be heretical before". To say that is to abdicate responsibility as a Church with a doctrinal position. I am sure that on reflection you will see that our consecration pledges make such a line impossible for you or for me.

(2) I can say publicly, and invite the Bishops to concur, that in my judgment the thesis of the book is contrary to the doctrine of Scripture and the Creed. That is honestly my view of the matter if the question is answered in plain terms "on the face of it". I could with some ingenuity shew that the thesis somehow "meant the same thing" as the doctrine of God in the Creed, but this would require a good deal of subtlety: and, on that, I have no particular right to involve the Church's orthodoxy in my own subtleties. Furthermore, I would say that, on any shewing, the doctrine of the Trinity is out of place in the thesis propounded.

All this, of course, relates to orthodoxy. It is not to say that there is not value in the thesis: but that will not be the question at issue if members of Convocation take it up.

[f.127] (3) If I, and the Bishops, were to say that we did not regard the thesis as unorthodox it would be impossible to get away with such a declaration, in the eyes of intelligent orthodox people of all Churches, unless one also said that unfortunately the book had given an emphatic impression of unorthodoxy, and that this was due to deplorable muddle and irresponsibility. I should myself have to say, unless I said the thing in the previous paragraph (2): a Bishop promises

---

[6]   Mandell Creighton (1843–1901), historian and Bishop of London.

not only to be consistent with orthodoxy, but himself to teach orthodox faith unambiguously.

There may be other alternatives. I dread the handing of the matter to some Committee of inquiry, thereby dragging the matter on and on for the good of nobody: and there is no competent Court for such a matter.

As I have said I am grieved that the orthodoxy issue should arise, and whatever is done I shall be anxious to affirm the proper place of thought and freedom in our Church. But it is impossible for the Bishops of what claims to be a part of the Holy Catholic Church just to run away from their pledges, or else we cease to be a teaching Church and become a club for the discussion of religious opinions.

Any solution, *any* action or inaction, now is going to be unhappy in one way or another, and this need not have been so if there had been at the outset a sense of responsibility about these matters, all of which could have been foreseen.

Yours ever,

Ramsey to all English Diocesan Bishops on *Honest to God*, 26 April 1963

[Ramsey Papers, vol.50, f.137]

My dear Bishop,

I have in these last weeks realised that you must have had, like myself, great trouble and anxiety about the book of the Bishop of Woolwich, and perhaps still more the mode which he adopted of presenting his ideas to the country through the press. I have wished that there could have been opportunities of talk with my fellow Bishops, but the season of Easter and the great pressure which this matter has brought to me made that impossible.

You will have seen that a pamphlet by me entitled "Image Old and New" has been published to-day. My hope is that this will help people on the ground of the theological questions, and I have been very anxious to avoid any impression that as a Church we are obscurantist in the treatment of "new" ideas. I do not, however, feel that my pamphlet does all that is required from us as it does not speak specifically about the question of Orthodoxy, except by implication. My own view is that the book removes the conception of God known to us in the Bible and the Creed, and while some sort of doctrine about God and the Deity of Christ emerges, it is impossible to identify this doctrine with the doctrine of our Church which as Bishops we have promised to uphold.

Knowing that there is some threat of a heresy hunt in the Lower House of the Convocation of Canterbury, I am therefore making a brief statement in my

Presidential Address in which, while disclaiming any obscurantist attitude, I speak clearly about the Faith to which our Church is committed.

As I am about to leave for a short holiday, please forgive the absence of my personal signature from this letter.

Yours very sincerely,

A Second Letter from Ramsey to Stockwood on *Honest to God*, 29 April 1963

[Ramsey Papers, vol.50, f.144]

My dear Mervyn,

Thank you very much for your letter of April 19 in reply to mine. I am away this week for a short holiday.

First about William Temple, I readily agree that he was *suspected* of being unorthodox in his earlier years, but my point remains that there was no occasion of public complaint or accusation or abuse similar to what occurred in the case of Henson, nor were there any writings of Temple's which were or could be so attacked.[7]

Thank you for telling me of your proposed action within the Diocese in relation to the Bishop of Woolwich.[8] I have no doubt that the knowledge that you are intending so to act has done good, and I hope that in the event itself good will be done.

You suggest that I might myself take a course similar to that which you are taking. I do not think this is desirable or likely to achieve anything, for I could not fairly ask any theologians to constitute themselves a sort of Provincial "orthodoxy tribunal".

I had a long talk with the Bishop of Woolwich on April 23. I was grieved to find how lacking he is in responsibility; indeed he seemed to me to be

---

7 Stockwood had in reply cited the fact that the Bishop of Oxford had at one point advised Temple by private letter that he could not countenance ordaining him due to Temple's view on the Virgin Birth. The letter is given in full at Iremonger, *Temple*, pp.108–10. On the 1917 campaign against Henson's consecration as Bishop of Hereford on grounds of his apparent unorthodoxy, see Owen Chadwick, *Hensley Henson. A study in the friction between Church and State* (London, 1983), Chapter 6.

8 Stockwood was at the time arranging an informal meeting between himself, his examining chaplains, Robinson, and some of the evangelical clergy in the diocese, and suggested that Ramsey might do something similar at the level of the province of Canterbury. Stockwood to Ramsey, 19 April 1963, at Ramsey Papers 50, ff.128–32.

"adolescent" in his failure to grasp that actions have inevitable consequences and make inevitable impressions. He was "surprised" at things which should give no surprise at all to any intelligent adult. I thought he was in a good deal of muddle spiritually and more in need of help than he realised; and his adolescent limitation extends to his own realm of theological discussion where he fails to see what meaning is inevitably conveyed by words and phrases. He did however ask my advice as to what he should do. My advice to him was: (i) to avoid constant publicity; (ii) to take opportunities of making clear his acceptance of orthodoxy, if he is conscientiously able to do so, *but* (iii) if he is asked how he reconciles acceptance of orthodoxy with the thesis of his book, I do not know how he can set about it.

I told him, what I have told other people, that one must distinguish between saying that a *person* is unorthodox and saying that certain *statements* are unorthodox. Whether *he* is unorthodox is a question which possibly no one except the Almighty can presume to answer, as it involves interior states of mind and soul which words may not properly convey. But whether a *thesis* is unorthodox is another matter, and in my own view the doctrine which is *so far* made apparent in his reconstruction is palpably not the same as the doctrine which he rejects.

I enclose a copy of my booklet *Image Old and New* in case it has not yet reached you. At least it gives no ground for saying that the Church is "obscurantist". I wish I could leave it at that but I feel bound to say something briefly to Convocation about the doctrine to which our Church is committed.

Yours ever

Sermon at Requiem for Pope John XXIII, Lambeth Palace Chapel, 17 June 1963

[Ramsey Papers, vol. 46, f.270]

We are met today, in the words of our English Catechism, for the continued remembrance of the sacrifice of the death of Christ and for the benefits which we have received thereby, and it is in the service of our Prayer Book that we make our memorial. Amongst the fruits of Christ's passion none are more significant than saintly Christian lives. For one of them we bring today deep thanksgiving to God as we recall his servant Pope John, and commend him to God's light and God's rest.

The world is full of *doing*. Pope John has shewn us again the power of *being*, by being a man very near to God, by being a man who touched human hearts with charity. So there has come to many a new longing for the unity of all Christians, and a new knowledge that however long the road may be, charity already makes all the difference to it. "Rest eternal grant unto him O Lord, and let light perpetual shine upon him".

We pray today therefore that God will lead all Christians into unity in truth and holiness. Let us thank him for the one baptism in which we share already. Let us grieve that as today's liturgy here reminds us we are not yet one in the eucharistic feast. Let us pray for obedience to whatever Christ our Saviour wills for us, saying: *Da quod jubes et jube quod vis*, grant what thou commandest and command what thou wilt.[9]

Address to the Convocation of Canterbury after the Anglican Congress at Toronto, 8 October 1963

[Ramsey Papers vol. 45, ff. 321-4[10]]

The Anglican Congress in Toronto was not an official meeting with legislative powers, and for that reason it was able to reflect spontaneously any powerful tendency within the Churches of the Anglican Communion, composed as it was of lay people, priests and bishops from all our Anglican Churches with the exception, to our grief and loss, of the Church in China. If most of us who were delegates went to the Congress not knowing what they would find, they did find a spontaneous ardent desire within the Anglican Churches for a greater partnership with one another in the missionary task. This is perhaps the first of many causes of gratitude to the Canadian Church for making the Congress possible.

Giving and Receiving

It is fair to say that in its history the Anglican Communion has known three stages. The first stage was that of Churches in the British Isles with the beginning of a series of missionary outposts in other parts of the world, and of the Churches

---

[9] A phrase of St Augustine, from the *Confessions*, Book X.
[10] This edition is of the text issued by the Church Information Office to the press. The section headings are likely to be those of the CIO rather than Ramsey's own.

beyond the Atlantic. The second stage was that a group of Churches in many parts of the world divided consciously or unconsciously [f.322] into those which were old or parent or "sending" Churches and those which were young or native or dependent or receiving Churches. Toronto did not create so much as reflect the ardent desire to pass right away from that stage and to enter fully into a third stage, already begun, in which our Communion is a family of Churches equal in authority and in responsibility towards one another, all of them giving and receiving from one another, conscious that they are all missionary Churches and all eager to share the burdens and the privileges of mission to the world.

A month hence I shall be speaking in the Church Assembly about the practical proposals for our Anglican Communion which have gone to all the Anglican Churches from the meeting of the Metropolitans which preceded the Congress.[11] I will speak now rather of the role of the Anglican Communion which is implied by these proposals as also by the greater spirit of partnership which the Congress disclosed.

A fear has been expressed that the increase of Anglican consciousness and Anglican solidarity throughout the world may detract from oecumenical opportunity and obligation. I believe that the fear is wide of the mark. The strengthening of Anglican ties will enhance what our Anglican Churches can give in the cause of unity. Let it be noticed that the resolutions of the Metropolitans include a plea that when an Anglican Church or Province enters a church unity scheme, assuming it to be on principles with which the other Anglican Provinces will concur, the financial support to the Church shall continue undiminished. That is plainly not the plea of men interested only in Anglicanism, in a self-contained isolation. Furthermore, the new officers asked for (incidentally, let me say, not for the purpose of centralisation so much as for the diffusion of authority) will be as concerned with oecumenical relations as with the unity of Anglican activities.

Approaches to Other Churches

Furthermore, I believe we need as an Anglican Communion to have cohesion in our approaches to other Churches. Is it right that in Canada and in the United States there should be entirely separate approaches to the Presbyterians without knowledge or co-operation across the frontier? Is it right that we should

---

[11] This meeting of the metropolitans had produced a document on Mutual Responsibility and Interdependence in the Body of Christ; Jacob, *The Making of the Anglican Church Worldwide*, p.283.

approach the Methodists in this country without co-operation with the Church of Wales and such approaches that it may think right? Would it be better that my own nominees as observers at the Vatican Council should be a mere "Church of England" group, instead of – as is the case – a group of Anglican divines from England, America, Asia and (from next month) Africa as well? Let me add one more instance. It is hoped that when the Theological Commission on Eastern Orthodox and Anglican doctrinal questions is started again, just as the Oecumenical Patriarch will appoint a body drawn widely from the Orthodox Churches, so there will be a body of Anglican divines to meet them drawn [f.323] widely from the Anglican Churches.

Things are happening in this way because the world is very small, and Anglican partnership has become more vigorous. It has been fostered by the arduous journeys of my predecessor (a man never unmindful of oecumenical vision and duty), and latterly by the self-sacrificing work of Bishop Bayne as the servant of all our Anglican Churches.[12]

If it is not difficult to describe this partnership in theological terms, it will be harder for us all to practise it in terms of giving, for partnership will mean each of our Churches asking not merely "what are our needs for, let us say England", but "what are our needs as a world-wide mission and what share in them is the duty and privilege of us in our particular Church?"

Division "Must Disappear"

Just as each of our Churches is a part of the Anglican Communion so are all of them a part of the Holy Catholic Church of Christ into which we have all been baptised. What must disappear is division within that one Church of God, and separation between its portions, so that every portion will come to share with the other portions in a full communion based upon Apostolic and Catholic faith and order. When in any part of the world an Anglican Church joins with other Churches in creating a new United Church, it is understood (1) that the act of union involves humble receiving from others as well as giving to them, (2) that the resulting United Church will be of sure catholicity and the Anglican churches will have full communion with it.

Next April there will be a meeting at Canterbury of bishops from various Churches with which Anglican Churches have relations of full communion or

---

12   Stephen Bayne had become Executive Officer to the Anglican Communion in 1959. On Geoffrey Fisher's work in relation to worldwide Anglicanism, see Chandler and Hein, *Fisher*, pp.75–91.

something near to full communion, together with bishops from the Anglican Provinces. What is now called "the wider Episcopal Fellowship" is not an organisation but rather an exploring of the meaning of full communion and of the relation of various Churches to one another and to the See of Canterbury.

I see in these developments no sign of an Anglican isolationism or introversion, but rather a trend right away from such tendencies. Equally I see in these developments no abdication of our conviction that as Anglicans we have still a life to live and treasures of faith and order to conserve because they are true, and we believe in them. But the treasures are to be shared because they are not our own but Christ's, and the life is one of sacrificial partnership amongst ourselves for the sake of others.

[f.324] Anglican-Methodist Relations

The months which lie immediately ahead are full of opportunity in the quest of Christian unity. In this country there will be the urgent study of the Report on Anglican-Methodist Relations both by the Methodists and by our own clergy and laity in the dioceses. We must realise that if the decisions to be made by ourselves are hard, the decisions to be made by the Methodists are perhaps harder still. If it turns out that we of the Church of England are ready to go forward on the lines of the Report and hope that the Methodists will be ready too, it will be necessary for us to convey certain things to them in heart and mind. They know already that for us certain things in doctrine and in Church order are requisite for unity. What they must be assured wholeheartedly is that we shall expect them to enjoy no less liberty of interpretation of the facts of Church order than we enjoy ourselves, and that we are humbly and ardently desiring to learn from them and to receive from them those treasures of spirituality wherein they are strong and we are weak. There must be this heart and mind in us, conveyed with conviction and love from us to the Methodists, if it is our decision to endorse the Report.

Meanwhile the Second Session of the Vatican Council in Rome began on Michaelmas Day. Its agenda touches more nearly than ever upon those themes which relate to Christians outside the Roman obedience. Our prayers for the Council will not cease. The Gospel for the feast of St. Michael, common as it is to both the Roman and the Anglican liturgies, tells us all how we must regard all who believe on the name of Christ. "Take heed that ye despise not one of these little ones; for I say unto you, that in heaven, their angels do always behold the face of my Father which is in heaven".[13]

---

[13]   Matthew 18:10.

1964

Sermon on Anglican-Orthodox Rapprochement, Preached at the Greek Orthodox Cathedral[1] in London, 20 June 1964

[Ramsey Papers, vol.316, ff.144–7]

"From glory to glory". 2 Corinthians 3, v.18.

Orthodoxy is a characteristic of the Christian church. The word suggests at once 'true doctrine', for the Church is nothing unless it is filled with the spirit of truth and teaches the truth handed down from Christ and the Apostles. But a little knowledge of the Greek language at once sees that the word orthodoxy suggests not only true doctrine but also true glory. Within the Church, whose members are sinful, fallible, struggling men, women and children, there is present the glory of the risen Lord Jesus. Thus the Church's life is a perpetual Easter saying to us again and again "Christ is risen. He is risen indeed", and possessing the glory of the risen Jesus dwelling within us we are linked already with the glory of heaven where the blessed saints reflect the one unique glory of our Redeemer. Belonging to earth and to heaven the life of a Christian and the life of the Church advances "from glory to glory".

East and West: "The Roots of the Problem" [f.145]

Today the Anglican and Eastern Churches Association celebrates the centenary of one of its two parent bodies, and in essence therefore its own centenary. It has through a hundred years served a great cause, the mutual knowledge and friendship of the Holy Orthodox Church and the Anglican Churches.

This is a cause of far more than domestic importance; it is far more than a sort of ecclesiastical hobby. It is a cause which goes to the roots of the whole problem of Christian unity. Before and behind the divisions so familiar to us in the West (Roman Catholics, Protestants, divided Churches and denominations)

---

[1]   The cathedral of St Sophia, Moscow Road, Bayswater.

there is the old deep division between the East and the West. East and West needed one another, and the sad cleavage meant loss to both. But through the centuries there has been a constant reaching-out between them, and in this reaching-out Anglicans have long borne their part. The Orthodox Church and the Anglican Churches discovered one another as Churches making the same claim: to possess the faith of the Scriptures and the ancient Church, to possess the Apostolic Succession of episcopate and priesthood, the unbroken stream of mystical and sacramental life, a non-papal Catholic Christianity.

This is not to say that the Orthodox Church has recognised Churches outside its own unity. This is not to say that Anglicans have been without their critiques of Eastern Christianity. Yet amid a host of problems not yet solved and questions not yet answered, Orthodox and Anglican Christians have found themselves deeply sharing in something which draws them together, something neither Papal nor Protestant, older than either word yet now and vivid in mystical experience. Very significantly it is in the realm of worship that this drawing together is experienced most intensely, and worship is always 'from glory to glory' as we know our nearness to the worship of heaven.

Friendship, Worship and Prayer

In the movement of unity between Orthodox and Anglicans there have been great names and great events. Within the last century we [f.146] Anglicans recall John Mason Neale[2] who opened for English Christians the hymns and liturgies of the East, laymen like F.J. Birkbeck and Athelstan Riley[3] who were pioneers in the knowledge of Russian Christianity, priests like George Williams, Liddon, T.T. Carter, Pullan, J.A. Douglas and Fynes Clinton[4], bishops like

---

[2]   John Mason Neale (1818–66), Anglican clergyman, author, hymnologist and ecclesiologist.

[3]   This must refer in fact to William John Birkbeck (1859–1916), ecumenist, with a particular and lifelong interest in Russia. Both Birkbeck and the hymn-writer Athelstan Riley were leading lights in the production of *The English Hymnal* (1906), which contained several hymns of Orthodox origin.

[4]   George Williams (1814–78), Anglican priest, topographer and scholar with particular interests in Russian Christianity and the city of Jerusalem; Henry Parry Liddon (1829–90), priest and theologian, traveller and ecumenical diplomat; Thomas Thellusson Carter, rector of Clewer (Berkshire), Tractarian and leading figure in the English Church Union; John Albert Douglas, Anglican clergyman, author and translator, leading member of the Anglican and Eastern Churches Association, and author of *Anglican Relations with the Eastern Orthodox* (1921); Henry Joy Fynes-Clinton, rector of St Magnus the Martyr in the City of London from 1921, general secretary of the Anglican and Eastern Churches

Headlam, Frere, Nugent Hicks, Brent and Grafton of Fond-du-Lac.[5] And time would fail to recall more happenings than the presence of Eastern prelates at the Nicene celebrations in Westminster Abbey in 1925, the important findings of the Joint Commission on Doctrine in 1930–1931, the agreement between representatives of the Church of Rumania and the Church of England in 1935, the theological conference in Moscow in 1956.[6]

But the movement means far more than the official occasions. It means the practical friendship of Orthodox and Anglican Christians in many countries, the study of one another's writings, the sharing (as yet, alas, without sacramental communion) in one another's worship, and the constant, deep, sacrificial, joyful prayer in which soul is near to soul. Here in London the congregations of Orthodox Christians have been a blessing to us. I greet to-day the Greek Christians in their Cathedral who are celebrating their patronal festival. I greet you in the love of Christ. Peace be unto you, the peace of the risen Lord.

The Search for Unity

Today the rapprochement of Orthodoxy and the Anglican Churches can look beyond itself as it serves the ecumenical movement in West and East and everywhere. Within that movement are involved Christians of every tradition, by virtue of our baptism into the Triune Name of God and in virtue of the commitment of Churches to one another in the search of the unity which God wills and gives. Anglicans reach out in spiritual kinship towards the Protestant Churches with which they share the open Bible and many of the experiences of the Reformation. All of us welcome the new trends, scriptural, patristic, liturgical, within the Church of Rome, and feel these trends to be significant for us all. Unity must be the unity of all with all in the name and will of Christ.

[f.147] Yet within this great process, a process of theology, a process of prayer and spiritual life and a process of common practical service, too, a deep significance belongs to that Orthodox-Anglican friendship for which we thank

---

Association (1906-20), and of the Archbishops' Eastern Churches Committee (1920-24); probably Leighton Pullan (1865–1940), historian and liturgist.

[5] Arthur Cayley Headlam (1862–1947), Bishop of Gloucester; Walter Howard Frere (1863–1938), liturgist and Bishop of Truro; Frederick Cyril Nugent Hicks, Bishop of Lincoln from 1933, and Ramsey's bishop while at Boston: Chadwick, *Ramsey*, pp.51–2; Charles Henry Brent, Bishop of Western New York, and contributor to the World Conference on Faith and Order at Lausanne in 1927: Sachs, *Transformation of Anglicanism*, p.292; Charles Chapman Grafton (1830–1912), Bishop of Fond du Lac.

[6] Ramsey was himself among the Anglican delegates: Chadwick, *Ramsey*, pp.297–301

God to-day. This friendship gives us the vision of a catholicity not of East or West alone, but of East and West together. It is a catholicity into which we shall grow, for it is ultimately the fullness of Christ, true God and true Man, and it is a catholicity already given in Christ's indwelling life and truth to which the Apostles and the ancient Fathers witnessed. So the Church will advance from glory to glory, and so too must each of its members through the wounds of the Cross to the joy of the Resurrection. May Christ lead us from glory to glory as we bear His reproach and share His wounds in this world of pain and division until with Saints and Angels we may glorify Him in heaven and see His face.

1965

Sermon at a Service Marking the Anniversary of the Sealing of the Magna Carta, in St Paul's Cathedral, 10 June 1965

[Ramsey Papers vol.316, ff.252–53]

Zechariah 4.10. "Who hath despised the day of small things?"

Just seven-and-a-half centuries ago on the tenth of June a group of Barons made their way to the lovely meadow of Runnymede. They set up a tent with a throne in it ready for the King. Across from Windsor the King came, and with him amongst others Stephen Langton, the Archbishop of Canterbury. The Barons made their demands. The Archbishop – bravely, for the Pope was not behind him – supported the demands and urged their acceptance. King John agreed. And five days later with many more people on the meadow the parties swore to keep the agreement, and when the Charter was written it ends with these words, simple and final: 'Given under our hand in the meadow that is called Runnymede between Windsor and Staines in the fifteenth day of June in the seventeenth year of our reign.'

Small things. Yes, it was not a declaration in the name of all the people in the land. It was the act of one group, one order in the realm, asserting its own rights: and, in the words of G.M. Trevelyan, 'the barons were acting selfishly and class-consciously to just the same degree – no more and no less – as other English classes and parties who in successive centuries have taken part in developing our constitution by self-assertion ending in a practical compromise.'[1]

Foundation of Constitution and Civilisation

Again, it was not a declaration of universal principles or a proclamation of great ideals. It was a cold, business-like document, agreeing that certain practical abuses must cease. Small things: yes, limited aims, technical formulations, very

---

[1]   The passage is from Trevelyan's *History of England* (London, 1926).

business-like, very practical, very detailed. But these were based on law, and the sovereign will be bound by it like his subjects, and they in turn will be protected by it. And little could the Barons and the King have known that they were laying a foundation for great far-reaching ideals and principles upon [f.253] which not only a constitution but a civilization have come to stand.

A few weeks ago there was another scene in the meadow of Runnymede. The Sovereign was there, and Barons were there, but in and amongst a throng of citizens of every kind. And an agreement was made, to set apart a portion of the meadow as a memorial to a great statesman and leader of an English-speaking nation beyond the Atlantic.[2] Yes, the day of small things at Runnymede seven-and-a-half centuries ago led on to days when the Charter of Runnymede became a symbol of human rights, the rights of nations to live their own life, the rights of the man, the woman, the child to be free. 'The Charter' wrote Winston Churchill, 'was in future to be used as the foundation of principles of which neither King John nor his nobles dreamed.'[3]

A Lesson for All

Who hath despised the day of small things? The lesson for all of us is plain. When men do what is right in the particular circumstance, in the task in hand, in the details of what lies immediately before them, they may be building greater than they can ever know.

It is not given to most men to see great visions, or to construct grand conceptions. It is given to every man and every woman to make decisions about the matters immediately at hand, putting what is right before what is capricious, putting divine law before human wilfulness. When that happens God in His good providence gathers up our little actions of the moment and uses them in his design down the ages. Did not Christ say that he who is faithful in little shall have great riches? The riches may be in incalculable results in later times.

Man's Rights and Worth

The rights of a man: that was the issue on the meadow of Runnymede. It is the issue still. For all his seeming insignificance in the vastness of the world, in the long procession of events and people, each man has supreme worth. The Barons

---

[2] Sir Geoffrey Jellicoe's memorial to John F. Kennedy remains at Runnymede.
[3] From the first volume of Churchill's *A History of the English-Speaking Peoples* (London, 1956).

and the King faintly, dimly knew why our Christian faith plainly proclaims that each single man has rights because God made him in his own image with an infinite worth for all eternity. The prophet bade us not despise the day of small things. Christ bids us not despise the very least of God's children for each one of them has rights in this world and has been created for eternity and heaven.[4]

Speech in the House of Lords on Capital Punishment, 20 July 1965[5]

[House of Lords Debates, 5th series, 20 July 1965, vol. 268, cols 633–38]

My Lords, I support this Bill. My first speech in your Lordships' House was made in July, 1956, in support of the abolition of the death penalty. On that occasion, I followed the noble and learned Earl[6], Lord Kilmuir, who is to follow me to-day; and I remember that, although he and I differed on the main issue, I took common ground with him in the belief that retribution is a necessary and valid aspect of punishment. I should still wish to emphasise that retribution need not imply vindictiveness or hatred or vengeance. It does not mean that the wrongdoer suffers punishment because he deserves to; and the recognition on his part that he is getting something he deserves is a necessary step towards his reformation. And if the crime has been a terrible one, the penalty will be a terrible one. A terrible penalty: yes, my Lords. It must be so.

But in trying to set out what I believe to be Christian principles in this matter, I go at once to two other considerations. First, there ought to be beyond the penalty the possibility of reclamation. I mean the possibility of the person being alive, repentant and different. If this can happen in this world, and not only for the world to come, we should strive for that to be so. Secondly, there ought to [col.634] be recognition of the fact that the taking of life as a penalty does devalue human life. It means society saying, in effect: "This man has killed someone. Very well; we will kill him too." This does not enhance the sacredness of human life. I believe that it derates it further.

I am very conscious that these considerations have to be weighed against whatever weight there may be in the other consideration which has been

---

[4] Likely a reference to Matthew 18:10: 'Take heed that ye despise not one of these little ones; for I say unto you, That in heaven their angels do always behold the face of my Father which is in heaven.'

[5] Ramsey included much of this speech, with some emendations, in his *Canterbury Pilgrim*, pp.139–43.

[6] David Maxwell-Fyfe (1900–67), 1st Earl of Kilmuir.

so prominent in the discussion yesterday and to-day – namely, the need for deterrence. Terrible crime needs to be deterred. Victims must be protected, and all of us feel to the uttermost for victims and their families. If there were convincing evidence that any penalty is a unique deterrent, then I should feel obliged to let that consideration weigh very heavily in the scale against those basic considerations which I have tried to set out. I will come back to that issue later.

Now it is asked: if not the death penalty, then what? I take up my own phrase, "A terrible punishment for a terrible crime". Here the arguments seem to me to be very strong for the life sentence rather than a judicial sentence for a certain term of years. There is the argument that the Judge cannot know at the outset what the man is going to be like after 9, 10, 11 or 12 years, or how he should be best treated, both for public safety and for his own good, after that time. That consideration is a strong one, and it concerns both security and the protection of the people, as well as what is good in the reclamation of the criminal himself.

But I would add this consideration, too, in connection with the life sentence. The sentence for the crime of murder ought, I believe, to have what I call a retributive moral seriousness about it: therefore, I believe that the life sentence is right, even though it again and again, and perhaps almost always, be mitigated in practice. The life sentence says, in effect, to a convicted murderer: "You have outraged society by killing one of your fellows. You must expect no claim to your old place in society for a very long time, not, indeed, until society can be told that you are on the way to being an utterly different sort of person from what you are now." I believe that, thus understood, a life sentence carries with it a terrible moral [col.635] meaning. It can be a terrible deterrent; and, indeed, it is so.

Yesterday the noble and learned Lord, the Lord Chief Justice,[7] pleaded for far fuller consideration of the life sentence and the procedures in connection with it. Indeed, it should in some cases be a really long sentence for desperate types of criminal. That was the plea of the Lord Chief Justice. But he urged, also, that the penal methods ought to be such – and I am glad he said that he was sure they could be such – that personality should not rot in the process. But I wonder whether, in trying by Amendments to this Bill to give further definition to the content of a life sentence, we are any more likely to be successful than they were in another place. The life sentence is a deterrent because it can demand the custody of the person for a very long time, and it carries with it the right of the State to recall the person to custody. It should be reformative. There is ample

---

[7]   Hubert, Baron Parker of Waddington (1900–72), Lord Chief Justice 1958–71.

evidence that already it can prove reformative; indeed, we can most certainly hope for means in the future to make it so. For all these reasons, I believe that the alternative to capital punishment should be defined as the life sentence rather than the various alternatives which have been tried and pleaded for.

Those, my Lords, are the main considerations which determine my attitude. But let me come now to the special problem of the Homicide Act, and then to the matter of capital punishment as a deterrent. Previous to the Homicide Act there had been attempts to get at a classification of murders, with some moral distinction between those which were more loathsome or more morally vicious than others. In a debate here in 1947 my predecessor, searching as others at the time were searching, for some line of distinction between capital and non-capital murders, spoke of the distinction between "murder" and "murder most foul". But when the Homicide Act drew a distinction, it did not claim to be a moral distinction in that way. It drew a distinction, on lines of expedience and of public safety, between murder in circumstances where the death penalty might be a unique deterrent to violence or the use of arms, and murder in circumstances where that was [col.636] not so. It was the noble Lord, Lord Conesford,[8] who said in his speech on the Second Reading of the Homicide Bill that a moral issue was involved, and that the proposed distinction between capital and non-capital murders would be found to affront morality – though the noble Lord then made it clear that he was not an abolitionist. I said at that time, in a brief intervention, that I agreed with the noble Lord.

Now, in another place, two successive Home Secretaries, different in their politics and different in their initial approach to the abolition question, have told how they have found intolerable moral issues in the distinction of sentence between capital and non-capital murder. On the one hand, a murderer kills while stealing, perhaps on a sudden, delirious impulse – the death penalty. On the other hand, a murderer poisons after loathsome, vicious premeditation – not the death sentence. If, penalties other than the death penalty were involved, the moral arbitrariness of the distinction might be swallowed. But where the penalty is sometimes to kill the murderer, sometimes to sentence the murderer to death, and sometimes not, it seems that law and morality have gone apart on the very point where it is imperative for them to go together.

It was not surprising to hear from the Lord Chief Justice yesterday: "I have seen the complete absurdities that are produced, and have been completely disgusted at the result."[9] To be fair, these considerations may be construed as

8   The Conservative peer Henry George Strauss (1892–1974), 1st Baron Conesford.
9   In the same volume, col.481.

an argument for going back, as well as an argument for going forward to total abolition. But I was impressed to hear yesterday from the Lord Chief Justice the plea that to go back to the older system of general capital sentences, mitigated by frequent reprieves, was to put a quite intolerable burden upon the mind and heart of the one man on whom it falls to make those decisions.

I realise, and I feel deeply, that against all these considerations the argument of a unique deterrence in the death penalty might throw an overwhelming weight if it were an argument that had real validity. Like others, I have been very worried about this and ready to let the evidence have all the weight that it might have. I have not the training of a lawyer, [col.637] but I can read and listen, like any person who might be eligible to sit upon a jury in this country. After listening and reading a great mass of evidence, I feel that there is a dearth of convincing evidence that for murders by armed thieves the death penalty is a unique deterrent. There has been such opportunity for the production of that evidence, in weighty and convincing forms, in these last two days, and I do not feel it has been there. In its place, we have had generalisations and appeals to feelings – feelings, of course, which we all have, and which cannot help moving us.

There is the evidence, on the other side, of the former Home Secretary, Mr. Henry Brooke[10]: "By no means all those murderers who came before me because they had been sentenced to death were from the criminal classes". There is the evidence as to the proportionate increase in murders now capital and murders not capital since the Homicide Act became law. The figures here show that the increase has been in both categories, thereby combating the view that the death penalty is a uniquely powerful deterrent. We do not think to look to the evidence of foreign countries in order to be impressed by this evidence which we have at home, although I believe that some of the evidence from foreign countries is, when sifted, very weighty indeed. I could not help being impressed by the speeches yesterday of no fewer than three of Her Majesty's Judges who were, in a way, giving their own evidence and also summarising their weighing of the general evidence of people and situations, which is their life's work. I could not help being impressed by their conclusions, and it just is not shown that the death penalty is a uniquely powerful deterrent.

Let me end by referring to all those considerations of feeling which bear upon us, whatever our conclusions and opinions may be. No one can help feeling terribly for the victims of crime and their families. No one can help

---

[10]   Henry Brooke (1902–84), Conservative MP for Hampstead, was Home Secretary under Prime Minister Harold Macmillan between 1962 and 1964.

feeling terribly the fears which exist in many hearts since crime, and not least violent crime, has increased. Still more must our feelings go out to the members of the Police Force and to those who are in the Prison Service. The country owes so much – and there is no limit to what it owes – to its servants who are exposed to great dangers in serving [col.638] it. But, my Lords, again and again in the formation of judgments upon human affairs we have, on the one hand, a set of anxieties, and, on the other, the action or conclusion needed to answer those anxieties. So often in human affairs we tend to build a bridge from the one set of facts to the other set of facts by our feelings and our emotions, rather than by our reason. Not many years ago, at a time when the increase of violent crime was giving so much anxiety, we were urged to build the bridge between the anxieties and the conclusions by the re-introduction of flogging. It was really a method of substituting feeling and emotion for reasoned conviction about causes and effects.

I believe that the issue in this case is somewhat the same, and that here, too, it is not those emotional considerations but the conclusions of reason which should prevail. I believe it to be a completely reasonable conclusion that capital punishment is not a unique deterrent; that a sentence of life imprisonment is a terrible sentence, deterrent in effect, and capable of issuing in a wise, stern and human penology, and that to abolish the death penalty in this country will set us in the way of progress in this matter, and rid us from the wrong of a system which punishes killing by a penalty which helps to devalue human life. I therefore hope that the House will give a Second Reading to this Bill, and that it will soon become the law of this country.

Speech in the House of Lords on the Sexual Offences Bill

[House of Lords Debates, 5th series, vol. 269, 28 October 1965, cols.714–17]

My Lords, as a supporter of the Bill throughout the debates, I have listened with respect to the noble Lords who have opposed it, and in particular I have thought again and again about the cogency of two arguments which have [col.715] been put forward. If those arguments were cogent, they would carry considerable weight with me in the scales. The first argument has been that, as a result of the passing of this Bill, there would be given to adults an encouragement to practise homosexual acts, and that that encouragement would have a depraving effect upon the morality of the country. The second argument has been that the passing of this Bill would encourage young people to think that, because homosexual acts between adults were no longer criminal, therefore these acts could not really be so bad after all, and thus encouragement would be given to them.

Take the first point. I do not believe that the argument against the Bill is really cogent. I attach importance to some of the clauses which were added to the Bill – clauses of a protective kind – but I attach still more importance to the evidence given a good many times during our debates by noble Lords, some on these Benches and some on other Benches, with considerable experience of helping people: the evidence that the present law hinders men in difficulty from being helped and saved from those difficulties. It was stated several times in opposition to this Bill that if a man wants to avoid blackmail the thing for him to do is not to commit the offence for which he can be blackmailed. But I did not think, and I do not think, that to say that is at all helpful. It is no use saying to a man of homosexual tendencies, "Stop having homosexual tendencies." It is no use saying to a man who is tempted to homosexual acts, "Do not be tempted to homosexual acts, and then you will not be blackmailed." What matters is that such people should be more accessible to the means available to help them; and the evidence is, I believe, overwhelmingly strong that the present law makes it difficult or impossible for many to make themselves accessible to those forces of grace which would help them.

Secondly, there is the argument about young people: about how a change in the law will encourage them to think that homosexual behaviour cannot, after all, be so bad. I believe that the law should protect young people. The law does protect young people, and I believe that the present Bill, if it is carried, has in some [col.716] respects increased the protection which the law will give to young people. But if the law is to protect and help young people, it must be a law that wins their respect as being just. I think that the respect of young people for the law, and the morality which it tries to uphold, is at present hindered by the feeling of young people that the law is really unjust. More still, young people are going to be moral if we present to them a version of morality which is Christian and rational, which can win their respect, and is not a kind of lopsided presentation of morality.

My support of this Bill has been increased by hearing, among those who have opposed it during these debates, what I can only call a really lopsided presentation of morality – a presentation which quotes the Old Testament, which takes the line that sexual sins are apparently the worst of all sins, and that homosexual sins are invariably the worst sort of sins among sexual sins. I think that such a presentation of morality is lopsided and is going to be rejected by the people of the new generation, who need a better presentation of morality to win their respect and admiration.

The word "abominable" came into our debates rather as a key word. I agree that the acts which we have been discussing are abominable acts, but many other things also are abominable, and as the Old Testament has figured a good deal in the debates I make no apology for turning to the other Testament. I do not find in the teaching of Christ any use of the word "abominable" in classifying sins, but I do find a passage in which a term very near to "abominable" is used; namely, "sins which defile a man". Nothing could be more abominable than those. What are they? I use the best modern translation which I know: "Those acts of fornication, theft, murder, adultery, ruthless greed, malice, fraud, envy, slander, arrogance."[11] Those are the abominable sins which in the teaching of the Founder of Christianity defile a man. Some of those sins are sexual, some of them are not sexual; among the sexual sins there is not apparently an isolation of homosexuality as being more cardinally sinful than are the others. I believe that [col.717] it is a presentation of morality, balanced, Christian and rational, that can win the respect and the allegiance of the younger generation, hard task though it is. I believe that the law can play some part in the upholding of that morality, but it must be a law which young people are going to respect as being a just one.

So, my Lords, the effect of these long debates has been to make me more rather than less anxious to see the Wolfenden reforms on this matter carried into law, and I hope that in the next Session of Parliament Her Majesty's Government will help and facilitate the process. Meanwhile I am among those who hold my noble friend Lord Arran[12] in great honour for his initiative in this matter, and by the passing of this Bill I believe that your Lordships will be writing an honourable chapter in the pages of your Lordships' House.

Ramsey to Prime Minister Wilson on the Relation of Church and State, 4 November 1965

[Ramsey Papers vol.74, ff.104–6]

My dear Prime Minister,

The Archbishop of York and I were grateful for your confidential letter in reply to ours of 12th October, in which I wrote about the two ways in which,

---

11   This is taken from Mark 7:21–2, in the New English Bible translation.
12   Arthur Gore, 8th Earl of Arran (1910–83).

following the Report[13] of the Howick Commission, we hope to make progress on the subject of ecclesiastical appointments by means of administrative action within the Church.

As the result of the debates on the Report we have come to the conclusion that the Assembly will not agree to adopt all the Howick Commission's recommendations for legislation. Unless they are all adopted it does not seem advisable, or even practicable, to proceed with them.

A further proposal is, however, to be made in the Church Assembly next week. It would affect a much wider field than that of ecclesiastical appointments and I should like to explain to you the reasons for it.

The Archbishop of York and I have discussed with the Standing Committee of the Church Assembly the growth which we have noted in recent years of a desire for further modification of the relations between Church and State.

There has already been some modification and more is in view. The new system of Church Courts has abolished the final jurisdiction of the Privy Council as such.[14] The Prayer Book (Alternative and Other Services) Measure has secured limited freedom in public worship. You know, too, that I am grateful for the Government's promise to introduce early in the new Session a Bill embodying our wishes about the dissolution of the Convocations. The Church itself has already given much thought to the formation of a General Synod and I hope that Lord Hodson's Commission will bring out its report in 1966.[15]

Yet in spite of this we have sensed, perhaps especially during the debates on the Howick Commission's report, though not by any means only on account of it, a desire for greater [f.105] freedom. This has undoubtedly been influenced to some extent by the realisation that unity with other Churches has become a living issue. As you will know, we have reached a fairly advanced stage in our discussions with the Methodists. We are also having discussions with the Presbyterians and it must be remembered that in other countries the Congregationalists, too, have come, or are coming, together in a United Church with Anglicans, Methodists and Presbyterians. All this has sharpened the realisation that, if unity is to come, the relationship between Church and State needs consideration: for instance, the whole episcopate and Crown and Parliament; the full freedom of the Church to regulate its own liturgy.

I do not foresee a demand for dis-establishment so much as for a revision of the Establishment, possibly in the direction of the Scottish arrangement. We

---

[13] Crown Appointments and the Church (London, 1964).

[14] A result of the Ecclesiastical Jurisdiction Measure, passed by Parliament in 1963.

[15] The report *Government by Synod* did indeed appear in 1966.

believe that there is a desire on the part not only of the Church of England, but also of the other Churches to have a link with the State.

These considerations have led to the formulation of the following resolutions, which, at the request of the Standing Committee, the Archbishop of York is to move in the Church Assembly:-

> "That the Archbishops be requested to appoint a Commission to make recommendations as to the modifications in the constitutional relationship between Church and State which are desirable and practicable and in so doing to take account of current and future steps to promote greater unity between the Churches."

And

> "That further consideration of legislation concerning Crown Appointments be adjourned."

If this resolution is passed, the Church of England will be taking action on its own responsibility and its own behalf, but the increasing call for Christian unity should act as a stimulus and provide a focus for the work of the Commission.

[f.106] We should expect that it would be authorized to have consultations with other Churches. When the Commission reports, the Church of England, possibly through a new General Synod, will be free to formulate its proposals. One hopes they will be found acceptable by the Free Churches. It would then be for the State to take its decisions upon the proposals.

All this, of course, will depend upon the Church Assembly's decision next week, but I want you to know the reasons for putting forward the two resolutions which I have mentioned.

I have been so very grateful for all the help which has been given by the Government's advisers to the Church's representatives since the issue of the Howick Report, and indeed before that. The trend of opinion in the Church has changed more rapidly than one could have expected since that Commission was appointed and has led to the situation in which we are now placed. If you would like to talk this over after the Church Assembly I hope you will not hesitate to let me know.

Yours sincerely,

Speech to the House of Lords on Southern Rhodesia, 15 November 1965

[House of Lords Debates, 5th series, 15 November 1965 vol. 270, cols. 265–68]

My Lords, it falls to me to be the first to welcome to our debates the noble Lord, Lord Butler of Saffron Walden, and as he and I are old friends it is a special privilege to do this.[16] I know that we all hope that the noble Lord will frequently give us, as he has given us to-day, the great value of his counsel, coming, as it does, from such knowledge, experience and wisdom.

It is indeed a tragedy which we are facing, and, I would mention, not only a tragedy for countries but a personal [col.266] tragedy for many persons. The Rhodesian crisis has brought to many people grief between friends, and grief between relatives, too; and we cannot forget that among those on the other side in Rhodesia are people who, however mistaken we may think them, are God-fearing people who care for Christian values. We are very lacking in imagination if we do not have some understanding of the fears felt by some of the white people, who know about the violence, and even the chaos, which has occurred in some parts of Africa. But it is a tragedy in which there are clear moral issues, as the noble Lord, Lord Butler of Saffron Walden, has been telling us so clearly. I believe that the people of this country, after some inevitable bewilderment, are grasping what these moral issues are.

First, there has already been the issue of the wrongness of allowing independence to Rhodesia except on the basis of all the conditions which the Prime Minister has described in the five points. I think it is important for us to be clear that the issue is not just one of democracy: it was not, and it is not, an issue of, "One man, one vote". There are things which matter more than votes. The issue has not been that of immediate rule by the majority, but of a safeguarding for the members of that majority of real progress in education, in civil rights and in freedom from racial discrimination. It is in these matters that the obligation of this countries [*sic*] lies.

Next, now that U.D.I.[17] has happened, the issue for our country in the sight of the world, and not least in the sight of all the countries of Africa, is that our country should be seen to uphold law, order and justice with the same resolution everywhere, whatever be the race and colour of those in relation to whom law has to be upheld. Nothing could damage us more in the eyes of African countries –

---

[16]   R.A. 'Rab' Butler was a contemporary of Ramsey at Cambridge in the 1920s. Chadwick, *Ramsey*, p.vi.

[17]   A Unilateral Declaration of Independence.

and, I would add, in the eyes of the God of justice and righteousness – than that we should even seem to falter in this duty and obligation.

Now the matter of sanctions. What are they for? What are they designed to achieve? Many people in the country have been rather confused about the aim and ethics of sanctions. I do not believe that sanctions have very much [col.267] significance as a kind of gesture of protest. Gestures of protest may be right, but a mere gesture could damage people whom we least want to damage and could leave the final situation no better. Again, I do not believe in sanctions as a sort of punishment; and, in any case, they could, if prolonged, bring punishment to innocent people, Africans as well as white. But sanctions have, I believe, both moral validity and reason behind them if their aim is, as the Prime Minister has told us, to bring about the end of the illegal régime in Rhodesia. I would thus call sanctions not a moral gesture, nor a punishment, but an effective moral instrument to achieve a result. That is perhaps their sole justification.

Presumably sanctions can be effective partly by causing such difficulties for the Rhodesian régime as to disable it from carrying on, and partly by causing more people in Rhodesia to see that this régime offers just no way forward. But, my Lords, if sanctions are to do that, they must be really effective and as quick as possible in their effect. Only thus can they be the effective moral instrument. Otherwise, sanctions can drag on in embittering ineffectiveness. Perhaps, very soon, the question of oil may arise. It has been suggested that an oil embargo, if practicable and effective, might be the strongest form of pressure. The report in *The Times* to-day of what the noble Viscount, Lord Malvern,[18] has said is most significant.

As to possible action beyond economic sanctions, my own view is known as to what I believe Christian conscience should say if the lamentable necessity arose. It is good now to hear from the Government that any intervention to uphold order would be on request of the Governor and not on request of any Party on either side. I believe, therefore, that the actions already taken and now being prepared by Her Majesty's Government have behind them sound moral principle. I do not believe that the Government could, without dishonour, be acting differently. But it is a course with dangers on either side.

On the one side there is the danger that any vacillation or watering-down of sanctions would mean slow, ineffectual sanctions, leading to much prolonged [col.268] bitterness and no firm result. There is the danger that other countries, either within the United Nations or on African soil, should lose patience and go

---

[18] Sir Godfrey Huggins (1883–1971), first viscount Malvern, and former Prime Minister of the short-lived Federation of Rhodesia and Nyasaland.

to extremes – and nothing might more easily excite other countries to extremes than if they saw Britain, in contrast with some of her own actions in the past, in Africa and elsewhere, being unable to uphold law in a territory where there is, after all, a British Governor and judges whom we recognise.

My Lords, no Government could have a harder task than ours at this time: the task of steering between these two dangers and of being resolutely firm, yet looking for a law and order which must, in the end, go with reconciliation and with changes in outlook. In following this course I believe that the Government at this moment and on this issue deserve the support of all our citizens, if there are differences as to what particular sanctions are likely to achieve, no doubt these differences must be debated, but we can all surely hope – and, certainly so far, today's debate has encouraged us to hope – that these differences will not prevent all our leaders from being at one in stating clearly, and upholding, the moral duty of our country. There are at stake not only the future of Rhodesia and the future of much else beside, but also the honour of this country.

1966

Ramsey to Oliver Tomkins, Bishop of Bristol, on Relations with Roman Catholics in England, 26 January 1966

[Ramsey Papers, vol.107, ff.72–73]

My dear Oliver,

Thank you for your letter about my visit to Rome. I am going only in the capacity in which I was invited, namely as Archbishop of Canterbury and President of the Lambeth Conference. I note what you say about Cardinal Heenan[1] and R.C. relations. One has to act with the greatest caution in relation to moves made by Cardinal Heenan, and there is some conflict of purpose between his aims and ours. He is apt to use what he thinks are ecumenical gestures for the purpose of R.C. propaganda, and if we respond uncritically to the tune which he plays we may find ourselves doing more harm than good. The issues on which discretion needs to be exercised are, I think, these:

1. It is really important that our dealing with Rome should, on the Roman side, be dealt with and controlled by the Secretariat for Unity,[2] and not by the English Hierarchy. Of course the English Hierarchy has to be involved, but if it is allowed to control we find our Continental contacts kept out, and the propagandist element strengthened.

2. It must, therefore, be our line that dialogue is with the Roman Church as a whole and not only with the Roman Church in England, and that means that on our side the party to the dialogue is not only the Church of England but the Anglican Communion as a whole. Cardinal Heenan naturally does not like this line, and that it makes it the more necessary to stick to it.

3. The favourable treatment of the Anglican Communion in the Vatican Council scheme <u>De Ecumenismo</u> is a positive thing on which to build. It is right that we should build on it because we believe that our role in Christendom is not

---

[1]   John Carmel Heenan (1905–75), Cardinal Archbishop of Westminster.
[2]   The Secretariat for the Promotion of Unity amongst Christians was established by Pope John XXIII in 1960.

only that of "one of the Protestant churches". Cardinal Heenan does not like this and tries to play down the Church of England by lumping us with Protestants generally. That sounds very broad minded and ecumenical of him, especially when he says nice things about the Free Churches etc. but it is part of a device on his part, and I am not surprised that some of the B.C.C.[3] people are a bit taken in.

[f.73] I put these considerations to you as I am not sure how far they have been present in your own mind. That all Churches should get involved in dialogue with Romans is, I think, inevitable and right, as you found at Nottingham[4], but we do have to guard against this being used by Roman propagandists to block the distinctive progress which Anglican Communion relations with the Vatican can be making.

I was so glad to have passed on to you the news of the proposal to postpone the Canon B.15 section of the Prayer Book (Further Provisions) Measure until the Intercommunion Commission has done its main work.[5]

Yours ever,

Ramsey to E.L. Mascall[6] on Church Unity, 18 March 1966

[Ramsey Papers, vol.103, ff.111–13]

I am sorry to have kept you waiting for an answer to your letter.[7] It is indeed true that within the Roman Church there has been remarkable change and development and the emergence of what you call "Reformed Catholicism". It is also true that there is a good deal of frustration in our own Church, though I wonder whether in the history of our Church from the point of view of "Reformed Catholicism" 1966 shows a big deterioration upon 1866, when Tate[8]

3   British Council of Churches.
4   The British Faith and Order Conference, held at Nottingham in 1964 under the auspices of the British Council of Churches, at which there were Roman Catholic observers.
5   Canon B.15, governing the circumstances under which non-Anglicans might be admitted to communion, had been a matter of some dispute. Tomkins was chairman of the commission that was to produce the report *Intercommunion Today* (London, 1968).
6   Eric Lionel Mascall (1905–93), Anglican clergyman and theologian, and a regular correspondent of Ramsey of long standing.
7   E.L. Mascall to Ramsey, 1 March 1966, Ramsey Papers 103, ff.107–10. Ramsey's letter prompted a further letter from Mascall, 16 April 1966, Ramsey Papers 103, ff.114–16, and another in turn from Ramsey.
8   Archibald Campbell Tait (1811–82), Archbishop of Canterbury.

was Primate and the prosecution of Maconochie[9] was taking place, or 1766 in which year I do not recall who was Primate but I should not think there was much "Reformed Catholicism" in evidence. Furthermore, while the new spirit in Rome grows considerably we have to face the fact that in parts of Rome there is still a rigid intransigence in existence, not least in the Roman Hierarchy in this country where, apart from the putting of the Liturgy into the vernacular and a number of acts of public fraternising, there is so far very little essential change. Furthermore I find amongst Roman Catholics of the new outlook a good deal of desire that the Anglican Communion should continue for their sake as well as for everyone else's sake.

As to Protestantism and our relations to it, it has to be recognised that Protestantism is in a state of considerable change: some of it is static in its older members, some of it is ultra-liberal with not much principle at all, but a good deal of it is the scene of processes very much akin to those which you call "Reformed Catholicism". Indeed the way in which theological tendencies cut across old definitions has become very considerable. I find myself that amongst intelligent nonconformists in this country there is a perception of such Catholic doctrines as Eucharistic Sacrifice, the Communion of Saints, and the sacramental significance of Church Order, to an extent which is lacking amongst our own Anglican low churchmen. It is far from being true that union with Protestants is necessarily followed by a kind of Protestant swamping of ourselves: Roman Catholics perceive this and tell us, for instance, that the C.S.I.[10] Liturgy and Ordinal are, in their view, better than our own Ordinal and Liturgy. It seems to be to be both lacking in common sense, and doing despite to the Holy Spirit of truth, who is presumably at work amongst baptised Christians, always to assume the worst in connection with relations with Protestants.

[f.112] You mention certain Reunion schemes such as Nigeria: I have visited Nigeria and tried to see what is happening to Christianity in that country, and my impression is this: the Anglican Church is a very old fashioned Church of a rather Victorian C.M.S.[11] outlook. I believe that union with Presbyterians and Methodists will give it something of a theological stirring and awakening, bearing in mind the many kites flying in the ecumenical movement, so I should expect the United Church, which will be episcopal and retaining the Creeds,

---

[9]   Alexander Heriot Mackonochie (1825–87) was the subject of a series of prosecutions on account of the ritual practice at his church of St Alban, Holborn.

[10]   The Church of South India, created in 1945 by a union of the Anglican church with other Protestant denominations.

[11]   The Church Missionary Society, in the nineteenth century the principal missionary society of the Evangelical wing of the Church of England.

to have a good deal greater potentiality of "Reformed Catholicism" than the present Anglican Church has in isolation. In any case with the growth of African leadership the isolation of Nigerian Christianity from this country is likely to grow. I think it is rather nonsense to suppose that by preserving a group of low church C.M.S. Dioceses in isolation, both from this country and from other Churches in Nigeria, you are conserving "Reformed Catholicism".

Well, you may disagree but I have at least tried to study the question in terms of the total development of Christianity in the country concerned, and I do not think that any sound judgment can be formed simply by the scrutiny of paper documents. The African mind is not capable of the sort of definitive processes of the Western mind, and it is necessary to study the potentialities of the African mind in developing Christian forms and not to judge everything by Western concepts. It was from you that I learned long ago that Christian Unity has to be seen in these total sociological terms.

As to orthodoxy in our Communion, unless we are to run our Churches by heresy trials, it is simply a part of our history that we have eccentrics like Bishop Barnes[12] and Bishop Jim Pike[13] in America, and mutual reproaches between Anglican Churches about this are, I think, unhelpful. I should myself resist trying to maintain orthodoxy by heresy trials, and when one says that one has to accept its consequences.

I put these considerations to you because I believe they are true and relevant. I do not think that the way of an Anglican nowadays is at all easy, but I doubt if it was at any time easier, and if you were to pick any other dates, besides 1866 and 1766, you would, I think, very rarely find "Reformed Catholicism" as the easily assumed version of Anglicanism. Nor, I think, could you name a time at which more was being done to bring about better relations with the Patriarchates in East and West. The problem we are discussing is, I think, only one instance of the continuing problem of the relation between the divine and the human factors in the Church of God. The human factors are provided by the sinfulness and fallibility of the Church's members, and the divine factor is provided by the presence of the Risen Lord and the Holy Spirit: our belief that the divine factor continues to overcome the vagaries of the human factor can be helped by the sort of [f.113] calculating consideration which I have set out, and it can be hindered by the sort of gloomy pessimism of which your letter is full, e.g. predicting in advance that we are going to be "swallowed" by error. But the belief

---

[12]   E.W. Barnes (1874–1953), Bishop of Birmingham.

[13]   James A. Pike, Bishop of California, and one of the most controversial figures in American Anglicanism, being the subject of heresy proceedings on several occasions; Sachs, *The Transformation of Anglicanism*, pp.307–10.

is surely at bottom an act of faith that the Church is God's and not ours, and that He is taking care of it.

Ramsey to Chad Varah on Sex, 8 November 1966

[Ramsey Papers vol.91, ff.365–66]

Thank you for your letter.[14] I think you are under a good deal of misunderstanding. I have never singled out the act of intercourse as the sole human action which is to be judged. I am entirely aware that there can be marriages in which love has perished and the relationships of man and woman are in many ways wrong and sex is therefore robbed of its true sacramental meaning. That is a very wrong state of affairs, and it is not made right by the mere fact of there being intercourse within marriage. It is the will of God for a marriage that there should be the fullest love and partnership and that sex should find its true meaning in that context. Similarly, as to the unmarried, it is true that between unmarried lovers who have intercourse there can be a genuine love and unselfishness which may be lacking in the kind of poor marriage which I have described. But what do we conclude from this? We conclude that we must not judge people and must specially avoid comparative judgments. But we do know as Christians something about the purpose and design of God, and all that deviates from that purpose and design of God is wrong, however much or little the blame may be and however much there may be good motives. It is the design of God that the married should enjoy the fullest partnership with sex as its expression, and marriages that deviate from that are imperfect and sinful. So too it is the design of God that the unmarried should keep their relationships in a state of chastity and know that the truest and best use of sex is in marriage. We have to say what is the perfect will of God and that all that deviates from that is somehow sinful.

---

[14]   Chad Varah (1911–2007), rector of the church of St Stephen Walbrook in the City of London, and founder of the charity The Samaritans. He had written in response to reports of comments made by Ramsey to the Canterbury Diocesan Conference on 29 October. Ramsey had said: 'We believe as a Church that in God's purpose and design the right use of sex is within marriage, and sexual intercourse outside marriage is always wrong. This week the British Council of Churches has reaffirmed this. I have not the slightest doubt that all of us here in this Conference believe this. We have however to commend this standard to those who are perplexed and to shew real understanding of their problems. That is the task to which we must be pledged.' Ramsey Papers vol.91, f.356; Varah to Ramsey, 6 November 1966, at Ramsey Papers vol.91, f.363.

To say this is not to single out any one sin as being the worst or to single out any one action as being the thing by which we are judged.

I think, therefore, that your letter does reveal a certain amount of muddle. My view of the Sex and Morality Report is this.[15] It is a laudable attempt to do something which we need to do, namely to discuss this moral issue empirically from the position in which people find themselves, and starting from a position which they can understand, namely the meaning of love and mutual respect, work back from that position towards the Christian affirmation as that which gives it its true meaning.

[f.366] I think the attempt in the pamphlet was very laudable and nearly achieved a considerable success. In some quarters I think it has done a lot of good in commending the essence of Christian morality in the sort of terms which perplexed non-Christians can understand. It ought, however, to have gone more deeply into the ethical issues and treated divine law, a very different thing from rule making, more seriously. Because of this lacuna in its treatment, while it did good in some circles, it did harm in others by suggesting that there is an attempt to water down the fundamentals.

The B.C.C. was trying (a) to commend for its own purpose the kind of method of the pamphlet, and (b) to affirm that there is a design of God about the use of sex and that fornication is contrary to that design. It might also have said that loveless and selfish conduct within marriage is also contrary to that design however sex is used.

I hope you will think that this amplification of my view makes sense and is one to be made intelligible to your clients. You will also see that there is considerable difference between my thesis and Shillinglaw's.[16]

Yours always affectionately,

---

[15]   A report prepared by a working party appointed by the British Council of Churches in 1964 to examine 'the Christian case for abstinence from sexual intercourse before marriage and faithfulness within marriage, taking full account of responsible criticisms, and to suggest means whereby the Christian position may be effectively presented to the various sections of the community.' *Sex and Morality. A report presented to the British Council of Churches* (London, 1966), p.5.
[16]   I have been unable to identify this person.

'The Proposed Canonisation of the English and Welsh Martyrs of the Reformation Period. A Note by the Archbishop of Canterbury'. 8 November 1966[17]

[Ramsey Papers vol.107, f.24]

I have been asked a number of times what I think would be the consequences for ecumenical work of the proposed canonisation. I am increasingly convinced that the canonisation would be harmful to the ecumenical cause in England and that it would encourage those emotions which militate against the ecumenical cause. I set out below my reasons for this view.

I believe that it is in the context of the Communion of Saints that we go closer together in the ecumenical way. Thus I believe that it is right for Anglicans to acknowledge and revere sanctity where it is seen in the Roman Catholic Church, and it is equally right for Roman Catholics to honour and thank God for sanctity as it has been seen in Anglican and other Churches outside the Roman obedience. It is, however, very important that in this process polemical associations should be avoided. In England I am sure that it is good that Roman Catholics and Anglicans should together honour and thank God for those Saints whom they believe that they share in their own history, like the Venerable Bede, St. Cuthbert and St. Anselm in England and St. Benedict too. This is how I would positively relate the cause of ecumenism and the Communion of Saints to one another.

In England our past history creates inevitable difficulties for ecumenical progress. Nobody familiar with our English history need be surprised at this. There is not only the prejudice of ultra-Protestant people but there is also the "siege mentality" which is still apt to possess Roman Catholics in England. By "siege mentality" I mean a kind of polemical self-consciousness which is far different from the spirit of the meeting between His Holiness the Pope and myself in March 1966. The "siege mentality" is, I believe, bound up psychologically with a kind of martyrdom complex deeply, and of course intelligibly, rooted in history. Ought we not on both sides to be getting away from this? My fear is that devotion to the English Martyrs on either side has been and still is a focus for this kind of mentality in its polemical form.

Such being my general uneasiness about the proposal to canonise the English Martyrs, I have tried to look with fairness of mind at the proposals themselves

---

[17] This private memorandum was prepared for the information of the Vatican Secretariat for Promoting Christian Unity, in response to discussion of the matter between Ramsey and Roman Catholic representatives in England.

as set out by the promoters of the cause. I have read the "Manifesto for Martyrs' Sunday 1965" and also the "Biblical Service for the Feast of the Martyrs of England and Wales". I find in these documents confirmation of my fear that the canonisation all too readily lends itself to the continuance of the polemical spirit. While some ecumenical language is used, the final outcome is that the Martyrs are to be invoked so that with the aid of their prayers non-Roman Catholic Christians in England may be brought within the Roman obedience.

I cannot therefore help thinking that the proposed canonisation will in the historical circumstances of England encourage on both sides the kind of emotions of which we are anxious to be rid and retard the development of that spirit and approach which the meeting between His Holiness the Pope and the Archbishop of Canterbury tried so much to set forward.

1967

Memorandum on the Visit to Lambeth of Cardinal Suenens, 19 May 1967

[Ramsey Papers vol.120, ff.283–85]

On Saturday, 19th May, 1967, the Cardinal celebrated Mass in the Post Room, at a table specially arranged, with his two chaplains con-celebrating. Much of the service was in English and easy to follow, and the canon said in Latin was also easy to follow. The Mass was very simply celebrated, and I noticed specially the absence of much of the minor ceremonial which used to be prominent amongst both Romans and Anglo-Catholics. After the consecration the Cardinal gave me the kiss of peace. Besides his two assistant priests the service was attended by myself, my wife, two Chaplains and two C.F.R.[1] clergy.

Subsequently the Cardinal attended Holy Communion celebrated by myself in the Chapel. The Series 1 form of Interim Rite was used.[2] I gave the Cardinal the kiss of peace after the consecration. There was no "inter-communion" at either service.

After breakfast the Cardinal had a long talk with me alone in the study. I record my recollection of all the subjects discussed, though not the order of the conversation.

1. The Cardinal wanted me to know that the visit to Lambeth, in return for my visit to Malines, was the chief object of his coming to England. He had come for that in response to my invitation, and his going to Liverpool for the consecration of the Cathedral was in his mind secondary.[3]

2. He spoke frankly about the progress of ecumenical action in England and was afraid that the English hierarchy was not as forthcoming as it might be. I commented on this and said that the English hierarchy was full of genuine friendliness but had hardly begun to grasp the real meaning of the ecumenical

---

[1]   Council for Foreign Relations, the department at Lambeth responsible for interactions between the Church of England and non-Anglican churches overseas.

[2]   Series 1 was the first set of experimental revised liturgies enabled by the Prayer Book (Alternative and Other Services) Measure of 1965.

[3]   The metropolitan cathedral of Christ the King in Liverpool.

movement. The Cardinal readily understood that the Apostolic Delegate[4] was more helpful. (The Cardinal did not refer to the fact but may have noticed that none of the English hierarchy had come to Evensong the night before or to the dinner. Both Cardinal Heenan and Bishop Butler[5] had excused themselves with no suggestion of a substitute.)

3. The Cardinal asked me my view of the decrees of the Vatican Council and which of them I thought most helpful. I said that much was helpful at many points but I could specifically refer to the Decree on Revelation with its emphasis biblical and patristic rather than scholastic; the Decree on the Church with its emphasis upon Holy Baptism, the unity of all the baptised and the collegiality of Pope and Bishops; also the Decree on Ecumenism [f.284] with its much warmer attitude to Christians outside the Roman obedience; and statements in the Decree on Religious Liberty. He agreed that all these things were significant.

4. We spoke of Anglican Orders, and the Cardinal was evidently for a new examination which might be expected to yield a result different from Pope Leo XIII. We agreed in the wrongness of isolating Holy Orders from the general subject of ecclesiology.

5. The Cardinal spoke very frankly about the Pope whom he knows intimately. He has had much talk with him, advising him to take a more openly progressive attitude. The difficulty is that the Pope, while full of human sympathies, has a mind largely trained by Canon Law and does not easily grasp other theological conceptions. The Cardinal had specially urged the Pope to come out sympathetically about birth control, but without success. The Cardinal was evidently keen for a new line on birth control. I asked whether in view of authoritative statements in the past about the total sinfulness of contraceptives it would not be very difficult to Rome to announce a new line. The Cardinal said it would not be so difficult as the theology which condemned birth control was itself a rather arbitrary development and not the fundamental theology of the Church. The fundamental theology could find a new understanding and expression called out by the thought of the times. These were not the Cardinal's exact terms but it was clearly his view, put here in my own way.

6. The Cardinal asked me about the most important practical steps and I mentioned two, (a) a better line about mixed marriages and (b) the uninhibited growth of Roman Catholics and Anglicans worshipping together at one another's Liturgies as well as on special occasions. I mentioned joint Retreats, which the Cardinal welcomed, and I told him of the joint Retreat of Anglican

---

[4]   Igino Cardinale.

[5]   Bishop Christopher Butler, auxiliary Bishop of Westminster since 1966.

and Roman Catholic Prison Chaplains which I had taken, and he was delighted. On the two main issues which I mentioned he said (a) the most hopeful medium for tackling mixed marriages might be the new Synod of Bishops summoned by the Pope, as it could air views held in different parts of the world: (b) as to joint services, the Directory not yet published would prove a great help. I asked what had happened to the Directory and he said that it had been completed some time ago and was very good but "someone had put it in a drawer". He hoped however that it was about to be published. (It was in fact published in Rome on the very next day, Whit Sunday.)

7. The Cardinal told me of his great interest in the theological questions concerning revelation, history, myth etc. These [f.285] questions were now prominent in the Belgian universities and their handling was of the utmost importance. To test my attitude he asked what I thought about the elements of history and non-historical symbolic writing in the Fourth Gospel, and asked specifically did I believe in the historicity of the turning of water into wine at Cana? I said that I did not feel I knew the answer for certain and was ready to think that the Fourth Gospel contained narratives which were pieces of symbolic interpretation of the Gospel rather than strict history, though I was sure that the Fourth Gospel did contain historical traditions and that the writer valued history as well as symbolic interpretation. I sensed that the Cardinal thought much the same. I told him that in my view revelation comprised events and symbolic images, that both were essential but the borderline between the two was not always certain. He said he was glad that my book on the Resurrection had been translated into French, though he had not yet read it in either English or French. Was it a new book? I said "No, I wrote it more than twenty years ago and it goes on selling." Unfortunately I did not have a copy at hand to give him but I promised to send him one. He wanted to know the line I took about the historical question, and I told him briefly what my line was. He thanked me for my book *The Glory of God and the Transfiguration of Christ* of which I had given him a copy in French.

8. The Cardinal asked about plans for unity with Protestant Churches, e.g. the Methodists, and I told him of my belief that these were so far compatible with the kind of Anglican-Roman Catholic progress which we cared about.

9. We spoke about the Marian dogmas. I said that while many Anglicans were timid about the Communion of Saints through sheer Protestantism and reaction, many Anglicans were more appreciative and ready to honour Mary in virtue of her place in the economy of salvation, but were unable to accept (a) the modern dogmas as being *de fide* and (b) any violation of the unique glory of the Son of God as Redeemer. I quoted to him words from Bishop Pearson's Exposition of

the Creed:[6] "Let her be honoured and esteemed, let Him be worshipped and adored", and said that much modern practical Mariology seemed to transgress that distinction. I said I was very sorry that the Pope had gone to Fatima[7] as it seemed to encourage the wrong sort of Mariology and to be insensitive to ecumenical considerations. The Cardinal clearly agreed and said that personally for his part he was happy with Lourdes and unhappy with Fatima.

10. We both expressed the hope that we would keep in touch with one another and that we would see positive advances in many of the matters which are at present moving slowly.

Sermon for the Opening of Human Rights Year in Westminster Abbey, 10 December 1967[8]

[Ramsey Papers, vol.317, ff.132–34]

Psalm 8.4. What is man that thou art mindful of him?

And what indeed is Man? People of many religions or of none, people of many philosophies or of none, will join in saying that Man is the being of highest significance in the world, and in echoing the old words of Sophocles: "Many things are marvellous, and nothing is more marvellous than Man." Christians, as indeed Jews, have their own belief about this, that Man is created by God in God's own image with fellowship with God in heaven for ever as the goal of his existence. God created the human race by an evolutionary process through many stages of nature, with a care for every one of us, each in his own individuality, a care for each of us so great that there might be no one else in the world for him to care for. And he cares so much for each one that – quite simply – he wants each one to be with him in the perfect fellowship of heaven for ever. If we think rightly about heaven it is not remote from the concerns of today and tomorrow. Rather is it the supreme assertion of how greatly God cares about every human person today and tomorrow. It is a caring with an eternal significance and an eternal goal.

---

6   John Pearson (1613–86), English theologian and later bishop of Chester.
7   The Marian pilgrimage site in Portugal.
8   Reproduced from a Church Information Office press release. The prefatory note for editors has been omitted, but the sub-headings which were probably inserted by CIO staff have been retained.

A Human Right

Here indeed is a human right which no cruelty in the world can snatch from any man, the right to be loved by God, the right to respond to that love and to reach the destiny. A man can rob himself of his heavenly goal by his own stubbornness. But others cannot rob him of it. However his fellows may treat him by cruelty or persecution they cannot snatch from him his right to live with God for ever. God will be his portion and his joy.

For us Christians this thought of the ultimacy, the everlasting weight of the individual, gives urgency to our concern for the rights of every single person here and now. This life or that life, this unimportant life or that unimportant life as some may call it, has itself the weight, the value of a universe. It is with the impulse drawn from that conviction that we proclaim human rights and set about to serve and protect them.

"Spiritual Warfare"

So today we begin a year of spiritual warfare for human rights. In this year we join with people in many countries to stir our concern and to use the ways available to put our concern into practice. Our heart goes out to those in prison without justice, because of their opinions or because of their religion or their dissent from the regime under which they live. Our heart goes out to those who are separated from their fellows or denied equal citizenship or a citizen's privileges because their skins are of a certain colour. Our heart goes out to those whom our world's economic failure condemns to poverty and hunger. Our heart goes out to all of these. We pray for them, and their families, and for those who injure them. And from today on, in the human rights year now beginning, our prayers will be more constant, caring, more imaginative, as by our intercession we become channels of the outgoing compassion of God.

Practical Service and Community Relations

So too will our actions be more urgent. Is there some part of the field of human rights where we can best give our practical service? Of course there is, and we dare not stand idly by. I think of those in this country who are working to help the best community relations between citizens of Anglo-Saxon stock and citizens of other races living beside them. The [f.134] building up of community relations is the best answer to actions which are contrary to human rights. And beside our prayers and our actions there must be our voices, protesting against what is unjust and stating the principles of the rights of every man.

Alas, the trampling on human rights can happen in ways more near at home, more easy and familiar than the great issues of the world. Every insensitive action towards another man or woman, every unkindness or thoughtlessness is an act of violence to a fellow creature; it is treating a person like a thing, and to do this is to crucify Christ afresh.

The Christian Message

"Inasmuch as you did it not to the least of one of these, you did it not to me."[9] So speaks Christ to us. Inasmuch, he says, as you neglect the divine image in the other man and do not care about him you are doing this to me. The crucifixion of Jesus stands as the divine judgment upon every man's insensitivity to every man. And we today are living in an hour of divine judgment. The vast increases in civilisation, in culture, in the use of the sciences, in the astonishing development of man's powers, have not eradicated from Man his readiness to trample the rights of others. So we proclaim our Christian message. Return to God, we say, return to your creator and your saviour.

Yes, but the God to whom we summon Man to turn must always be shewn as the God whose image is in every man. To turn to God is to turn to this man or that woman who is oppressed. To turn to God is to turn to this man or that woman in whom Christ suffers. Christ is the Christ who is found there. God is the God who is found in every one who possesses his image. It is when our religion and compassion, are utterly one, it is when our sense of God and our care for humanity are utterly one, that things begin to happen, for our God is no one unless he is the Christ who suffers in and for humanity. "What is Man that thou art mindful of him?"[10] Man is a being, every man is a being, who has the weight and worth of eternity. And what is required of Man? Let the prophet's words tell us. "He hath shewed thee, O Man, what is good, and what doth the Lord require of thee, but to do justly and to love mercy and to walk humbly with thy God."[11]

---

[9]   Matthew 25:45.

[10]   Psalm 8:4.

[11]   Micah 6:8.

1968

Speech to the House of Lords on the Race Relations Bill

[House of Lords Debates, 5th series, 15 July 1968, vol. 295, cols. 56–61.]

My Lords, I welcome this Bill because I am impressed by the evidence that a bit of legislation helps in a task [col.57] of this kind. I want also to say how wholeheartedly I welcome and agree with the plea made by the noble Lord, Lord Brooke, that this Bill – be it as some of us believe a good Bill, or be it, as he suspects, perhaps not quite so good a Bill – is but one item in a far greater process: the process of education, and indeed the process of dealing comprehensively with all the practical problems of community relations in this country. I believe that the Bill is necessary, but I see it only as an item.

I should like to say a word or two about that larger context within which I see the Bill as an item. Centuries hence our successors may be astonished at this phase in human history, that there was so much trouble and discussion about the colour of human skin. If one looks at the matter in that way, it is altogether astonishing. Why should the colour of human skin be such a tremendous issue, any more than the difference between blue eyes and brown eyes and grey eyes, or between the different colours of hair? But we know that it is not just the colour of skin; it is the colour problem intermingled with a legion of other problems concerning culture and ways of life, and whether people have always lived in a place or are new arrivals. A whole tangle of social and economic problems develops, and, as well as the frank colour prejudice which certainly exists, there are the prejudicial troubles caused when colour becomes a symbol for things more complex than itself. That, I believe, is part of our contemporary tragedy in this country.

I see the Bill as a necessary item in the immense efforts that we need to be making to get good community relations, which have been described as "equal opportunity accompanied by cultural diversity in an atmosphere of tolerance"[1].

---

[1]   The phrase is that of Roy Jenkins, Labour Home Secretary, cited by Anthony Lester in Andrew Adonis and Keith Thomas (eds), *Roy Jenkins. A retrospective* (Oxford, 2004),

If that is to be, it calls for a delicate balance between the readiness of newcomers in any community to adapt themselves to that community and the readiness of those already in the community to accept differences of outlook and to be very sympathetic and tolerant. In the past three years I have seen something of the efforts made by many voluntary bodies in the sphere of community relations, through the part which I have in the work of the National Committee for Commonwealth Immigrants.[2] I should like to commend the Report of that [col.58] Committee for 1967, as it gives a full and fascinating picture of work done in community relations in many parts of the country; and, indeed, it describes vividly something of this human scene which is the context of the Bill.

The N.C.C.I. now has 64 voluntary liaison committees working in different parts of the country. The term "liaison committee" here is very significant, because there is an immense variety of bodies in the country dealing with community relations, and those bodies are of very different sorts. They range from militant groups which exist for the purpose of protesting and making a noise about grievances to groups of white citizens, right at the other end of the scale, trying very hard to do good but being rather paternalistic and sometimes rather surprised when they do not quite meet the feelings of immigrant communities or communities of people of other races. But the best work is, I believe, done when you get a group of citizens, including persons of different races, working together in a common understanding, realising that the problems are common to both of them and doing their best to help with them in practical ways.

The work of the N.C.C.I. has included specialist panels whose researches have been able to give the Government information and advice about the needs of particular localities. It has also included training courses for professional people whose work increasingly involves them in matters of race relations, though their professional training may not have specially prepared them for those problems. The police officer, the magistrate, the school teacher, the educationist in other spheres, and many kinds of social worker, have not necessarily been trained in race relations matters and they, perhaps, find themselves suddenly involved in them. The N.C.C.I. has been giving help by skilled educational courses, warmly welcomed by professional people, about the racial problems which they encounter in their work. In this present month of July there are taking place some 30 classes for talks of this character in different parts of the country. Of course, the work of education includes helping the immigrant communities

---

p.142.
2   Ramsey had become the first chairman of the NCCI at the invitation of Prime Minister Harold Wilson.

to understand things about this country which they badly need to know and understand, and also helping our community generally to [col.59] know what is the contribution that some immigrant communities have been giving to our economy and our culture.

Before I leave the work of the N.C.C.I. I would mention one very interesting activity; that is, the provision of pre-school age playing groups for children. Playgrounds are provided where children, before they have quite reached the age for going to school, can play together and get to know one another, which of course they usually do without any inhibition about the colour of one another's skin. The provision of these playgrounds has been found to help greatly when children go on to school, and the difficulties of school problems can be very much lessened by them.

I welcome greatly the fact that the N.C.C.I. is now to give place to a new body called the Community Relations Commission, because the work will now be not with those correctly called "immigrants" but with the second or third generations who are now our fellow citizens. I hope that the new Commission will have in its membership men and women with really scientific knowledge of the problems to be tackled. I hope it will have a chairman, not who cares more about these matters than I do – because one will not be found – but who will be able to give a great deal more time to what will be an immensely growing work than I have been able to give to the work of the N.C.C.I. I hope, also, that the Government will realise that £200,000 is a small budget for these immensely important operations. If this work is to grow as it should grow, it will cost more; and I am sure the Government know they must face that.

It is in the context of all this that I see the present Bill as designed to help, and I believe that it will help. But I want to make three criticisms of it. My first criticism is with regard to the definition of "discrimination" in Clause 1. I am glad that on the Report stage in another place the definition was enlarged, but I agree with the noble Lord, Lord Byers, that it is a great pity that the definition was not carried further still. Is it possible to improve upon the words used in the International Convention document of 1965: "any distinction, exclusion, restriction or preference based on race, colour or national or ethnic origin"?[3] [col.60] Those words make it clear that discrimination may include not only the provision of unequal services, but also the provision of services in separation.

---

[3]   The International Convention on the Elimination of all forms of Racial Discrimination, article 1. It was adopted by the United Nations in 1965; www.ohchr.org, accessed 14 Mar 2014.

The Home Secretary, when tackled about this, gave personal assurances that of course he entirely agreed that it was inconceivable that separation could slip in without being banned as discrimination. He said that his advice was that there was no loophole in the new clause, and that it was inconceivable that the Race Relations Board could take a different view. But if that is so, is it not possible to make it quite clear in the definition of discrimination that there is no loophole, especially, as we have been told so often that the purpose of this first clause is not only to make the law but also to enunciate a principle for all to understand? May I put the matter thus? When the Government spokesman replies, will he tell us whether it would be bad law or impossible law to use the words: "any distinction, exclusion, restriction or preference based on race, colour or national or ethnic origin"? My second criticism is about the powers of the Race Relations Board. Together with a good many other people, I regret that the Board are not given power, when they deal with a complaint, to compel the presence of witnesses and to require the production of papers and statistics. I think that the lack of those powers by the Board may mean two things. The first is that complaints may just cause irritation and be inconclusive if the information for dealing with them is not available. I think that it may also mean that matters might find themselves going to the courts when they need not otherwise do so just because recourse to the courts is the only way of getting the necessary information. I do not think that to give these powers to the Board turns them from being a conciliatory body into a judicial body. I should have judged, rather, that the lack of these powers weakens the Board's capacity to do the very thing that they are meant to do; namely, conciliation.

In this discussion, again and again dental language has been used: it has been discussed whether there are enough teeth or too many teeth in the Bill. I would see the matter rather as where [col.61] teeth are to be located. Courts always have teeth, and we do not want too many matters going to the courts for the teeth of the courts to bite on. I believe that in this particular matter, if the Race Relations Board have just these few more teeth they would do their conciliatory work better and the teeth of the courts would be less likely to be employed in a serious matter of where there was a complaint and yet the information was not available.

My third criticism concerns racial groups in employment. I feel a bit uneasy about this kind of situation. A well-qualified man applies for a job, but it has to be said to him: "Mr. X, we are sorry. You are the best qualified applicant for this post, but we cannot give it to you because the quota requires that we should give the post to another racial group." These are matters about which perhaps the Government may even now have, I will not say second but third or fourth thoughts. But for all these criticisms I welcome the Bill, believing that it will be a help in the great ongoing work of education in community relations.

My Lords, it is not only a matter of how in this country we can get the most just and peaceful arrangements for our own community. It is also a matter of what contribution this country can be making to what indeed is a world crisis. Race relations are a crisis in the world: whether in the world as a whole there is to be racial conflict or racial harmony. And what happens in any one country can have immense effects for good or for ill upon other countries – far more than we commonly realise. I believe that the help which this Bill gives to the building up of good community relations in this country will be a contribution which our country can make to racial harmony in the world at large.

Ramsey to Margaret Deanesly on Anglican-Methodist Unity, 15 July 1968

[Ramsey Papers vol.143, ff.10–13]

I am grateful to you for having written to me so fully about Anglican-Methodist unity because I have been perplexed by letters you have written to the papers from time to time, and being myself a Catholic Christian no less than you I am grieved that you should imply that I and others are advocating any kind of undermining of the Catholic faith.[4] I am very glad to have this opportunity of discussing the matter with you.

1. I must say first that I think that it is a great over-simplification historically to maintain a sharp contrast between on the one hand the Church of England as upholding the apostolic faith and apostolic commission and on the other hand the Free Churches upholding "God's illumination of each individual soul as the sovereign authority". This latter view is characteristic of a good deal of the liberal Protestantism from the time of Schleiermacher onwards but it is far different from the main theological trend of the Churches of the 1662 ejectment and of the Methodists in this country. That sort of ultra[-]theological liberalism is to be found in our own Church as well as in the Free Churches, and we have to judge religious bodies by their formularies and their best teachers and not by their aberrations. The Methodist[s] were affected by the kinds of liberalism which affected the Free Churches generally in the last century, but in my experience they

---

Deanesly was by this time Professor Emerita of the University of London, after a career in medieval history. She was amongst the most vocal opponents of the Anglican-Methodist unity scheme, in works such as Deanesly and Geoffrey G. Willis, *Anglican-Methodist Unity. Some considerations historical and liturgical* (London, 1968).

represent a pretty solid body of credal orthodoxy seen in the use of the Creeds in their services and their use of deeply orthodox hymns. The proposed basis of union includes the Creeds, and when people say they accept them we should trust them as we trust ourselves. May I give you a bit of personal experience from my own ecumenical contacts? I have often found myself taking part in theological discussion at conferences with a big variety of participants from many Christian traditions and I have usually found that English Methodists are ranged with ourselves and the Eastern Orthodox on the main theological issues as against Protestants of the Reformed tradition and also against the ultra[-] liberal Christianity of an American sort. I believe that union with the [f.11] Methodists would on the whole reinforce the more theologically conservative elements in our English Christianity, even perhaps the more unthinking kinds of conservatism.

2. As to belief concerning the ministry and the sacraments I think that it is within our own Church in Evangelical circles that the "lowest" views are to be found (if I may use such a loose expression), and in the Anglican-Methodist discussions it is not from the Methodists but from some of the Anglicans that the most disturbingly "Protestant" notions have emerged. The Methodists include a trend which is deeply sacramental, as is illustrated in Wesley's eucharistic hymns which I am sure you know, and there are also elements which are "low" about the sacraments and indeed quite vague – but that in fairness must be said of our own Church too. It was by the pressures of evangelistic fervour that the Methodists originally broke with the traditional episcopal order, but in this country the Methodists are keen to come back to it, as the present plan for unity shows. It is not true that their view of ordination at present is purely individualistic and interior, though they have as we do a very lay anti-clerical wing. They practise already a ministerial succession of a kind inasmuch as ordination is from the hands of ministers already ordained. The great thing is that they are in this scheme ready to adopt episcopal ordination in a succession shared with ourselves as their future invariable practice. Is that not a great thing? This scheme also pledges them to the disappearance of lay celebrations of the Eucharist, though it may take a little time for these to disappear completely – but that will be before the actual union of the Churches.

3. The Ordinal proposed for the use of both Churches in the scheme is, I am convinced, an Ordinal sound on Catholic principles. I think it is an improvement on our existing Ordinal in (a) its formulation of the office of the presbyter or priest in relation to the Word and the Sacraments, and (b) in its formulation of authority as being that of both Christ and the Church. I wonder if you have studied e.g. in recent articles in the *Tablet* the judgement of sympathetic Roman

Catholic theologians about this Ordinal. I beg you to study Roman Catholic opinions on it before hurrying to the conclusion that it is an unsound Ordinal.

[f.12] 4. Future ordinations under the plan being invariably episcopal the tricky problem is about the existing Methodist ministers. Frankly with entirely regular Orders ensured for the future it would not shock me to have something anomalous happening in the case of this one generation of ministers, and I believe that God could and would overrule such anomalies. Do you remember the period in Alexandria in, I think, the third century when the continuity of the ministry was for a time through presbyters and the strictly episcopal succession was interrupted, but the Church did not go to pieces through this irregularity if it was one? I wonder if you remember an article about this by Dr. Telfer in an early number of the *Journal of Ecclesiastical History*.[5] But the scheme provides something unprecedented to deal with the unprecedented situation of the two churches coming together. I think that something unprecedented is not so surprising or shocking for this reason. We know that our own Orders are completely regular and valid from a Catholic standpoint. We do not know the exact relative status and value in God's eyes of the existing Methodist ministry, i.e. it is impossible to equate it with what we call "the apostolic ministry" but it is equally impossible to say that it is just nothing as it is an orderly ministry used and blessed by God through the continuous life of a Christian community. I should therefore be entirely ready as a Bishop to take part in the laying on of hands on the Methodist ministers of this generation asking God to give to them what he knows they need in grace and authority in order that their ministry may be in status, office and authority identical with our own. It is in a sense agnostic but it is not a novel kind of agnosticism as I am frankly agnostic already about the standing of a Methodist minister. For my part I should be ready to receive the laying on of hands from Methodist ministers asking God to give me not indeed apostolic authority (because I believe I already possess that) but an added significance to my ministry which will come to it through the divided Churches being made one.

5. If the proposed act is "agnostic" I think it is so in a sense that is entirely right and wholesome, and for me it would certainly be honest. As to "ambiguity", I would not call the proceedings ambiguous as I believe they are [f.13] clear in what they affirm and clear in what they shrink from affirming. If, however, you are convinced that they are ambiguous, then I would say that there is a fair amount of ambiguity already in the historic position of our English Church.

---

5   Ramsey is most likely referring to W. Telfer, 'Episcopal succession in Egypt', *Journal of Ecclesiastical History* 3 (1952), 1–13.

There is ambiguity in the understanding of some of the doctrines included within the Elizabethan settlement, and there are phrases in the Prayer Book and the Articles which have notoriously lent themselves to alternative interpretations. I think it is unfair if we tax this scheme with ambiguity as if it was something we never practised as Anglicans. What matters is the uniformity and continuity of essential practice, and I believe that Anglican-Methodist unity will achieve this. I wonder how closely you have studied the Church of South India. There was much lamentation when it started about the decay of Catholic faith and practice that would ensue, but in fact in respect of things which were left indeterminate it has been shown that Catholic faith and practice win their way by their inherent truth and value.

I ask you therefore to consider with sympathy the considerations which I have set out, to weight them even though you may be inclined to be doubtful about them. You struck a personal note in your letter, and I will for once strike a personal note myself and say that I am rather hurt at the allegation by such a one as yourself that I am in some way playing with infidelity. Anyhow I do ask that before you again write in public in that sense you weight carefully what I have said in this letter and if need be come and have a talk with me.
With kindest regards,
Yours sincerely,

Sermon at the opening of the Lambeth Conference, Canterbury Cathedral, 25 July 1968

[Ramsey Papers vol.317, ff.178–85]

[f.178] Hebrews xii, 27–29. "This phrase 'yet once more' indicates the removal of what is shaken … . in order that what cannot be shaken may remain. Therefore let us be grateful for receiving a kingdom which cannot be shaken, and thus let us offer to God acceptable worship with reverence and awe, for our God is a consuming fire."

Today we have all come to Canterbury with hearts full of thankfulness for a place, a man and a history. This place means very much to us as we think of St. Augustine and his monks coming here from Thanet with the Cross borne before them, preaching the Gospel to king and people, and inaugurating a history which includes not only the English Church in its continuity through the centuries but a family of Churches of many countries and races which still see in Canterbury a symbol and a bond. Today we thank God for all this, and for the witness within Christendom of a tradition of ordered liberty and scriptural Christianity which the name Anglican has been used to describe. Thanks be to God for his great goodness.

No part of the early history is more interesting than the questions which St. Augustine sent to Pope Gregory about some of his perplexities and the answers which the Pope gave to him. One of the matters which bothered St. Augustine was the variety [f.179] of customs in different churches, and Pope Gregory told him that if he found anything in the Gallican or the Roman or in any other Church acceptable to Almighty God he should adopt it in England, because – and here comes the great principle – "things are not to be loved for the sake of places, but places for the sake of good things". "Non pro locis res, sed pro bonis rebus loca amanda sunt".[6] How suggestive, how far reaching, is this principle, how applicable to other issues and to other times. "Non pro locis res, sed pro bonis rebus loca". The local, the limited, the particular is to be cherished by Christian people not for any nostalgic attachment to it for its own sake, but always for the *real thing* which it represents and conveys, the thing which is catholic, essential, lasting. So our love for Canterbury melts into our love for Christ whose shrine Canterbury is; our love for what is Anglican is a little piece of our love for one Holy, Catholic, Apostolic Church; the love of any of us for our own heritage in country, culture, religious experience or theological insight, all subserves the supreme thing – the reality of God who draws men and women and children into union with himself in the fellowship of his Son. Not things for the sake of places, but places for the sake of good things: let that be a guiding principle, and the good things which concern us are what the apostolic writer calls the things which are not shaken.

[f.180] Today the words of the Epistle to the Hebrews come home to us, in cadences which seem to roll like thunder. Follow the thought of this tremendous passage. The voice of God shook the earth when the divine law was given on Mount Sinai, a divine law which, reinterpreted by our Lord, still stands and must be proclaimed. Then, in the new covenant, the voice of God shakes heaven as well as earth, since the Incarnation at Bethlehem and the resurrection from the tomb belong to both earth and heaven. Today the earth is being shaken, many things are cracking, melting, disappearing; and it is for us who are Christians to distinguish the things which are shaken and to receive gratefully a kingdom which is not shaken, the kingdom of our crucified Lord. Within this kingdom, the writer goes on, we offer to God the worship he can accept – but as we do so

---

6   The exchange is related in Bede's *Ecclesiastical history of the English people*, chapter 27.

we are never in cosy security, we have awe in our hearts, for we are near to our God, and our God is blazing fire.

Today the earth is being shaken, and there can be few or none who do not feel the shaking: the rapid onrush of the age of technology with the new secularity which comes with it, the terrible contrast between the world of affluence and the world of hunger, the explosions of racial conflict, the amassing of destructive weapons, the persistence of war and killing. And Man, they say, has come of age. Indeed he has, in the height [f.181] of the powers the Creator gave him, in the fulfilment of the Psalmist's words "thou has put all things under his feet"[7] but without, alas, Man learning to say with the Psalmist "O Lord, our Governor, how excellent is thy name".[8] That is the nature of Man's triumph, and Man's utter frustration.

Amidst a shaken earth we who are Christians receive a kingdom which cannot be shaken, and are called so to enjoy it that others are led to find it and receive it with us. How is God today calling us to do this? God calls us to faith, to ministry, to unity.

Faith. The faith to which we are called will always be folly and scandal to the world, it cannot be in the usual sense of the word popular; it is a supernatural faith and it cannot adapt itself to every passing fashion of human thought. But it will be a faith alert to distinguish what is shaken and is meant to go, and what is not shaken and is meant to remain. When men today tell us that they revere Jesus but find God or theism without meaning, it sometimes is that the image of God that we as Christians in our practice present it is the image of a God of religious concerns but not of compassion for all human life, and it is just not recognisable as the God and Father of Jesus Christ. So too when men reject theism it sometimes means that they cannot accept in this [f.182] shaken world any easy, facile assumption that the universe has a plan, a centre, a purpose. It is for us Christians to be sure that our faith is no facile assumption but a costly conviction that in Christ crucified and risen, in suffering and victorious love and in no other way, there is a plan, a centre, a purpose. In dying to love, in losing life so as to find it – there is the place where divine sovereignty is found and theism has meaning and vindication. The Bishops who will lead our thinking about faith at this Lambeth Conference will help us to see that faith means standing near to the Cross in the heart of the contemporary world, and not only standing but acting. Our faith will be tested in our actions, not least in our actions concerning

---

[7]   Psalm 8:6.
[8]   Psalm 8:9.

peace, concerning race, concerning poverty. Faith is a costly certainty, but no easy security as our God is blazing fire.

Ministry. The ministry to which we are called is described in our text. It is "to offer to God acceptable worship". We know that the only worship which God accepts is the expression of lives which reflect God's own righteousness and compassion. Yet amidst all the energies of serving humanity which so rightly concern Christian people let there be a deep revival of the priestly spirit, the spirit of loving God for God's own sake who made us for himself. The [f.183] Bishops who will lead our thinking about ministry will help us to recapture this priestly spirit while they show the way to new forms of practical service in every community where Christian people are. That service must not only inspire individuals, it must go on to affect states and nations in their policies, rich and poor, developed and undeveloped, one towards another.

Unity. Here Christendom is feeling the first tremors of a shaking which would have seemed incredible a few years back. What has been shaken? Much of the old complacency, much of the old contentment with our divided condition, much of the sheer ignorance of one another in theology and practice, and above all much of the self-consciousness which gave absurdity to the dealings of Christians with Christians. But the shaking has gone deeper still. Christendom has begun to learn that unity comes not by combining this Church with that Church much as they are now, but by the radical altering of Churches in reformation and renewal. It is here that the Vatican Council has had influence far beyond the boundaries of the Roman Catholic Church. We all are stirred to ask God to show us what are things rightly shaken and the things not shaken which must remain.

As Anglicans we ask ourselves: "Quo tendimus?"[9] This Lambeth Conference faces big questions about our relations [f.184] with one another as a world-wide Anglican family and about our role within a Christendom which is being called to unity in the truth. Can we do better than take to heart and apply to our tasks the counsel which Pope Gregory gave to St. Augustine "non pro locis res, sed loca pro bonis rebus". We shall love our own Anglican family not as something ultimate but because in it and through it we and others have our place in the one Church of Christ. The former is a lovely special loyalty: the latter is the Church against which our Lord predicted that the gates of death would not prevail. Now, as the work of unity advances there will come into existence United Churches not describably Anglican but in communion with us and sharing with us what we hold to be the unshaken essence of Catholicity. What then of the

---

[9] This may be translated as 'To what do we aspire?'

future boundaries of our Anglican Communion? We shall face that question without fear, without anxiety, because of our faith in the things which are not shaken. Perhaps the Anglican role in Christendom may come to be less like a separate encampment and more like a colour in the spectrum of a rainbow, a colour bright and unselfconscious.

"See that you do not refuse him who speaks." The writer to the Hebrews has his urgent message for us, telling us of the removal of what is shaken in order that what is not shaken [f.185] may remain. Therefore let us be grateful in receiving a kingdom which cannot be shaken. It is the kingdom of Christ crucified, our king who was crowned with thorns. And his Cross is the secret of our faith, the heart of our ministry and the source of our unity as we live not to ourselves but to one another and to him. Each of us at this time will want to say from his heart: –

> Thanks be to thee, O Lord Jesus Christ
> For all the benefits thou hast won for me,
> For all the pains and insults thou hast borne for me.
> O most merciful redeemer, friend and brother,
> May I know thee more clearly,
> Love thee more dearly,
> And follow thee more nearly.[10]

Speech in the House of Lords on Reform of the House

[House of Lords Debates, 5th series, 21 Nov 1968, vol.297, cols.1040–45.]

My Lords, listening to the [col.1041] debate for many hours, and conscientiously reading the speeches made at hours when I was not present, I have found myself reminded of the words of an old hymn, a hymn not very often sung nowadays, which contains the lines: "There is room for fresh creations / In that upper home of bliss".[11] Without arrogating to ourselves the claim that we are a "home of bliss", we have been spending three days discussing how fresh creations can best be made and how undesirable modes of creation may be eliminated. Listening to this debate has for me confirmed my own initial suspicions. They are three suspicions: first, that reform along the lines of an elected Chamber is

---

[10]   A prayer of St Richard of Chichester.
[11]   From the hymn beginning 'There's a wideness in God's mercy', by F.W. Faber (1814–63).

no road; second, that a nominated Chamber, despite all the dangers attaching to nomination, is the best way; and, third, that the two-tier system proposed does give a chance of conserving some of the present values of the House of Lords as a Chamber and of carrying those values over into the new reformed régime.

First as to the possibilities of reform along the lines of an elected Chamber. I believe that to look that way is really to ask for the moon and that there is no possibility of agreement as to how an elected Chamber would be elected, even if it were true that an elected Chamber or Senate were the desirable course. I believe that to dream of an elected Chamber is probably to postpone the reform of our House indefinitely.

Second, I think that facts adduced during this debate have made it clear that the proposals of the White Paper would not involve any considerable increase in patronage and would, indeed, introduce certain restraints and restrictions on patronage. That being so, I believe that the bogey of enlarged patronage of the Prime Minister ought not to deter us from looking favourably at these proposals. But in the discussions that we have had it is very clear that the Cross-Bench Members of the House, the primarily non-political Members of the House, are going to have an important role, not as politicians in disguise but as persons representing many aspects of skill and knowledge of value to the country.

As Her Majesty's Government regard this debate as an opportunity for the collecting of opinions and advice, it [col.1042] might be worth while saying that the Prime Minister, or any Prime Minister, is likely to need a good deal of advice, possibly of advice that he does not normally get, in the appointment of Cross-Bench and non-political Peers. A Prime Minister inevitably knows a great deal about politicians and who are good politicians to pick; but a Prime Minister does not necessarily know about the qualifications of scientists, men of letters, educationalists, industrialists or those in many, many walks of life whose wisdom is valuable to us already and is going to be still more valuable in a reformed Chamber. The modes of advice collected by the Prime Minister in that field seem to me to need very important consideration.

Thirdly, I come to the matter of two tiers. I think it has been unfair to liken the proposed two tiers to two classes, a first class and a second class, because in considering the categories of Members of our House we have to consider the categories of our debates. This House, as at present constituted, has influence and authority through the variety of the character of debate which it conducts. There are the legislative debates which commonly include a good deal of voting; there are also the debates on big social issues and issues of public concern, commonly on a Wednesday, which generally include no voting at all. We have been told that if we were indiscreet enough to press for a vote on a Wednesday debate on a Motion for Papers nobody would know in the issue what Papers would need to be moved from where to where in fulfilment of the vote that was conducted.

It seems to me important that the influence of this House, both as a legislative Chamber and as a Chamber concerned with debates on big issues – non-voting debates, but nevertheless very authoritative – should be carried into a reformed Chamber. It seems that the two-tier system proposed will facilitate that; and in that way it will be a good thing. Furthermore, I believe that the two-tier proposals will facilitate something about which strong desires have been expressed again and again in this debate; namely, the recruiting to the House of Lords of a good many younger Members. Many of us feel that to be of the very first importance. If a young man is deeply politically inclined, his [col.1043] thoughts are likely to go first towards another place. If a young man is not deeply politically inclined – and, indeed, if he is – he is likely to be heavily employed earning his living, and the possibility of his qualifying to be a voting Member by a one-third attendance is rather precarious. Therefore I believe that the two-tier proposal will enable, or could enable, a good many more younger Members to be brought into this House for its great good and with the advantage to all of us of listening to younger Members, able to speak with knowledge and authority but possibly unable to give enough time to qualify as voters without jeopardy to their professions and careers.

Again, as the purpose of this debate is not only to make a decision but also to enable the Prime Minister to collect advice, let Her Majesty's Ministers take note of the advice given a good many times in this debate about the desire to see younger Members in this Chamber. It is no use saying that the two-tier system will facilitate that unless the powers-that-be act upon it and see that that is so. On those three counts, my Lords – dismissing the possibility of an elected Chamber as asking for the moon; seeing on balance the disadvantages of an elected Chamber and also seeing the advantages of the two-tier proposal – I greatly hope that the White Paper will be approved and that legislation will follow which I believe will give us a more effective and more authoritative House of Lords than we have at present.

The House will forgive me for adding a few words about the position of Bishops in your Lordships' House. My words need only be very few, because my right reverend friend the Bishop of Chester[12] dealt with that subject very fully in his speech on the first day of the debate. I want to say how greatly I appreciate the consideration given to the Bishops' Bench by the members of the Inter-Party Conference in considering our role within the House of Lords; the great

---

[12] Gerald Ellison had been Bishop of Chester since 1955.

sympathy and understanding with which they listened to our views and also their understanding of our position as Spiritual Peers within your Lordships' House. In the course of the debate the preoccupation with the central issues has been so large that only a few references have been made to the role of the [col.1044] Bishops within a reformed Chamber. The noble Earl, Lord Iddesleigh, made some kind remarks about the Episcopal Bench. I want to thank him for those remarks which I appreciate greatly, coming as they did from a distinguished layman of a Church other than my own.

The noble Lord, Lord Reith – if we may round a little in the ecclesiastical spectrum – in a very brief intervention, asked why should not the Established Church of Scotland be represented in a reformed Chamber. I do not spy the noble Lord, Lord Reith, in his usual place, but let me say to my noble friend and neighbour and tenant that his remarks pose a dilemma. If representation of the Church of Scotland means ministers of the Church of Scotland in virtue of their ministerial office having a seat in the House of Lords, that may raise awkward questions for him, concerning the mode of nomination of those ministers to their office. On the other hand, if he desires, not the representation of the Church of Scotland through Ministers holding positions *ex officio* but through the exercise of nomination to Life Peerages, then I would say that I most heartily welcome the nomination to Life Peerages of members of other Churches than mine – of the Church of Scotland and of Churches in England as well – to play their part in this House.

This, my Lords, leads me to the remarks made by the noble Lord, Lord Sorensen. He said the most kind and appreciative things about us and our performance, but then went on to ask, "But why must we have these Bishops in our House at all?" My Lords, I am ready to discuss why we have these Bishops in our House at all if, at the same time, we can discuss such matters as the nomination of Bishops to their Sees by the Crown; the role of Parliament in relation to Church legislation and the whole complex of balanced factors that constitute our Church and State relationship. I should be very glad indeed to discuss that matter at any time, and it is my belief that considerable changes in the form of Church and State relationship are desirable. But it is obviously impossible to deal with those matters in the context of these proposals concerning the reform of the House of Lords.

In that context it is only reasonable that in a reformed House diminished in [col.1045] number, the number of Bishops who are Members should be diminished. But I will end by saying that, diminished in number, whether as speakers or as voters, we shall still want, within the Constitution, to go on giving our service to the House, sharing that desire, I believe, with many noble Lords;

and that we shall all give our service to the House with greater effectiveness within the general pattern of reform that the White Paper has set out.

1969

Ramsey to David L. Edwards on Anglican-Methodist Unity, 20 February 1969

[Ramsey Papers vol. 165, ff.185–86]

My dear David

I am glad to hear that the Chapter are fixing your Collation and Installation to be on Saturday, 26th April when you will be coming to Canterbury in any case.[1] I am very sorry indeed that I shall not able to be there as we are going to be kept in London for a function on that Saturday afternoon, but as we shall be in Canterbury for the rest of the weekend I greatly hope there will be a chance of seeing you during your visit. Just now we are about to set off on a visit to the West Indies for a month.

You asked me for some reflections about the Anglican-Methodist proposals. I have been saddened by the unimaginative and negative attitude into which many of our fellow churchmen have fallen, although I am not without hope that in spite of everything there may be a rallying to good sense which will enable the decision to come right. If it does not come right this time my strong inclination is to renew the same proposals say a couple of years hence and to stick to it.

The opposition involves, I think, a blindness on the part of certain people to the possibility of gaining the very things which they most care about. The Anglo-Catholics, or rather the less understanding of them because the more understanding of them significantly favour the proposals, are fearful of losing the things which they cherish. I believe that these proposals are perhaps the last chance of a unity scheme towards the Free Churches which conserves in essence the very things which the Catholic movement has borne witness to. To reject the proposals is, I think, to throw that away and to expose ourselves to the trend of inter-communion quite unrelated to historic order, i.e. the very things which the Anglo-Catholics most dislike. At the same time the Conservative Evangelicals are ready to throw away the prospect of being in full communion

---

[1]   A prolific author and former editor of the SCM Press, Edwards was at this time Dean of King's College, Cambridge. He was about to join the college of Six Preachers at Canterbury.

with their Methodist cousins in the Gospel through dislike of tolerating within the proposals a view of episcopacy and priesthood other than their own. They can only have the full communion with the [f.186] Methodists as a Church if they are ready to do it in a way which carries their fellow churchmen with them, and this they will not stomach. Hence the double tragedy of two sections of our Church being ready to throw away the things which they most care about through fear of losing their theological tidiness.

That is how I see the matter, though besides those whom I have mentioned there is a large number of those who are purely conservative and cannot face change or disturbance. But if I am allowed to have any particular hope in connection with what you wrote it is that you will help some of the two sections on the "wings" to see how greatly they may be damaging the very things they care about.

I look forward to seeing you and hearing more about your doings.

With very best wishes,

Yours ever,

Ramsey's Foreword to a Pamphlet Explaining the Changes Wrought by the Advent of General Synod[2]

[Ramsey Papers vol.171, ff.127–8]

What difference will the new forms of Church government make to all of us who are members of the Church of England? And what difference can we make to the effectiveness of their working? This booklet helps to answer these questions, and I hope therefore that it will be widely read.

It will be a great gain that the chief decisions on behalf of the whole Church will be made by bishops, clergy and laity sitting and discussing *together* in a national Synod. But the quality of the Synod's work will owe much to the touch which its members have with the thinking and the work of the Church in diocese and parish.

It will also be a great gain that in place of Diocesan Conferences where there is much speaking but little power of decision there will be in each diocese a Synod with an effective share in the making of all important policies. But the work of the Synod will be at its best if it is supported by Ruri-decanal bodies in which there is a lively sharing of clergy and laity in the mission of the Church.

---

2   This edition is made from a final draft typescript, dated May 1969.

In all these ways there will be a new opportunity for *partnership* in the life of our Church. "Synodical Government" [f.128] is designed to be the expression in constitutional forms of the spirit of partnership in every portion of the Church's activity, in its worship, its evangelism and its service of God and mankind. As we take our part in these changes in Church government we shall pray that the Holy Spirit will help us to use them as opportunities to be more than ever "members of one another" in our obedience to Christ as the Lord of the Church.

Ramsey to Eric Kemp[3] on the Anglican-Methodist Reunion Scheme, 11 July 1969

[Ramsey Papers vol.166, ff.190–91]

Thank you for your kind letter and for the gift of the book which I am delighted to have. Thank you also for your helpful remarks about the Anglican-Methodist debacle.

It is certainly true that there was a deterioration in attitudes within our Church between 1966 and 1969. I think this was helped a bit by the character of the final report which included far too much in the way of theological exposition which proved vulnerable to one side or the other. But I do not think that the report itself was the cause of the deterioration. I see the cause rather in the realm of the psychology of fear of change deepening and becoming obsessive and making use of various phenomena as a means for excusing itself, e.g. certain defects in the report, the myth that there was a better alternative, the myth that Rome was antagonistic, and for some the excuse that as Lord Fisher disliked the proposals there must be something fishy about them. When once the psychology of fear became really obsessive it was, I think, beyond the power of argument to help the situation. Now, however, the fact of the Methodist acceptance at the same moment as our own rejection has given a big shock, and I think that the shock may already be beginning to have its effects upon people's attitudes.

I am sure it is quite impossible now for our Church to put something different up to the Methodists or to ask the Methodists for any reconsideration of details, even if we agreed about what we wanted in such respect. Now that they have said "yes" and we have said "no" the leadership and initiative are theirs

---

[3] One of the Church of England's leading experts on canon law, Eric Waldram Kemp had been chaplain and fellow of Exeter College, Oxford since 1946. In 1969 he became Dean of Worcester.

and it is for us either to continue to say "no" or have another try at saying "yes".
It is hard at the moment to foresee when the best moment for this attempt will
come. Ordinarily one would have said "after the General Synod is set up", but it
may be that the pressure of new opinion in the dioceses will start indicating that
the propitious [f.191] moment may be sooner, and it may be right to try again
in the life of the present Convocations. The one thing I feel quite clear about is
that it is both morally impossible and quite impracticable to start talking about
modifying the proposals.

The Bishops will need as soon as possible to give some lead in the purely
pastoral sphere about the problems which are going to be pressing hard in
dioceses and parishes where things have already gone very far in Anglican-
Methodist co-operation. When this is done it will, I think, be see that the
problem of behaviour at the parochial level cannot be solved apart from an act by
the Churches which will reconcile the ministries and establish full communion.

Those are only my first thoughts.

Yours ever,

Speech at Dinner on the Commemoration of Guru Nanak, 6 November 1969

[Ramsey Papers, vol.169, ff.243–44]

Five hundred years ago the Wars of the Roses were being fought in England,
and barons and knights were killing one another on one battlefield after
another. At the same time far away in the Punjab Guru Nanak was teaching
his contemporaries. What was he teaching them? There is one God, present
everywhere, beyond us, within us, utterly loving.

> Wherefore the Lord in the forests you seek?
> All-pervading and purest light is he.
> Know ye, the Lord ever dwells in thee,
> As fragrance in the flower sweet,
> As image clear in mirror neat,
> So the Lord ever dwells in thee.
> A great truth the Guru has revealed.

Anywhere, everywhere men and women can commune with the living God
and have his peace in their lives. Therefore brotherhood is the true way of life,

unselfish brotherhood. Guru Nanak repudiated all distinctions of caste, and he repudiated the subjection of women. He spoke five hundred years ago, and he speaks for today. We are honouring a great teacher of mankind.

[f.244] Now, I am a Christian, and you know that means I believe Jesus Christ to be the only perfect, complete revelation of God. No Christian can surrender the uniqueness of Jesus Christ. But we Christians believe that the light lightens every man, and it is fitting for us to honour in sincerity Guru Nanak and to revere the Sikh people. Would that we all put into practice the love and the brotherhood which Guru Nanak taught. Would that we all realised the nearness of God as he and his followers did, and had the bravery which Sikh people have had through the ages, ready to give their lives for their faith, and more than once in history to give their lives alongside the lives of Christians of this and other countries in the cause of freedom.

Today no country, no race, no culture can live to itself or by itself. Sikh people are found in many countries far beyond the Punjab. They are found in this country, with their hard work, their courage and their ideals which go back five hundred years. All of us in this country who care for sound community relations, based on mutual respect and understanding, will salute the Sikhs with honour as they commemorate their founder whose words all humanity would be the better for hearing and putting into practice.

1971

Speech in the House of Lords on Northern Ireland

[House of Lords Debates, 5th series, 22 September 1971, vol. 324, cols.28–30]

My Lords, I share what I believe is the general view, that it was right for your Lordships' House to be recalled for this debate, and there seems already to be considerable hope that the debate will demonstrate one thing; namely, the immense desire that Ireland should not become a matter of conflict between the political Parties in this country. The situation is tragic enough, and I believe that we are all anxious to do the utmost we can to avoid the additional tragedy of acute political conflict over Northern Ireland in this country. But is it really necessary that there should be political conflict or even thought of it? Is there not considerable agreement in a policy that might be described as a triad of three co-equal propositions? First. that Northern Ireland remains a part of the United Kingdom; secondly, that considerable reforms should be made concerning the role of minorities in Northern Ireland – and some of the reforms are sadly overdue; and, thirdly, that terrible violence must be made to cease. I should be very surprised if at the end of your Lordships' debate there were not pretty general assent to the necessity for accepting those three propositions, all forming part of a single policy: and I believe that all citizens can rightly rally behind a policy on those lines.

Concerning internment, of course it utterly offends my own liberal instincts. Yet I believe that internment was unavoidable. When there is in a country an organisation, existing partly in that country and partly elsewhere, persisting, and boasting that it persists, in killing soldiers and civilians, it is hard to see what alternative there could be – though I share the general hope that, as soon as may be, internment may cease. It goes without saying that I share in the feeling of being not only moved, but very moved indeed, in admiration for the soldiers in the role which they are bearing.

I want now, my Lords, to say a few words about some factors which make for hope, and those factors have to do with religion. It is sometimes assumed that because the words "Catholic" and "Protestant" are so often used in this context the conflict is about religion. I believe the noble Lord, Lord Gladwyn, was right in saying that it is not really [col.29] a conflict about religion. It is about religion when religion gets entangled with a great many other things as well: because we have to distinguish between what I would call real religion, on the one hand, and bigotry, on the other. I would briefly put the distinction thus. Real religion is a condition of faith however great the adversities to faith may be; a condition of faith which results in compassion, humility and other lovely qualities. Bigotry, on the other hand, is religion, which may be ardent and sincere, entangled with other things, and particularly with fear for the security of one's own group, whether religious, social or political; and, further, the entanglement with fear about those things easily goes with the banging of the drums and historical memories, so that people can actually be living as if Oliver Cromwell, William of Orange and Guy Fawkes were their contemporaries with whom they were in daily conversation.

This tragic entanglement of religion with bigotry is no monopoly of Ireland in human history. It has existed considerably in other parts of the world. It has existed at different times and in different degrees in our own country. But the striking phenomenon of our time is the way in which the wave of recovery of real religion, in the spirit of fellowship and brotherhood, is undermining the old forces of bigotry. Recently, one small symbol of it happened in this country when an Archbishop of Canterbury was welcomed into the pulpit of Westminster Cathedral, and a Cardinal Archbishop was welcomed into the pulpit of St. Paul's. That would not have happened decades or so ago. And there are parts of Ireland where that kind of thing is already beginning to happen.

Now, to-day in Ireland, alongside the horrible things of which we hear daily on the radio and see on television, there are things of a different sort happening. There are places in Northern Ireland where Protestants and Catholics are joining quietly in one another's churches, praying together for reconciliation. There are Catholic priests and Protestant ministers taking part in such proceedings. It might not help them if I were to give names and places at this time; but this activity goes on quietly. Such things do happen. Much publicity was given to the strong condemnation of violence made by Cardinal Conway[1] and his [col.30] colleagues of the Roman Catholic hierarchy. Less publicity was given to the strong plea by my fellow Anglican Primate, the Archbishop of Armagh,[2] and his

---

[1]   William Conway (1913–77) was the Roman Catholic Archbishop of Armagh, Cardinal, and Primate of all Ireland.
[2]   George Simms (1910–91).

colleagues urging Protestants not to condemn Catholics as such for the horrible violence that is taking place.

Let me mention an instance of a hopeful trend which moved me more than anything else. The question of schools in Northern Ireland is bound to have a deep place in any settlement of a constructive kind. My illustration is not exactly about schools, but is about something in a similar context. The North of Ireland Ecumenical Youth Service arranges summer camps where boys from different schools, Protestant and Catholic, spend several weeks together. They play together, discuss together, and plan acts of social service together. Some such camps have been held in Northern Ireland even during these months of horrible tension. How much better, indeed, for boys and girls to grow up learning to enjoy the friendship of boys and girls of the other sort, rather than learning to take part in marches and counter-marches and to live and think in the seventeenth century! If developments of that kind were to grow, is it too much to hope that there might be a generation of boys and girls who know the word "orange" only as the name of a delectable fruit which no part of the British Isles is capable of producing?

I mention these signs that forces of hope in the name of religion are present in Ireland because things which are small in one decade often become very much larger in the next, and if only there can be a diminution of the present terrible crescendo of violence and political impasse these forces of moderation in the sphere of religion and elsewhere may have a chance of growing. So, my Lords, I am sure that Christian people everywhere at this time pray fervently that the coming discussions of the Prime Ministers will have some success, and that there may be a chance at once for the ending of loathsome violence and for a real change in the role of minorities in Northern Ireland.

1972

Address in Westminster Cathedral, 14 March 1972, on Northern Ireland

[Ramsey Papers, vol.319, ff.63–65]

Friday is St. Patrick's Day. On that day thousands of Christian people in every part of the world will be remembering Ireland's saint and missionary. Let them not forget, let none of us forget, how it was that St. Patrick won people throughout Ireland, far and wide, to Christ and to Christian faith. What was it in his character which marked and gave him such power? History leaves us in no doubt. Patrick was a forgiving man, a man of reconciliation. As a youth he had been kidnapped and held in Ireland as a slave, and for some years he had suffered terribly. In the course of those years he became a Christian; and later, living on the continent, he was called to be a missionary. He goes back to the people who had ill-used him. He will care for them, win them, serve them in Christ's name. "Who compelled me?" he says, "I am a slave to Christ for the unspeakable glory of the eternal life that is in Christ our Lord". A man of forgiveness, a reconciler: can we doubt that his prayers are with us tonight, as we pray for the miracle of reconciliation. Miracle? Yes, that is what Christianity is about, miracle in human relationships.

It is Christianity which brings us all here tonight. We have come here because we are all Christians. Many here are Roman Catholics, many are Anglicans, many are Free Churchmen. And we all acknowledge Jesus Christ as our divine Lord, our saviour: that is what brings us together, Christians and therefore brothers.

Here tonight we all have on our hearts Northern Ireland. We pray for it, and that means we have it on our hearts in God's presence. As always in Christian prayer we begin with God. We recall God's greatness, God's integrity, God's righteousness, God's compassion for all our human sin and folly, God's power of reconciliation seen on the hill of Calvary, seen in the lives of many of his servants, seen in St. Patrick's mighty work. And then we lift up to God those who need him: those who share in government, [f.64] in Westminster, in Stormont, in Dublin, that they may have wisdom beyond their wisdom, courage beyond their courage; the soldiers, that they may be upheld amidst unspeakable strains in their duty; those in sorrow and bereavement, that they may have comfort; those who in any place are blind and cruel, that they may have their eyes opened; those in the Churches and their leaders who strive for reconciliation, that their loyalty may be only to Christ himself: "Christ in quiet, Christ in danger; Christ in mouth of friend and stranger."[1]

Our prayers are full of grief. Yet we can have thankfulness in our hearts. Why thankfulness? Because there are those who long for peace and try to serve it, those who put faith in Christ before the fears bequeathed by history and are striving for reconciliation. They are there: often little reported, little advertised, they are there. There are Catholics and Protestants who meet to pray together, there are Catholics and Protestants who together run schemes to rebuild homes which have been destroyed, there are Catholics and Protestants who together plan aid for those in distress. These things do happen, and when they happen a shaft of light pierces through the gloom of grief. Today's small things may be tomorrow's miracles, when the fears of centuries yield to a vision of Christ and of humanity: "Christ in mouth of friend and stranger."

Such is our prayer tonight, and such will be many prayers on St. Patrick's festival. This is how Patrick himself prayed during his days of captivity and loneliness. Listen to him:

> Now after I came to Ireland, tending the swine was my daily occupation, and constantly I used to pray in the daytime. Love of God and fear of him increased more and more, and faith grew and the spirit was moved in me. There the Lord opened my understanding that even though late I might call my faults to remembrance and that I might turn to the Lord my God.[2]

Let that be our prayer, that fearing God and submitting our own lives to him we may become both in our actions and in our prayers channels of his tremendous power in the affairs of men.

---

[1] Words from the hymn known as 'St Patrick's Breastplate', translated by Mrs C.F. Alexander. It was included in the *English Hymnal*, first published in 1906. The text quoted here is the conclusion of the eighth and final verse, later omitted from the *New English Hymnal* of 1986.

[2] Words from the *Confessio* of St Patrick.

I bind unto myself today
the power of God to hold and lead,
His eye to watch, his might to stay,
His ear to hearken to my need;
The wisdom of my God to teach,
His hand to guide, his shield to ward,
The word of God to give me speech,
the heavenly host to be my guard.[3]

[f.65] So, trying to submit our own selves to God's will for us, we pray that the light of his wisdom may bring light into the dark scenes of the world, as we bind unto ourselves today the strong name of the Triune God, Father, Son and Holy Spirit, to whom be praise and glory from saints in heaven and sinners on earth now and ever.

---

[3]   'St Patrick's Breastplate'.

1974

Farewell Sermon, Canterbury Cathedral, 2 November 1974[1]

[Ramsey Papers, vol. 320, ff.287–89]

[f.287] Genesis 28:12. He dreamed, and there was a ladder set up on earth, and the top of it reached to heaven, and the angels of God ascended and descended upon it.

Poor Jacob, it was only a dream; but at a time of loneliness and distress it gave him the assurance that heaven was near, and this assurance must have meant much to him in the tumultuous years that followed. We who are Christians in the new covenant know a ladder between earth and heaven which is no dream, but fact and reality. We remember Our Lord's conversation with Nathanael. Nathanael was astonished that Our Lord knew him under the fig tree, and he became a disciple.[2] But our Lord at once promised that he would see greater things and there would be a ladder between earth and heaven which would be the Son of Man himself, with the angels ascending and descending upon it.

How near Our Lord was to heaven throughout his life on earth, for heaven is not far away, heaven is where God is and where love is perfect. How near Jesus always was to the heavenly Father, near in close communion day by day, near in adoration, near in exultant thanksgiving, near in his total obedience; and once on the Mount of Transfiguration three apostles saw him in heaven's own glory. Yes, the top reached to heaven. But, because love is one and indivisible, Our Lord was at every moment "down to earth": we see him the friend of publicans and sinners, we see him as one who consorts with the outcasts of society, as one who bears our sorrows and sins. He teaches, he heals, he feeds the hungry, he is one with all of us. And in the Garden of Gethsemane he shares in man's fear of death, and on Calvary he is deep in the darkness of a world darkened and tormented by sin and tragedy. On this ladder the angels were coming up and down.

Now Christ was and is the ladder, divine and human, in order that with him and through him men and women might become parts of it, themselves rungs

---

[1]   This sermon was delivered again three days later in Westminster Abbey.
[2]   John 1:45–49.

in a ladder which is Christ. Such are the saints. On All Saints Day last Friday we were commemorating the great company of the saints of every century; and on the coming Friday we shall commemorate the saints, martyrs, and doctors of the Church in this country. Among the martyrs there were several who sat in St. Augustine's throne, and while these were men as down to earth as ever men could be, immersed in [f.288] the affairs of a nation as well as a Church, they were also men who witnessed that "we have here no continuing city."[3] But the company of the saints includes men and women of many different kinds. All of them were down to earth: down to earth in their awareness of their own sins, down to earth in the humility which asks for God's forgiveness, down to earth in their caring for their fellows and bearing their troubles – yet all the while with a heavenly serenity and joy which bring peace and healing. There is a ladder, and the top reaches to heaven.

It is not however only the saints whom we commemorate who are rungs in the ladder which is Christ. All of us who are Christians have the same calling. It is for us, as parts of Christ's ladder, to help people to come a bit nearer to heaven and to help the good things of heaven to come down into the world for its healing. The catholic faith possesses the rhythm of this double movement, at once other-worldly and this-worldly, at once beyond and here. It is hard for us Christians to grasp both aspects of this. It is possible for us to be caught upwards into a rather unreal realm of piety which misses some of the hard realities of Christian responsibility. It is no less possible for us to be caught into a kind of Christian social activism which forgets the top of the ladder. The Church in the past decade and more has seen much of the tensions between these one-sided graspings of the truth. May Christ teach us to be faithful to the indivisible reality of which Jacob dreamed and of which Christ spoke to Nathanael. A ladder of love which can pierce deep into our world is a ladder whose top reaches heaven.

This is for me a moment of goodbye and thank you. As I take leave of the office which has been mine for the past thirteen years I thank you, my fellow Christians of many Churches, who have all been in different ways my fellow workers. Your comradeship and love and generosity have for me made an impossible task possible, and a burdensome task happy. We thank God together for what we have shared together as we have tried to serve Christ. And we thank God that in years when the world has been darkened by wrong and tragedy there have in every country been Christians who have witnessed to God's righteousness with joy and courage; and we thank God that in striking ways the unity of Christians has seen new realisations.

---

3   Hebrews 13:14: 'For here have we no continuing city, but we seek one to come.'

[f.289] But when Christians say goodbye to one another they do so always as those who belong to the family of the communion of saints, that is our family, that is our home – a family and a home which knows no severances. We are always in the mansions of our one Father's house. The Eucharist in which we are sharing this evening is itself Christ's ladder. In truth we are now about to join in the worship of heaven, for it is the risen Jesus, the bread of heaven, on whom we shall be feeding. But as love is one and indivisible it is no less true that we meet here Christ Crucified, the Christ who suffers in our world of division and cruelty and frustration. And he feeds us so as to go out and find him in our fellows, to meet him there and to seek him there. And sometimes when the darkness seems to be very dark, and the pain and struggle of the Christian life seem most intense, we rejoice because there is a ladder and the top of it reaches to heaven.

Speech in the House of Lords, moving the Church of England (Worship and Doctrine) Measure 1974

[House of Lords Debates, 5th series, 14 November 1974, vol. 354, cols 867–74]

My Lords, this is, I believe, the most important Church Measure which has been presented to Parliament for a good many years. It passed the Church's General Synod in February of this year, and it was then hoped that the Measure would come before Parliament before Easter, but two General Elections and other factors have delayed the possibility of its introduction until to-day, which is the last day before my own retirement from Office.

First, let me mention that this Measure comes with overwhelming support in the Church's General Synod. The vote in favour was 340, and the vote against numbered only eight of the clerical members and two of the lay members. I see that your Lordships have been circularised with a Statement that the Synod fails to represent the laity because it is elected by 36,000 people, while there are nearly 2 million people entered on parish rolls. But the 36,000 electors are themselves members of Deanery Synods who are themselves elected by the parish meetings. This procedure ensures that important issues for the Church are discussed in the deaneries as well as the dioceses throughout the country, so that lay discussion, linked with lay representation, [col.868] exists at all these levels. I believe it is impossible to maintain with any justice that the lay support for this Measure is not very strong indeed. There was indeed only one Diocesan Synod which did not declare its support for these proposals in one form or another, and that was because it desired more radical proposals.

My Lords, let me first say what this Measure is not. It is necessary to say what it is not. It is not a Measure for the disestablishment of the Church of England, nor a step towards separating the Church of England from the Crown. I would claim rather – I hope to show so in the course of my argument – that this Measure provides a way in which the link between the Church of England and the State can continue in a form which enables each to fulfil its distinctive role for the benefit of the other, with greater effectiveness in the life of the Church. Again, it is not a Measure for abolishing the *Book of Common Prayer*. As I shall presently show, it gives to the *Book of Common Prayer* a secure place which could be altered only by the action of Parliament itself.

This Measure is a chapter in a story which starts a long way back, but my allusions to this long story will be brief. In 1906 the Royal Commission on Ecclesiastical Discipline reported that the law of public worship was too narrowly drawn for the needs of the time and called for the initiation of liturgical reform. But how could this be brought about? The Enabling Act of 1919 gave the Church Assembly of Bishops, Clergy and Laity the power to propose Measures, including Measures concerned with liturgy, which could receive the Royal Assent after an Affirmative Resolution in each House of Parliament. As everyone knows, a Measure for an Alternative Prayer Book, submitted by the Church Assembly in 1927 and 1928, was rejected in the House of Commons and a deadlock followed. I will not describe now a number of abortive attempts which were made to overcome the deadlock in the years between 1928 and the 1960s, but I would describe the main issue as I see it.

Ought a Christian Church, through its own chief pastors, ministers and laity, to have the ordering of its own forms of worship? I do not believe that there is a single Church in Christendom which [col.869] would not answer, "Yes, a Christian Church ought to have the ordering of its own forms of worship". Certainly the Church of Scotland, established as it is, would say this. Certainly every province of the world-wide Anglican Communion would say this. But this is linked with another question. If being a citizen and being an adherent of another Church are no longer identical, as was assumed in Hooker's great work, *Laws of Ecclesiastical Polity*, is it possible for a particular Church to have the desired autonomy in its worship and doctrine, and at the same time to have the link with the State and the Crown which we know as Establishment? My answer is that it is certainly possible, and the status of the Church of Scotland shows that that is so.

But let it be recognised that certain conditions are necessary. One condition is that in the United Kingdom such a Church must uphold the position of the Crown in relation to the Papal claims of the past. Another condition is that such a Church should have a defined identity. In Scotland, for example, the Church is identified as a Reformed Church of Presbyterian order. In England, the Church is identified as an Anglican Church whose formularies are known as its standard of belief. A further safeguard is surely necessary; that such a Church should be one in whose government the laity participate fully in partnership with the clergy.

In England, I believe it is true to say that the desire for greater self-government for the Church was long vitiated by the failure to introduce the role of the laity effectively into a traditionally episcopal Church. Now, however, the Church's synodical constitution brings in the partnership of the laity at every level of the Church's government and, as I hope to show, the proposals in this Measure involve the full participation of the laity in decisions about the use of forms of worship.

Now, my Lords, unless the Church of England was to be the only Church in Christendom which did not tackle the revision of old forms of worship, a start had to be made somewhere. This start was at long last made when in 1965 the Royal Assent was given to the Prayer Book (Alternative and Other Services) Measure, which it was at the time my [col.870] privilege to introduce in your Lordships' House. That Measure, as noble Lords will remember, gave power to the Church's Convocations and House of Laity to sanction, by two-thirds majorities, forms of service alternative to those of the 1662 Prayer Book for limited periods, with the proviso that the use of an alternative service in any parish requires the consent of the Parochial Church Council.

The Church has now enjoyed for nine years the use of new forms of service under the 1965 Measure. I believe that in spite of the misgivings of those who love the old forms, misgivings which call for much sympathy, the new forms, and in particular what is called the Series II services of Baptism and Holy Communion, have helped many people in a more lively participation in worship without loss of reverence or mystery. I would make one claim in particular. I believe that the Series II service, which I have mentioned, has enabled something of a breakthrough in the drawing together of those whom in the old language we called High Church and Low Church. I believe it is true that in the years in which we have indeed had varieties and variations the spiritual unity of our Church is stronger than in the past, and the kind of illegalities which were so troublesome to Church and State alike some 30 to 40 years ago are very much less frequent than in the past.

I think that I would put the matter thus. When I first became a Bishop 22 years ago, the Bishop's pastoral work as reconciler was still to some extent concerned with the historic parties in the Church, Catholic and Evangelical as they are called, and the tensions between them. To-day I am quite sure that the need for that kind of reconciling activity has greatly diminished, and the kind of pastoral leadership called for is now rather different. It is to bring understanding between those who value what is archaic and mysterious and those who feel more the pressures of contemporary need. It is a delicate task, but it is surely just the kind of task which Anglican leadership ought to be able to perform. But the performing of it needs both short-term and long-term strategy, and I believe we lack the opportunity for that. This Measure would provide that opportunity; and I should be very [col.871] surprised if at the end of the day Parliament thought that this was a task that it could perform itself.

My Lords, the powers given under the 1965 Measure will be expiring round about the year 1980. What then? If there is no further legislation, then the only services possessing lawful authority will be those of the 1662 Prayer Book. Is it really possible or desirable to revert to that position? Is it likely that the Church would be able or willing to present to Parliament one Prayer Book – all at once – designed to last a long time? No, my Lords, I think it is most unlikely; and the Measure that I am introducing is the Church's attempt to find a solution. As your Lordships know, it is based upon the Report of the Commission on Church and State, which was presided over by Dr. Owen Chadwick, the Regius Professor of Modern History at the University of Cambridge. That Commission reported two variants, of which the proposals in this Measure are one variant, and, in fact, the more conservative and cautious of the two of them. The Measure provides that the General Synod will have, not only for limited periods but for indefinite periods, the power to sanction alternative forms of service as well as rubrics and forms of subscription. It gives to the General Synod thus considerably more power in the control of worship and doctrine. But in order to conserve both the Church's doctrinal identity and the place of the *Book of Common Prayer*, and the rights of the laity – all three of these needs, my Lords – there are important provisos built into the Measure and sometimes critics of the Measure have overlooked this.

In the Measure the *Book of Common Prayer* remains as one of the Church's standards of doctrine. This, affirmed already in the existing Canons, is reaffirmed within the Measure. Furthermore, it is laid down that in any parish where the PCC[4] desires that a service of the 1662 Book shall be used then it shall be used.

---

4   Parochial Church Council.

What if the PCC and the parish priest disagree in what they want? In the original draft of the Measure the Bishop was to be the arbiter in such a dispute; but in the final draft of the Measure, in order to make the role of the laity strong and unequivocal, it is laid down, as will be seen, that the PCC may insist either on continuing a form [col.872] which has been in use for the past two years, if it wishes, or on reverting to the 1662 form if it wishes. I believe that this retention of the Prayer Book, both as a standard of doctrine and as a set of forms available when the PCC desires them, is a right means of conserving the identity of the Church to which Parliament is asked to allow the considerable new powers. There were those who wanted something more radical. I believe that this restraint and the proviso is right for the reasons which I have mentioned.

Noble Lords will not be misled by talk about the destruction of the Prayer Book when they notice that the safeguards for its use are stronger than they are at present under the 1965 Measure, stronger than they were in the draft Measure appended to the Chadwick Report and stronger than what was proposed when the Measure first came to our General Synod. The place of the Prayer Book in the Church's standards and the availability of the Prayer Book in the parishes when desired will be alterable only if Parliament were to decide to alter it. Cannot we say, therefore, that this Measure offers a right balance between the role of the Church and the role of the State in a continuing partnership?

Under the Measure it will be for the General Synod to decide what is and what is not consonant with sound doctrine. Is it likely that the Synod will be rash or hasty or unreliable in the use of this power? Its constitutional procedure would seem to make this somewhat unlikely, for what is that procedure? It is quite lengthy. Let me describe it. There is a debate on principles in one session, followed by a Revision Committee, followed in turn by a further session with the findings of the Revision Committee before it, and then a revision stage again. After all that Article 7 of the Constitution of the Synod comes into play, and it lays down: "A provision touching doctrinal formulae or the services or ceremonies of the Church of England or the administration of the Sacraments or sacred rites thereof shall, before it is finally approved by the General Synod, be referred to the House of Bishops, and shall be submitted for such final approval in terms proposed by the House of Bishops and not otherwise". I hardly think that at the end of the day Parliament would wish to undertake that function itself. Further, in any proposal [col.873] of liturgy or arrangement affecting relationships with other Churches, non-Anglican Churches, Article 8 of the Constitution comes into play, and Article 8 lays down that in such cases a proposal shall be submitted to all the diocesan Synods before it becomes finally acceptable.

There is still one more plea against this Measure. It is urged that the Measure is premature and that we ought to wait until the Synod has become a more experienced body. But, my Lords, although the Synod is a young body in its constituent parts, the Houses of Bishops and Clergy and Laity have been engaged on these questions for a very long time. It is 54 years since the old Church Assembly set its hand to the problem. It is 46 years since the deadlock of 1928. It is nine years since the period of alternatives with lawful authority began. If it is suggested that I am an old man in a hurry, I would recall that at my enthronement in Canterbury 13 years ago I pleaded for the necessity of a Measure on these lines, and it has taken until the last few hours of my Primacy for its introduction to come about.

My Lords, so far from the Measure being hasty, I believe that its rejection would be very damaging. I think it would be damaging to the leadership of the Church of England in the rest of the Anglican Communion and to the cause of Christian unity for any hope of reconciliation with the Free Churches and the United Church in this country – and I still treasure that hope and I feel very sure indeed that many noble Lords do as well. Any such hope will require something like this Measure as regards the Church's ordering of its own affairs, but rejection would be damaging chiefly to the younger people to whom the Church's mission is so important.

I rejoice to say that in the present year there has been a striking increase in the number of younger men seeking and being accepted for Ordination. This is the first rise of that kind to occur for a good many years. I believe that to be a sign that, with all the country's present frustrations, there is spiritual vitality and renewal happening in the Church, but I believe that the rejection of this Measure would be deeply discouraging to those who want to see the Church more able to give the kind of leadership it ought. Here, too, I [col.874] believe, is a chance for a partnership between the Church and the State in which the role of each will be better expressed and more effective. I ask, my Lords, that you will be ready to commend this Measure for the Royal Assent.

1982

Sermon in Westminster Abbey at a Service Marking the Fortieth Anniversary of the British Council of Churches, 30 September 1982

[Ramsey Papers vol. 320, ff. 346–49]

Luke 24.48. You are witnesses of these things.

Tonight this great company of Christian people from many traditions thanks God in celebration of the ecumenical movement. The phrase 'ecumenical movement' is widely used to describe the stirrings of Christian unity in many parts of the world[1] in the present century, and these stirrings are not confined to any particular organisation. But through 40 years in this country the British Council of Churches has been the servant and the mirror of these stirrings, and the story of its witness evokes our deep thankfulness to God. Not least we remember with gratitude leaders no longer with us: William Temple, George Bell, Geoffrey Fisher, Hugh Martin[2], Ernest Payne[3] and others who led and inspired. Tonight our thanksgiving is deep.

No 40 years in human history can have been more tumultuous and frightening than these. Within these years Christians have found themselves facing in new and strange ways the two questions: Who in Christendom is my Christian brother? and Who in the world of nations is my neighbour? What we call Christian unity is about the first question, and what we call Christian witness in the world is about [f.347] the second.

---

[1]   The typescript at this point originally read 'Christendom', amended by hand to 'the world'.

[2]   Hugh Martin (1890–1964), Baptist minister, publisher and student leader, provided practical support to the nascent BCC in its earliest days, and later served as vice-president. Martin also chaired the preparatory committee for Temple's Conference on Politics, Economics and Citizenship.

[3]   Ernest Payne (1902–1980) was general secretary of the Baptist Union between 1951 and 1967, and chairman of the BCC executive committee from 1962 until 1971.

The recovery of Christian unity, obscured and maimed by centuries of history, has indeed begun. There are many factors in the story. Christians of different traditions come to know one another in a new way and together to witness and to pray. Some actual unions of churches have happened, some on other continents and one in this country not so long ago. Much theological exploration has been made[,] bringing new understanding of issues which had been divisive, important because Christian unity means unity in the truth. But in this country I believe that the most significant change in the scene has been this: the old denominational self-consciousness, often aggressive and always obtrusive, has largely yielded to awareness in our consciousness that we are all of us Christians. That change of consciousness has been wide-spread. The British Council of Churches has mirrored this change as in a hundred ways it has helped Christians to be Christians together. And not only the British Council of Churches. The recent visit of the Pope to this country[4] has stirred many minds and consciences with the question: Who is my Christian brother? The patterns of ecumenism are changing, and unpredictable.

Who is my Christian brother? As that question presses, so does this other question Who is my neighbour? The last 40 years have brought home the parable of the road to Jericho with new poignancy to so many. Where is my neighbour in the world of races and nations? Is he someone of another race? Is he hungry? and perhaps starving? Is he one who suffers cruelty and persecution? Is he one who is bitterly hostile to ourselves? Is he one who is frightened by the amassing of weapons of destruction? Christians face these questions *together*. The [f.348] British Council of Churches has helped us in the facing of them together. We see these questions not as a self-contained programme of Christian politics, but in the context of the gospel of man's redemption by the Cross and the Resurrection of Jesus. We see the coming of God's kingdom on earth always in the context of heaven, for heaven is the goal of man; and heaven tells of the eternal worth of every man, woman and child that exists.

So our unity as Christians and our witness to the world go together. Jesus at the end of the Last Supper prayed for their unity in himself and in the Father, for their consecration in the truth, for their mission to the world, for their coming to heavenly glory. Here is the indivisible theme, and authentic ecumenism can mean no less than the fulfilment of this prayer.

In the fulfilment of this prayer through the centuries of history and indeed today is not surprising that advances are sometimes followed by frustrations and there are many imponderables. The divine compassion and the divine judgment

---

4   Pope John Paul II visited the UK in May/June 1982.

together. Today because the experience of Christian comradeship is happening for Christians in many different contexts in Christendom, it may be that some are afraid lest to move in one direction may hinder moving in another direction. That is not surprising. It is for statesmanship to have the vision and the patience to see how different parts of the ecumenical scene may relate to one another. It needs both vision[5] and patience. But wherever there is slowness in the making[6] of unions the more necessary is it to heed the challenge of Lund made just 30 years ago,[7] the challenge that [f.349] churches do separately only those things that they find impossible to do together. Our thanksgiving to God for what has been happening in the work of unity will include our real penitence for our sloth and our complacency which may wound our Lord and delay his purpose.

You shall be witnesses. Witness is one of the great words of Christianity. St. John tells of Jesus in his life on earth bearing witness to the truth. The apocalypse tells of Jesus as still the faithful witness to the truth, the first-born of the dead.[8] Jesus said to the apostles: "You shall be my witnesses"[9]. They bore witness to his life and his teaching, his death and his risen life. Other Christians are drawn to share in this witness, and the witness is by preaching and by lives, and not seldom by suffering and death. The continuing witness of Christians is no merely human activity, for it is enabled by the Holy Spirit who gives courage because the witness is in living and dying and gives understanding because it is always a witness to the truth. And the theme to which we bear witness is always the death and resurrection of Jesus. Here is revealed the sovereignty of God as the sovereignty of sacrificial love and the way of life for man as losing life to find it.

---

[5]   In the typescript, the word used is 'wisdom'.

[6]   The word 'making' is struck out by hand, but the insertion is illegible.

[7]   At the 1952 Faith and Order Conference of the World Council of Churches, held at Lund, Sweden.

[8]   Revelation 1:5.

[9]   Acts 1:8.

Appendix: Ramsey's Staff

Ramsey had around him a small staff at Lambeth, several of whom are to be found acting on his behalf at various stages. On arriving at Lambeth in 1961 he inherited a lay chief of staff in Robert Beloe, who had arrived at Lambeth after a distinguished career in educational administration.[1] Beloe was succeeded in 1969 by Hugh Whitworth, who had been in the civil service. The lay chief of staff handled business that related to matters outside the internal running of the Church, including parliamentary business. (On Beloe's work in relation to law reform, see Chapter 3.)

For the internal business of the Church, Ramsey was served by a senior chaplain and a domestic chaplain. Holders of the latter office, who were responsible for travel and for the diocese of Canterbury, included John Andrew (who came with Ramsey from York) and John Kirkham. The senior chaplain was a clerical chief of staff to match the laymen Beloe and Whitworth. These included Noel Kennaby, John Andrew, and lastly Geoffrey Tiarks from 1969. Tiarks was also made Bishop of Maidstone when it was felt that the senior chaplain needed a greater seniority. Ramsey's team of secretaries was overseen first by Priscilla Lethbridge and then by Barbara Lepper.[2]

Other parts of the wider administration of the Church which appear in these pages include the Council on Foreign Relations. The CFR went through a number of incarnations, but it and its general secretary John Satterthwaite appear here in connection with international and domestic ecumenical relationships. For public relations, Michael De-la-Noy served as Ramsey's press officer between 1967 and 1970.[3]

---

[1]   H.G. Judge, 'Beloe, Robert (1905-84) in ODNB.
[2]   Chadwick, *Ramsey*, pp.116-18.
[3]   De-la-Noy's colourful picture of the Church of England's public relations operation is given at *A Day in the Life of God*, pp.43-59.

Bibliography

Manuscripts

London, Lambeth Palace Library: the Ramsey Papers

Printed primary sources

Abortion: an Ethical Discussion. London, 1965.
Anglican-Methodist Unity. Report of the Anglican-Methodist Unity Commission. Part 2: The Scheme. London, 1968.
The Archbishops' Committee on Church and State. Report. London, 1918.
The Canon Law of the Church of England. Being a Report of the Archbishops' Commission on Canon Law [...]. London, 1947.
Catholicity. A Study in the Conflict of Christian Traditions in the West. London, 1948.
The Chronicle of Convocation. Being a Record of the Proceedings of the Convocation of Canterbury. London, 1858-.
Church and State. Being the Report of a Commission appointed by the Church Assembly in June 1949. London, 1952.
Church and State. Report of the Archbishops' Commission on the Relations Between Church and State. London, 1935.
Church and State. Report of the Archbishops' Commission. London, 1970.
The Convocations and the Laity. Being the Report of the Commission Set Up by the Church Assembly to Consider How the Clergy and Laity Can Best be Joined Together in the Synodical Government of the Church. London, 1958.
Crown Appointments and the Church. London, 1964.
The English Prayer Book 1549–1662. London, 1963.
Intercommunion To-day, being the Report of the Archbishops' Commission on Intercommunion. London, 1968.
Joint Committee on Censorship of the Theatre. Report etc. London, 1967.
The Lambeth Conference 1968. Resolutions and Reports. London, 1968.

Lambeth Essays on Faith. London, 1969.

Lambeth Essays on Ministry. London, 1969.

Lambeth Essays on Unity. London, 1969.

Oxford Dictionary of National Biography. Oxford, 2004; online edition.

Putting Asunder. A Divorce Law for Contemporary Society. London, 1966.

Baxter, Kay M. *Speak What We Feel. A Christian Looks at the Contemporary Theatre*. London, 1964.

Bayne, Stephen F. *An Anglican Turning Point. Documents and Interpretations*. Austin, Texas, 1964.

Bray, Gerald (ed.). *The Anglican Canons, 1529–1947*. London, 1998.

Crossman, Richard. *The Diaries of a Cabinet Minister. Volume One: Minister of Housing 1964-66*. London, 1975.

De-la-Noy, Michael. *A day in the life of God*. Derby, 1971.

Devlin, Patrick. *The Enforcement of Morals*. London, 1965.

Dicken, E.W. Trueman. *Not This Way. A Comment on Anglican-Methodist Unity*. London, 1968.

Duffield, Gervase. *Admission to Holy Communion*. Abingdon, 1964.

Edwards, David L. *The Honest to God Debate*. London, 1963.

Fisher, Geoffrey. *Covenant and Reconciliation. A Critical Examination*. Oxford, 1967.

Heenan, John Carmel. *A Crown of Thorns. An autobiography 1951–1963*. London, 1974.

Heenan, John Carmel (ed.). *Christian Unity: A Catholic View*. London, 1962.

Howe, John and Colin Craston. *Anglicanism and the Universal Church*. Revised edn., Toronto, 1990.

Loukes, Harold. *Teenage Religion*. London, 1961.

Macintyre, Alasdair. *Secularization and Moral Change*. London, 1967.

Martin, Christopher (ed.). *Great Christian Centuries to Come. Essays in Honour of A. M. Ramsey*. Oxford, 1974.

Packer, J.I. (ed.). *Fellowship in the Gospel. Evangelical Comment on Anglican-Methodist Unity and Intercommunion Today*. Abingdon, 1968.

Pawley, Bernard. *An Anglican View of the Vatican Council*. London, 1962.

Ramsey, Michael. *The Gospel and the Catholic Church*. London, 1936.

—— *The Church of England and the Eastern Orthodox Church. Why Their Unity is Important*. London, 1946.

—— *Durham Essays and Addresses*. London, 1956.

—— *From Gore to Temple. The Development of Anglican Theology between Lux Mundi and the Second World War 1889–1939*. London, 1960.

—— *The Authority of the Bible*. Edinburgh, 1962.

—— *Image Old and New*, London, 1963.

—— *Canterbury Essays and Addresses*. London, 1964.

—— *God, Christ and the World. A Study in Contemporary Theology*. London, 1969.

—— *Holy Spirit*. London, 1977.

—— *Be still and know*. London, 1982.

—— *The Christian Priest Today*. Second edn. London, 1985.

—— *The Anglican Spirit*. London, 1991.

Ramsey, Michael and Leon-Joseph Suenens. *The Future of the Christian Church*. London, 1971.

Riley, H and R.J. Graham (eds). *Acts of the Convocations of Canterbury and York 1921–1970*. London, 1971.

Robinson, John A.T. *Honest to God*. London, 1963.

Underwood, George W. *Intercommunion and the Open Table*. London, 1964.

Wansey, Christopher. *The Clockwork Church*. Oxford, 1978.

Secondary sources

Atherstone, Andrew. '"A Mad Hatter's Tea Party in the Old Mitre Tavern?" Ecumenical Reactions to *Growing into Union*.' *Ecclesiology* 6 (2010), 39–67.

Atherstone, Andrew. 'The canonisation of the Forty English Martyrs: an ecumenical dilemma.' *Recusant History* 30 (2011), 673–88.

Atherstone, Andrew. 'Christian family, Christian nation: Raymond Johnston and the Nationwide Festival of Light in defence of the family.' *Studies in Church History* 50 (2014), 456–68.

Atherstone, Andrew. 'Evangelical Dissentients and the Defeat of the Anglican-Methodist Unity Scheme.' Wesley and Methodist Studies 7 (2015), 100-16.

Bates, Stephen. *A Church at War. Anglicans and Homosexuality*. London, 2004.

Beaken, Robert. *Cosmo Lang. Archbishop in War and Crisis*. London, 2012.

Bell, G.K.A. *Randall Davidson. Archbishop of Canterbury*. (London, 1935).

Brewitt-Taylor, Sam. 'The invention of a "Secular Society"? Christianity and the sudden appearance of secularization discourses in the British national media, 1961-4.' *Twentieth Century British History* 24 (2013), 327-50.

Brown, Callum. *The Death of Christian Britain. Understanding Secularisation 1800–2000*. Second edn., Abingdon, 2009.

Bruce, Steve. *God save Ulster! The religion and politics of Paisleyism*. Oxford, 1986.

Carey, George. *Development and Change: an Examination of Michael Ramsey's Response to Honest to God and its Implications Today*. Durham, 1993.

Carpenter, Edward with Adrian Hastings. *Cantuar. The Archbishops in their Office*. Third edn., London, 1997.

Chadwick, Owen. *Hensley Henson. A Study in the Friction between Church and State*. Oxford, 1983.

Chadwick, Owen. *Michael Ramsey. A Life*. Oxford, 1990.

Chandler, Andrew. *The Church of England in the Twentieth Century: the Church Commissioners and the Politics of Reform, 1948–1998*. Woodbridge, 2006.

Chandler, Andrew. *Piety and Provocation. A Study of George Bell, Bishop of Chichester*. Chichester, 2008.

Chandler, Andrew and David Hein. *Archbishop Fisher, 1945–1961. Church, State and World*. Farnham, 2012.

Chapman, Alister. 'Anglican evangelicals and revival, 1945–59.' *Studies in Church History* 44 (2008), 307–17.

Chapman, Alister. *Godly Ambition. John Stott and the Evangelical Movement*. Oxford, 2012.

Chapman, Mark, Judith Maltby, and William Whyte. *The Established Church: Past, Present and Future*. London, 2011.

Clarke, Peter. *Hope and Glory. Britain 1900–2000*. London, 2004.

Clutterbuck, Ivan. *Marginal Catholics*. Leominster, 1993.

Cook, Hera. *The Long Sexual Revolution. English Women, Sex and Contraception 1800–1975*. Oxford, 2004.

Cramer, Jared. *Safeguarded by Glory: Michael Ramsey's Ecclesiology and the struggles of contemporary Anglicanism*. Lanham, MD, 2010.

DeGroot, Gerard. *The Sixties Unplugged*. London, 2008.

De-la-Noy, Michael. *Michael Ramsey. A Portrait*. London, 1990.

De-la-Noy, Michael. *Mervyn Stockwood. A Lonely Life*. London, 1996.

Dorey, Peter and Alexandra Kelso. *House of Lords Reform since 1911. Must the Lords Go?* Basingstoke, 2011.

Ferguson, Ronald. *George Macleod. Founder of the Iona Community*. London, 1990.

Gallagher, Eric and Stanley Worrall. *Christians in Ulster 1968–1980*. Oxford, 1982.

Garnett, Jane, Matthew Grimley, Alana Harris, William Whyte and Sarah Williams (eds). *Redefining Christian Britain. Post 1945 Perspectives*. London, 2007.

Gill, Robin and Lorna Kendall (eds). *Michael Ramsey as theologian*. London, 1995.

Grimley, Matthew. *Citizenship, Community, and the Church of England: Liberal Anglican Theories of the State between the Wars*. Oxford, 2004.

Grimley, Matthew. 'Law, Morality and Secularisation: The Church of England and the Wolfenden Report, 1954–1967.' *Journal of Ecclesiastical History* 60 (2009), 725–41.

Grimley, Matthew. 'The Church and the Bomb: Anglicans and the Campaign for Nuclear Disarmament, c.1958–1984' In: Stephen G. Parker and Tom Lawson (eds), *God and War. The Church of England and Armed Conflict in the Twentieth Century* (Farnham, 2012), 147–64.

Grimley, Matthew. 'The Church of England, race and multi-culturalism, 1962–2012' In: Jane Garnett and Alana Harris (eds), *Rescripting Religion in the City. Migration and Religious Identity in the Modern Metropolis.* (Farnham, 2013), 207–21.

Hastings, Adrian. *A History of English Christianity 1920–1990.* Third edn, London, 1991.

Hitchens, Peter. *The Abolition of Britain.* London, 1999.

Holloway, David. *The Church of England. Where is it going?* Eastbourne, 1985.

Hughes, Robert. *The Red Dean.* Worthing, 1987.

Iremonger, F. A. *William Temple, Archbishop of Canterbury. His Life and Letters.* London, 1948.

Jacob, W.M. *The Making of the Anglican Church Worldwide.* London, 1997.

James, Eric. *A Life of John A.T. Robinson. Scholar, Pastor, Prophet.* London, 1987.

Jasper, R.C.D. *George Bell. Bishop of Chichester.* London, 1967.

Jones, Ian. *The Local Church and Generational Change in Birmingham 1945–2000.* Woodbridge, 2012.

Jones, Timothy W. 'Moral welfare and social well-being: the Church of England and the emergence of modern homosexuality.' In: Lucy Delap and Sue Morgan (eds), *Men, Masculinities and Religious Change in Twentieth-Century Britain.* (Basingstoke, 2013), 197–217.

Kent, John. *William Temple.* Cambridge, 1992.

Kirby, Dianne. 'The Church of England and the Cold War.' In: Stephen G. Parker and Tom Lawson (eds), *God and War. The Church of England and Armed Conflict in the Twentieth Century.* (Farnham, 2013), 129–35.

Layton-Henry, Zig. *The Politics of Immigration.* Oxford, 1992.

Lewis, Jane and Patrick Wallis. 'Fault, breakdown and the Church of England's involvement in the 1969 divorce reform.' *Twentieth Century British History*, 11 (2000), 308–32.

Machin, G.I.T. *Churches and Social Issues in Twentieth-Century Britain.* Oxford, 1998.

Maiden, John. *National Religion and the Prayer Book Controversy, 1927–8.* Woodbridge, 2009.

Maiden, John and Peter Webster. 'Parliament, the Church of England and the last gasp of political Protestantism, 1961-4.' *Parliamentary History* 32 (2013), 361–77.

Marwick, Arthur. *The Sixties. Cultural Revolution in Britain, France, Italy and the United States, c.1958–c.1974*. Oxford, 1998.

McLeod, Hugh. 'God and the gallows: Christianity and capital punishment in the nineteenth and twentieth centuries.' *Studies in Church History* 40 (2004), 330–56.

McLeod, Hugh. *The Religious Crisis of the 1960s*. Oxford, 2007.

McLeod, Hugh. 'Homosexual law reform, 1953–67.' In: Melanie Barber, Stephen Taylor and Gabriel Sewell (eds). *From the Reformation to the Permissive Society*. (Woodbridge, 2010), 657–78.

Mews, Stuart. 'The trials of Lady Chatterley, the modernist bishop and the Victorian archbishop: clashes of class, culture and generations.' *Studies in Church History* 48 (2012), 449–64.

Morris, Brian (ed.). *Ritual Murder. Essays on Liturgical Reform*. Manchester, 1980.

Morris, Jeremy. *The Church in the Modern Age*. London, 2007.

Nicholls, David. *Church and State in Britain since 1820*. London, 1967.

Nicholson, Steve. *The Censorship of British Drama, 1900–68*. 3 vols, Exeter, 2003–09.

Norman, Edward. *Anglican Difficulties. A New Syllabus of Errors*. London, 2004.

Pawley, Bernard and Margaret Pawley. *Rome and Canterbury Through Four Centuries*. London, 1974.

Phillips, Melanie. *The World Turned Upside Down. The Global Battle over God, Truth and Power*. New York, 2010.

Pimlott, Ben. *The Queen*. London, 1996.

Potter, Harry. *Hanging in Judgment. Religion and the Death Penalty in England*. New York, 1993.

Purcell, William. *Portrait of Soper*. London, 1972.

Roodhouse, Mark. 'Lady Chatterley and the Monk: Anglican radicals and the Lady Chatterley trial of 1960.' *Journal of Ecclesiastical History* 59 (2008), 475–500.

Rowbotham, Sheila. *A Century of Women. The History of Women in Britain and the United States*. London, 1999.

Sachs, William L. *The Transformation of Anglicanism. From State Church to Global Communion*. Cambridge, 1993.

Sandbrook, Dominic. *White Heat. A History of Britain in the Swinging Sixties*. London, 2006.

Simpson, James B. *The Hundredth Archbishop of Canterbury*. New York, 1962.

Smith, Mark. 'The roots of resurgence: evangelical parish ministry in the mid-twentieth century.' *Studies in Church History* 44 (2008), 318–28.

Stock, Victor *Taking Stock. Confessions of a City Priest*. London, 2001.

Twitchell, Neville. *The Politics of the Rope: the Campaign to Abolish Capital Punishment in Britain, 1955–1969*. Bury St Edmunds, 2012.

Webster, Peter and Ian Jones. 'Anglican "Establishment" Reactions to "Pop" Church Music in England, c.1956–1991.' *Studies in Church History* 42 (2006), 429–41.

Webster, Peter. 'The archbishop of Canterbury, the Lord Chamberlain and the censorship of the theatre, 1909–49,' *Studies in Church History* 48 (2012), 437–48.

Webster, Peter. 'Archbishop Michael Ramsey and evangelicals in the Church of England' In: Andrew Atherstone and John Maiden (eds). *Evangelicalism and the Church of England in the Twentieth Century: Reform, Resistance and Renewal*. (Woodbridge, 2014), 162-82.

Webster, Peter. 'Race, religion and national identity in Sixties Britain: Michael Ramsey, archbishop of Canterbury and his encounter with other faiths.' *Studies in Church History* 51 (2015), 385–98.

Welsby, Paul A. *A History of the Church of England 1945–1980*. Oxford, 1984.

Williams, Rowan. *Anglican Identities*. London, 2004.

Williams, Rowan. *Why Study the Past? The Quest for the Historical Church*. London, 2005.

Williamson, Philip. 'State prayers, fasts and thanksgivings: public worship in Britain 1830–1897' *Past and Present* 200 (2008), 121–74.

Williamson, Philip. 'National days of prayer: the churches, the state and public worship in Britain 1899–1957.' *English Historical Review* 128 (2013), 324–66.

Wolffe, John. 'Judging the Nation: Early Nineteenth-Century British Evangelicals and Divine Retribution.' *Studies in Church History* 40 (2004), 291–300.

Yates, Nigel. *Love Now, Pay Later? Sex and Religion in the Fifties and Sixties*. London, 2010.

Index